IMAGES
of America

MAITLAND

I0809006

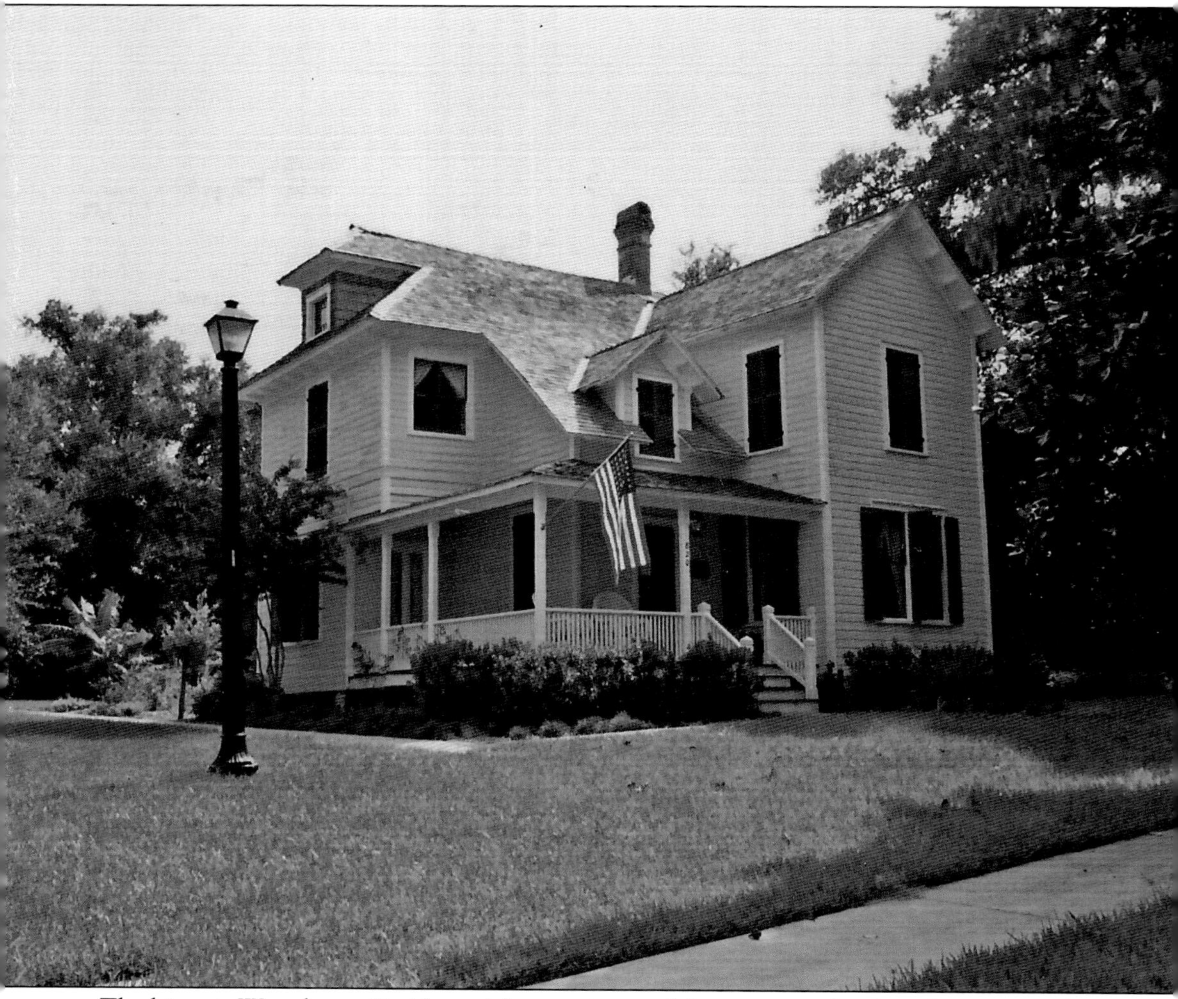

The historic Waterhouse Residence Museum is one of the treasures that have been restored and preserved by the Maitland Historical Society. Sitting on the shores of Lake Lily, the home was built by Maitland resident and carpenter William Waterhouse in 1884. Visitors can get a glimpse of the lifestyle of a middle-class Victorian family during the city's early days. (Courtesy Maitland Historical Society.)

On the Cover: The Seminoles first called it "Fumecheliga"—the place where muskmelons grow. The Seminoles and melons are gone now, but the residents of Maitland, the modern city now found in the same location, still enjoy the fruits of the land. In this photograph from 1962, youngsters enjoy a watermelon-eating contest as part of Maitland Day, a city celebration that was held every Fourth of July and featured a parade, exhibits, shows, and fireworks.

IMAGES
of America

MAITLAND

Leslie Kemp Poole and
the Maitland Historical Society

ARCADIA
PUBLISHING

ISBN 978-0-7385-6606-1

Published by Arcadia Publishing
Charleston SC, Chicago IL, Portsmouth NH, San Francisco CA

Printed in the United States of America

Library of Congress Control Number: 2009924092

For all general information contact Arcadia Publishing at:
Telephone 843-853-2070
Fax 843-853-0044
E-mail sales@arcadiapublishing.com
For customer service and orders:
Toll-Free 1-888-313-2665

Visit us on the Internet at www.arcadiapublishing.com

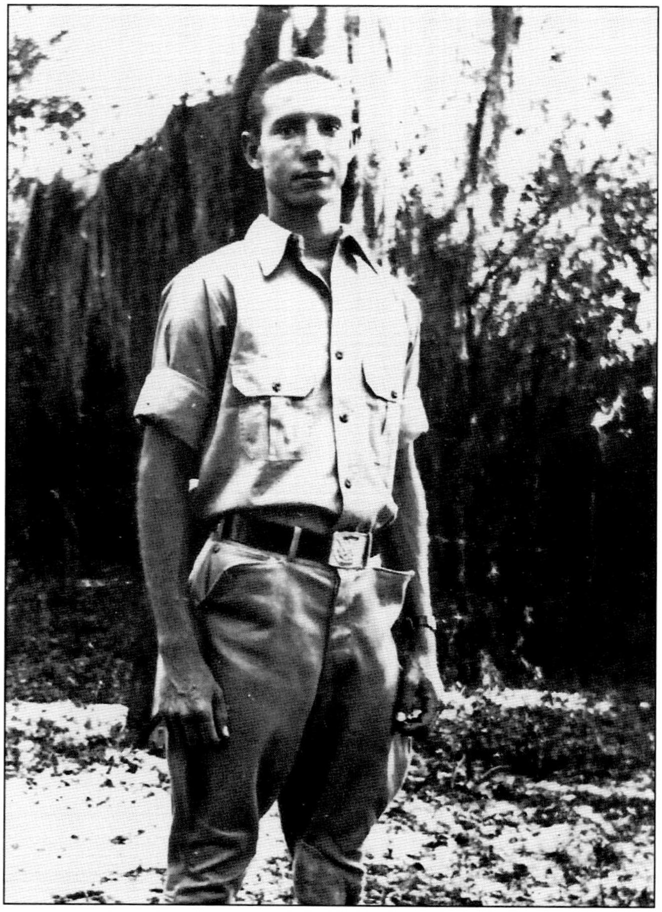

The Maitland Historical Society dedicates this book to longtime members David Kilbourne, pictured here in 1937, and Irene Logan. Their dreams of publishing a book about Maitland have become a reality because of the vision, time, talent, and passion they put into the organization and this project. (Courtesy Maitland Historical Society.)

Contents

ACKNOWLEDGMENTS

Although this book is a joint effort of the author and the Maitland Historical Society (MHS), several people must be credited for their assistance in making it a success. Andrea Bailey Cox, MHS executive director, provided much guidance and expertise in all things related to technology. Betty Sample, curator, was an invaluable guide to the MHS archives and in helping to choose the best photographs for this book. Layla Bellows served as assistant photo editor. In many ways, Irene Logan was the inspiration for this book, as her intimate knowledge of the city's history was vital to its writing and ensured the accuracy and integrity of this project.

Most of these images came from the files of the Maitland Historical Society (unless otherwise noted), but help came from a few others: the Florida State Archives; Jim Hulbert, who shared his family's keepsakes; the Hames-Dreisbach family; the Department of College Archives and Special Collections, Olin Library, Rollins College, Winter Park and Gertrude Laframboise and Wenxian Zhang, who made seven photographs and many files available; the Maitland Art Center for paintings and a photograph of Andre Smith; and the Sloane Gallery Collection, which granted the use of an archival photograph of women's "bird" fashions. Special thanks go to volunteer photographer Steve Clinton, Maitland City Hall, Mary Hodge and the Maitland Chamber of Commerce, and the Church of the Good Shepherd.

Many thanks to Luke Cunningham, at Arcadia Publishing, who enthusiastically suggested this project, and especially to Arcadia editor Lindsay Harris, who saw it through to the end, offering encouragement, advice, patience, and good humor when it was greatly needed.

Finally, I must thank my wonderful husband, Michael, and my sons, Blake and Preston, for their support.

Introduction

From its tranquil setting amid lakes and stately cypress trees, Maitland has witnessed a colorful history that spans more than a century and includes a whirlwind of change from settlers on horseback to railway commerce to a residential haven. It is a vision few early residents could have imagined.

The Pre-Columbian natives of this area, the Timucua, lived along the area's scenic lakes, using the waters' rich bounty for food. By the 19th century, the Timucua had disappeared, replaced by the Seminoles, who gave the area its first remembered name—Fumecheliga, meaning "place where the muskmelons grow." It was a way to remember a rich, nourishing landscape that would attract future settlers.

Florida became a U.S. territory in 1821, and three years later, Central Florida would be included in the newly created Mosquito County. By 1838, the federal government was embroiled in hostilities with the Seminoles, leading to the construction of several military forts, including one on the shores of Lake Fumecheliga. Lt. Col. Alexander Fanning named it Fort Maitland in honor of Capt. William Seton Maitland, one of Fanning's officers who had battled in an earlier conflict and died from his wounds. The lake also received the Maitland name—a tribute to a soldier who never saw it.

With the end of the Second Seminole War in 1842, settlers began moving into Central Florida. They were encouraged by the Congressional Armed Occupation Act that granted 160-acre tracts to the heads of families who met a number of criteria. Settlers agreed to build homes, clear 5 acres, and occupy them for five years in order to establish ownership. With the close of the Civil War, more settlers moved into the area, mostly farming, raising cattle, and growing citrus.

Early pioneers moved into the area known as Lake Maitland in the postwar years, coming by way of steamship from Jacksonville up the St. Johns River to Mellonville, near present-day Sanford. From there, they traveled to the area by foot or in primitive horse-drawn wagons. In 1871, with only 25 families in the area—13 of them within 2 miles of town—Christopher Columbus Beasley applied for permission to establish a post office that operated out of his property. A year later, James Erwin Hill arrived by horseback from Alabama, becoming one of the earliest settlers. With his four sons, Hill built a log cabin on the north side of Lake Hope, and the family became important community members, planting the first orange grove in the area.

Other pioneers soon followed. George Horatio Packwood left his business in Louisiana, bought 39 acres, and erected a large town hall on Maitland Avenue that served as the budding settlement's social and commercial center. Two years later, Beasley homesteaded 160 acres and built the first house in Lake Maitland. By then, only charred ruins remained from the fort that had brought the community its name.

Lake Maitland was laid out as a town in 1876 by far-seeing city founders who lined its streets with sturdy oaks, creating an arboreal beauty that remains. Four years later, the railroad arrived with its connection to Northern markets and cities, heralding an era of change and growth. The railroad became a centerpiece of the community, bringing mail, merchandise, and visitors, and the city became a vital link along its tracks.

The city was incorporated in 1885, and Josiah Eaton became its first mayor. He also helped establish nearby Eatonville, which became the oldest incorporated African American city in the United States. A directory the following year reported a number of businesses in Maitland, including a sawmill, a newspaper, an ice manufacturer, hotels, a physician, and a livery and stables. The city was home to several churches as well.

By the late 1800s, the city had attracted a number of wealthy winter visitors who built large homes on big tracts of land, often bordering the nearby lakes. Many grew citrus in the area or in nearby counties—important business interests that occupied their time while they enjoyed a respite from cold Northern climes. Much of the tasty citrus grown in these groves was shipped by railroad to Northern markets, sporting labels with local names and images. A number of notable people also visited the area, including author Louisa May Alcott, *New York Times* correspondent William Drysdale, and Julia Ward Howe, author of "The Battle Hymn of the Republic."

With an increase in population, Lake Maitland naturally developed into a cultural and social center. In 1896, the Maitland Public Library was created, thanks to a gift of 360 books from Clara Dommerich, who with her husband, Louis, a wealthy New York merchant, owned a large lakefront estate called Hiawatha Grove. Four years later, their home would be the organizing site for the Florida Audubon Society. Many early city leaders were part of this group, which tirelessly worked to save Florida's birds by educating the public and pressing for avian protection.

By the turn of the 20th century, Lake Maitland was becoming a modern city. In 1910, Carl Hill Galloway installed the town's first switchboard at his father's grocery store and then placed 10 telephones in customers' homes so they could order goods, which were delivered by horse and buggy. Soon after, Galloway and James H. Hirsch built an electric light system, which brought new conveniences to residents' lives. The first grouted, brick road in Florida, called the Dixie Highway (now Maitland Avenue), was built along the city's Lake Lily in 1915, and by 1924, there were 5 miles of brick-paved roads in the city. New residential subdivisions sprouted to accommodate Florida's boom period, the city's first taste of things to come.

Noted artist, architect, and author Jules Andre Smith visited the area in the early 1930s while traveling to South Florida. He was so captured by the area's beauty that in 1938 he founded the Maitland Art Research Studio, a unique facility built in Aztec-Mayan style where guest artists could live and work. It is now the site of the Maitland Art Center.

Although freezes in the 1890s devastated many crops, the citrus industry rallied and remained a cornerstone of the local economy, along with tourism and transportation. After World War II, the city joined Florida's unprecedented growth with the creation of many roads and subdivisions to serve an exploding population. In the 1950s, the Martin Marietta Corporation in Maryland opened a new Orlando division to participate in the state's growing space industry. Many company employees chose to live in Maitland, which led to the conversion of many citrus groves into housing tracts that exist today.

The city's modern "face" began taking shape in the 1950s, with its name shortened to "Maitland" in 1959. Businesses and retailers moved into new shopping centers along its bustling streets. When Interstate 4 was proposed, many residents worked hard to keep the highway from bisecting the city, leading to rejoicing when its current path west of the city was approved. By the 1970s, the city boasted several banks, 12 new subdivisions, and Maitland Center, one of the leading office parks in the southeastern United States. The city had come a long way—from a fort to a thriving business, cultural, and residential area, always carrying with it the dreams and visions of a hardworking, vibrant citizenry while maintaining its picturesque setting amid cypress and lakes.

One

Early Settlers

An abundance of lakes, trees, rich soil, and a mild climate likely drew the first inhabitants to the area now known as Maitland. Approximately 10,000 years ago, humans migrated into Florida, gathering plants and hunting its abundant wildlife. The earliest named natives in Central Florida were the Timucua, who encountered the first European colonists, but by the 1800s, the area was home to the Seminoles, who fought federal troops until the end of the Second Seminole War in 1842. Those hostilities brought the first known large structure to the area—a wooden fortress called Fort Maitland. With peace and the encouragement of federal homestead offers, a number of pioneers left other parts of the United States and settled in the Maitland area, raising cattle and growing the new Florida "gold"—citrus. City leaders drew up a town plan in 1876, after the post office arrived in 1872. With the coming of the railroad in 1880 and the commercial promise of its steel connections to Northern markets—and tourists—the community would never be the same.

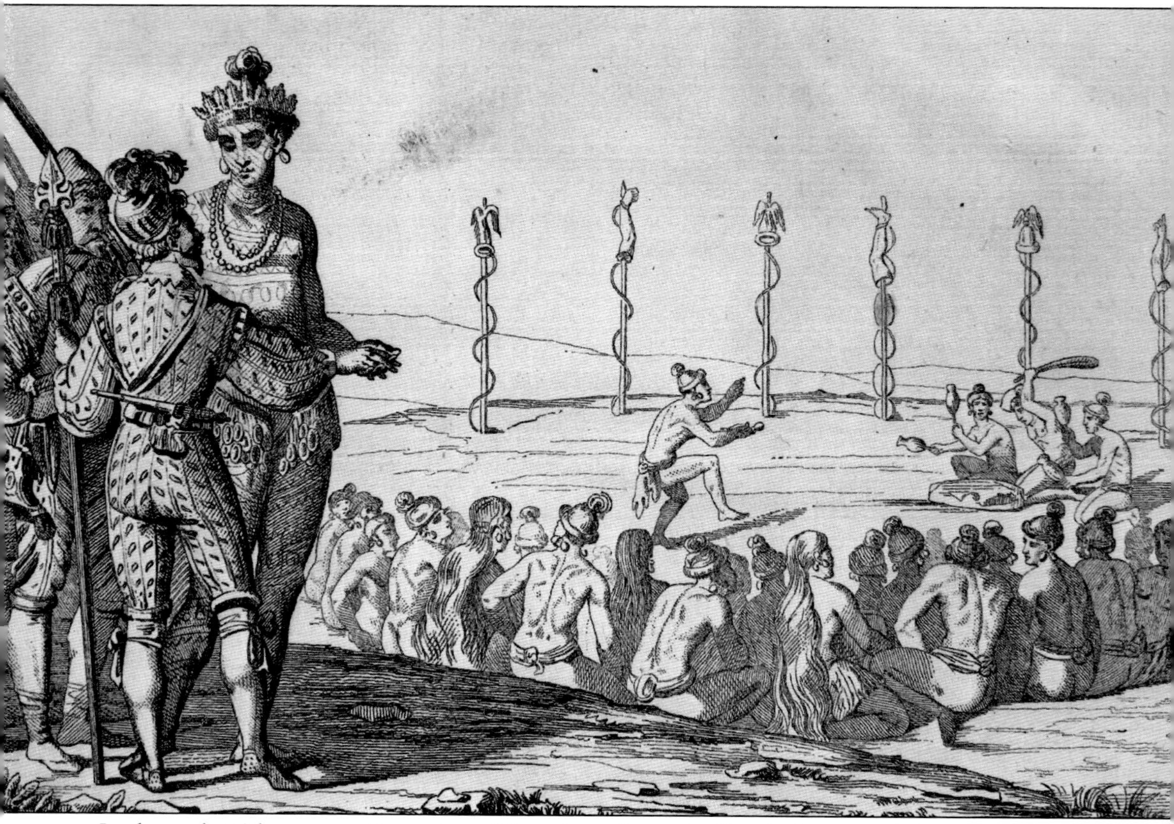

In the early 16th century, Spanish and French explorers in Florida discovered the native Timucua, whose territory extended across South Georgia and North Florida, including what is now the Maitland area. With an estimated population of 200,000 in 1492, these people, who spoke a common language, lived in at least 510 villages. As this image shows, the Timucua were taller than Europeans and decorated their skins with intricate tattoo patterns. They wore pierced earrings and gathered their long hair in elaborate buns on top of their heads, sometimes decorated with feathers. In 1564, French artist Jacques LeMoyne de Morgues made numerous drawings of these people, later turned into engravings and a 1591 book by Dutch engraver Theodore DeBry. This scene depicts a group of Timucua participating in a celebratory meeting with the spoils of war displayed on poles. (Courtesy State Archives of Florida.)

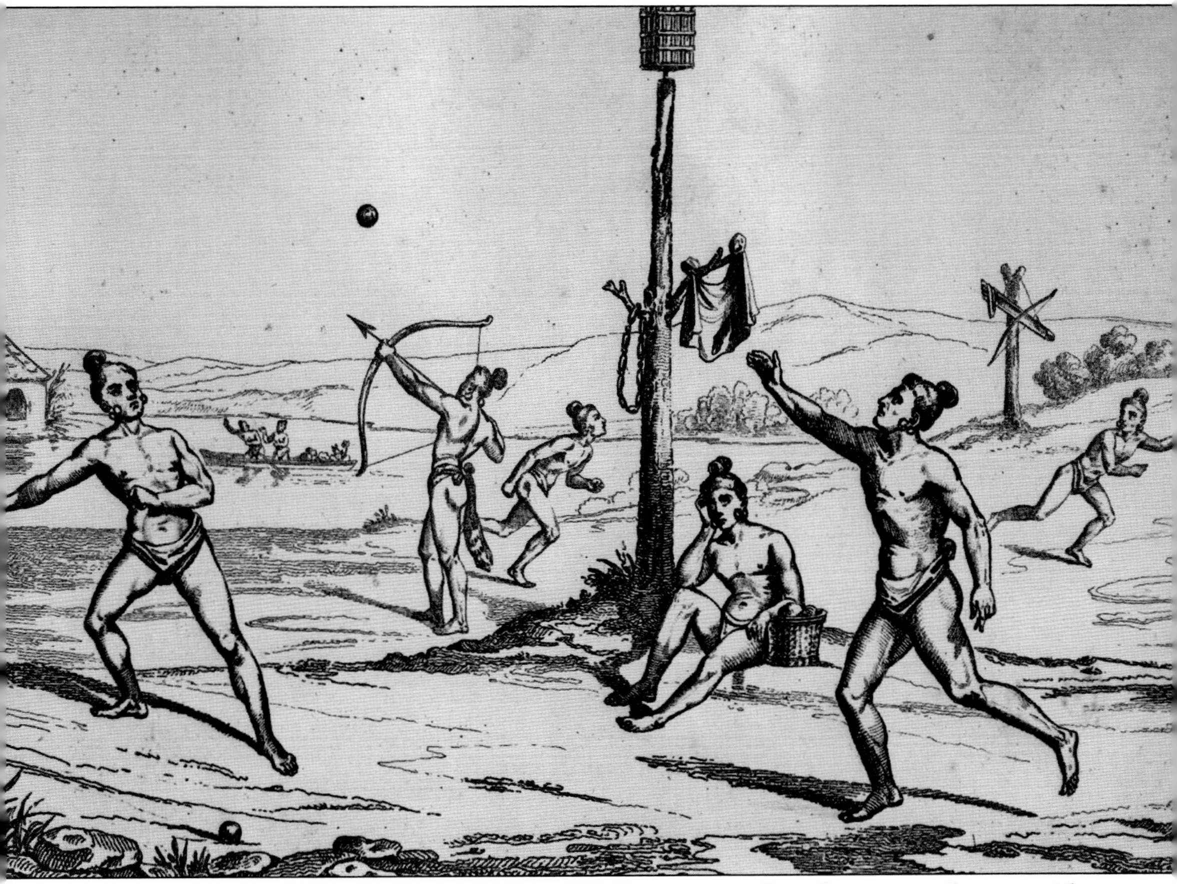

This LeMoyne drawing depicts male Timucua participating in archery, boating, and games with a tall pole as a central feature. The Timucua were expert hunters, and Spanish explorers reported that their accuracy with bow and arrow was remarkable. Contact with Europeans, however, took an enormous toll—by the end of the 16th century, only 25 percent of their population remained, the result of slavery, warfare, and European diseases that ravaged native people throughout the Americas. By 1700, only 1,000 Timucua were counted, and by 1763, when the Spanish left Florida in British control, only one Timucua accompanied them to Cuba. (Courtesy State Archives of Florida.)

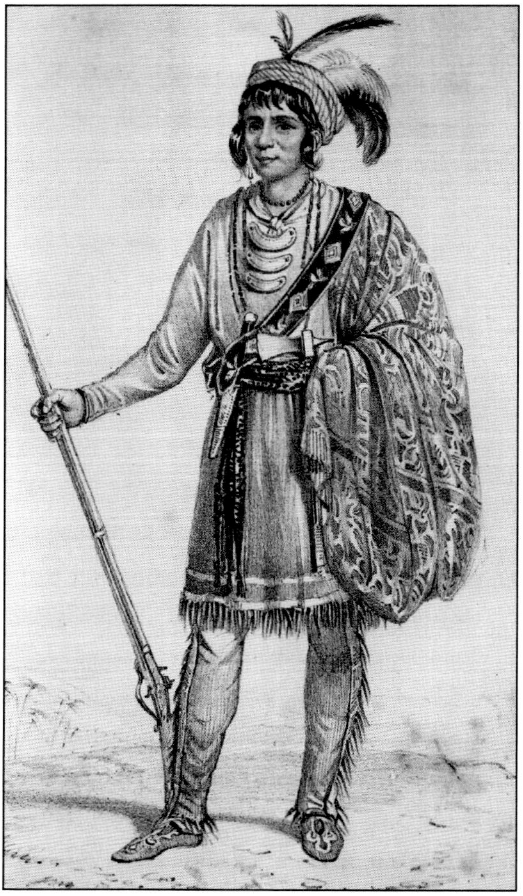

Chief Osceola, one of the greatest Seminole leaders, is depicted in this drawing. The name Seminole comes from the Spanish term *cimarron*, meaning "wild men." Many came to Florida under Spanish rule, escaping British slavery. The Seminoles supported themselves by hunting, fishing, gathering fruit, growing crops, and raising cattle. They called Maitland "Fumecheliga," meaning muskmelon place or place where the muskmelons grow—a name that extended to its largest lake. As shown in this accompanying photograph, the lake, with its towering pines and cypress, provided food and recreation for early inhabitants. By the early 19th century, the Seminoles became involved in a series of wars with American forces, which brought federal troops into Central Florida. Osceola was tricked into capture in 1837 and died three months later. (Left image courtesy State Archives of Florida.)

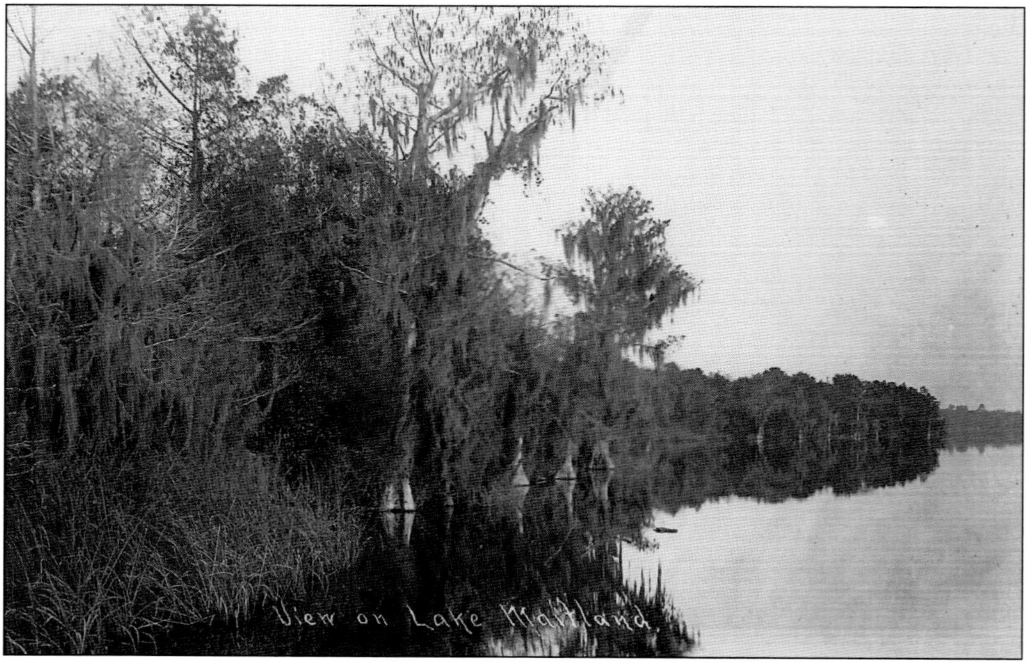

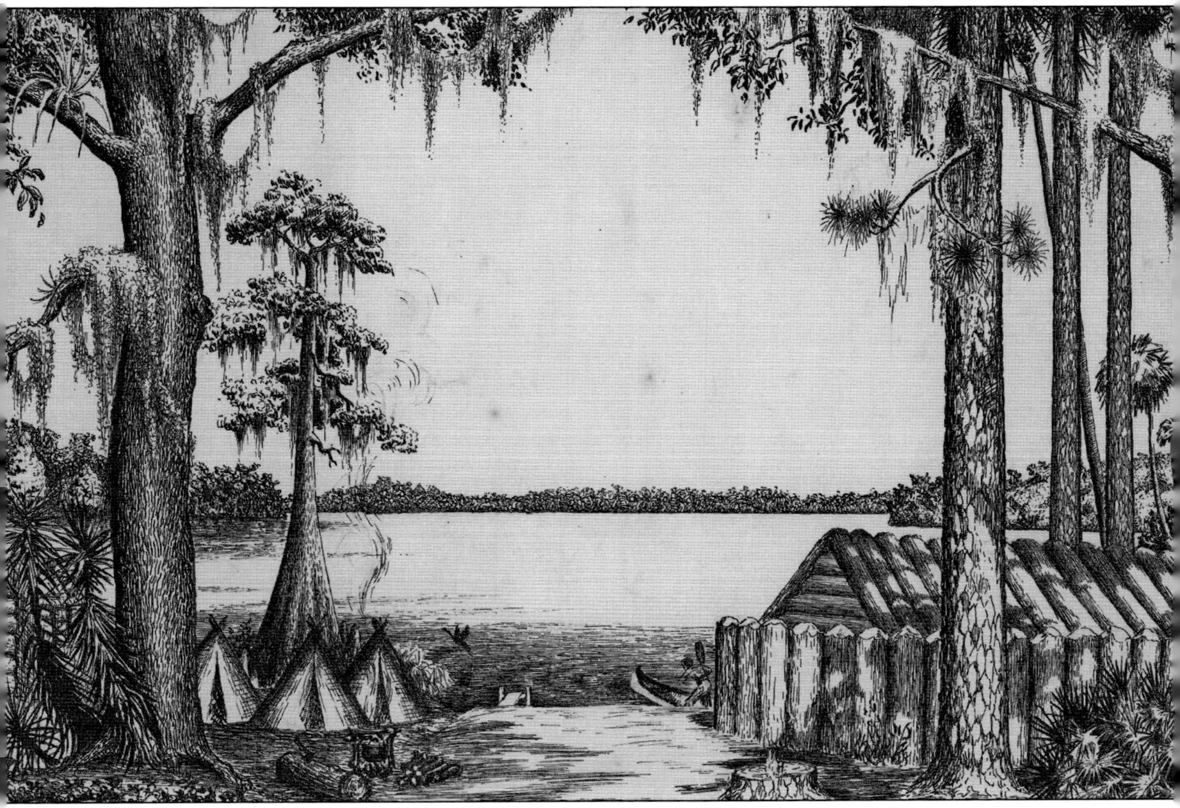

During the Second Seminole War, 1835–1842, U.S. forces built a series of forts across Florida, including Fort Mellon, near present-day Sanford, and Fort Gatlin, near Orlando. In October 1838, a wooden fort, depicted in this 1935 drawing by Georgianna Stone, was built on the western bank of Lake Fumecheliga to serve as a secondary post in the fort supply line and defense system. It was erected by Lt. Col. Alexander Fanning and named to honor Capt. William Seton Maitland, one of Fanning's officers who had died two years earlier after another Florida battle. Fort Maitland was occupied briefly, from October 1838 to April 1839, but never was involved in any armed conflicts. However, the name of a fallen soldier would become the new identity for the area for generations after his death.

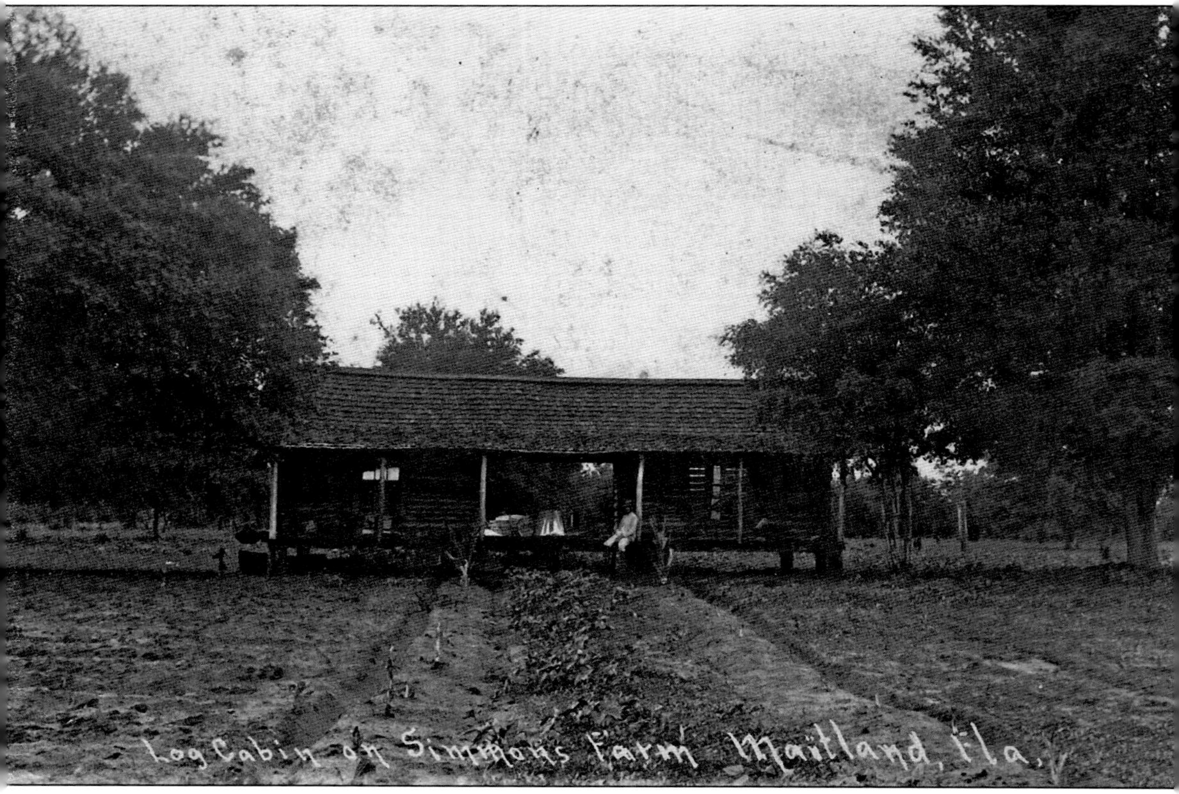

A lone man, possibly Maj. John S. Simmons, sits on the porch of an airy dog-trot-style log cabin built in the late 1800s by the Simmons family. Crops are visible in the sandy yard next to the cabin, located near the shore of Lake Charity. Simmons purchased his property, but many families acquired land with the help of federal homestead laws that allowed them 160 acres if they agreed to clear the land and improve the property for five years. The cabin likely was constructed from longleaf pine trees that previously occupied the Simmonses' acreage and much of the area.

Maj. John S. Simmons, a Confederate veteran of the Civil War, came by oxcart from Mississippi with his wife, Margaret, in 1876. They bought property on the north shore of Lake Charity (now Druid Hills). Their first home was a log house where they farmed and grew citrus. Eventually they lived in this home located on Vanderpool Avenue, now U.S. Highway 17-92. Simmons was the first teacher in Maitland School, a one-room schoolhouse located on Maitland Avenue. He served several terms as city alderman in the late 1890s and early 1900s. The Simmonses helped found the First Presbyterian Church in Lake Maitland. (Both courtesy of Jim Hulbert.)

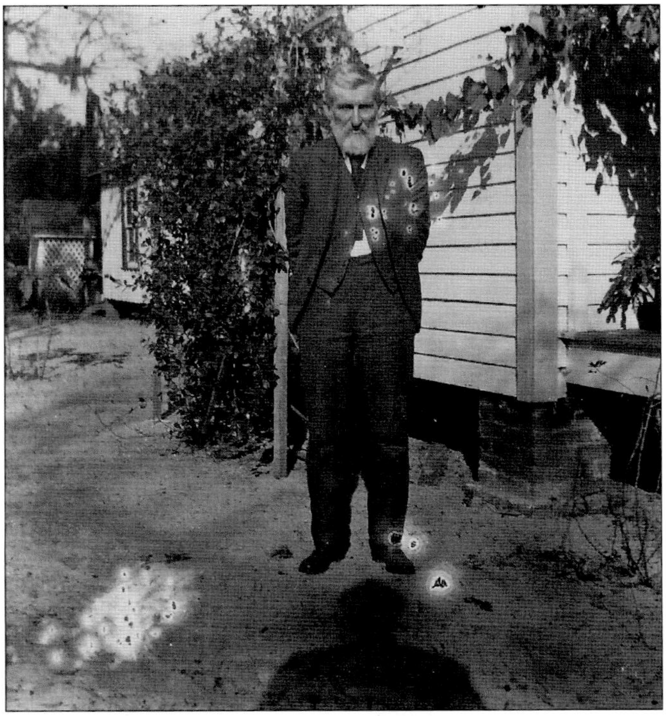

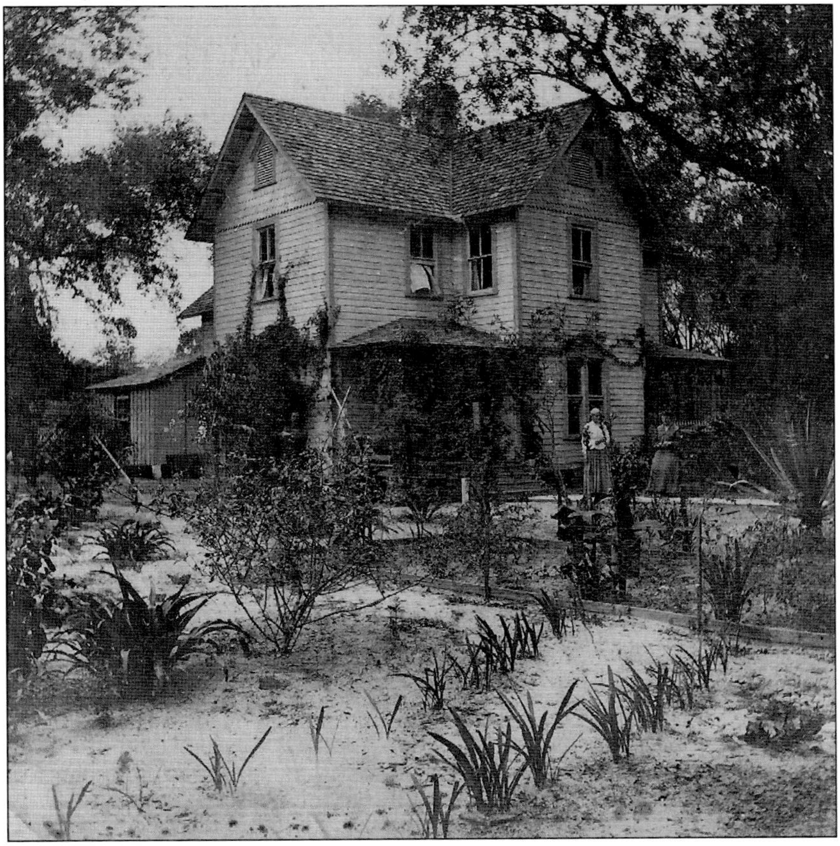

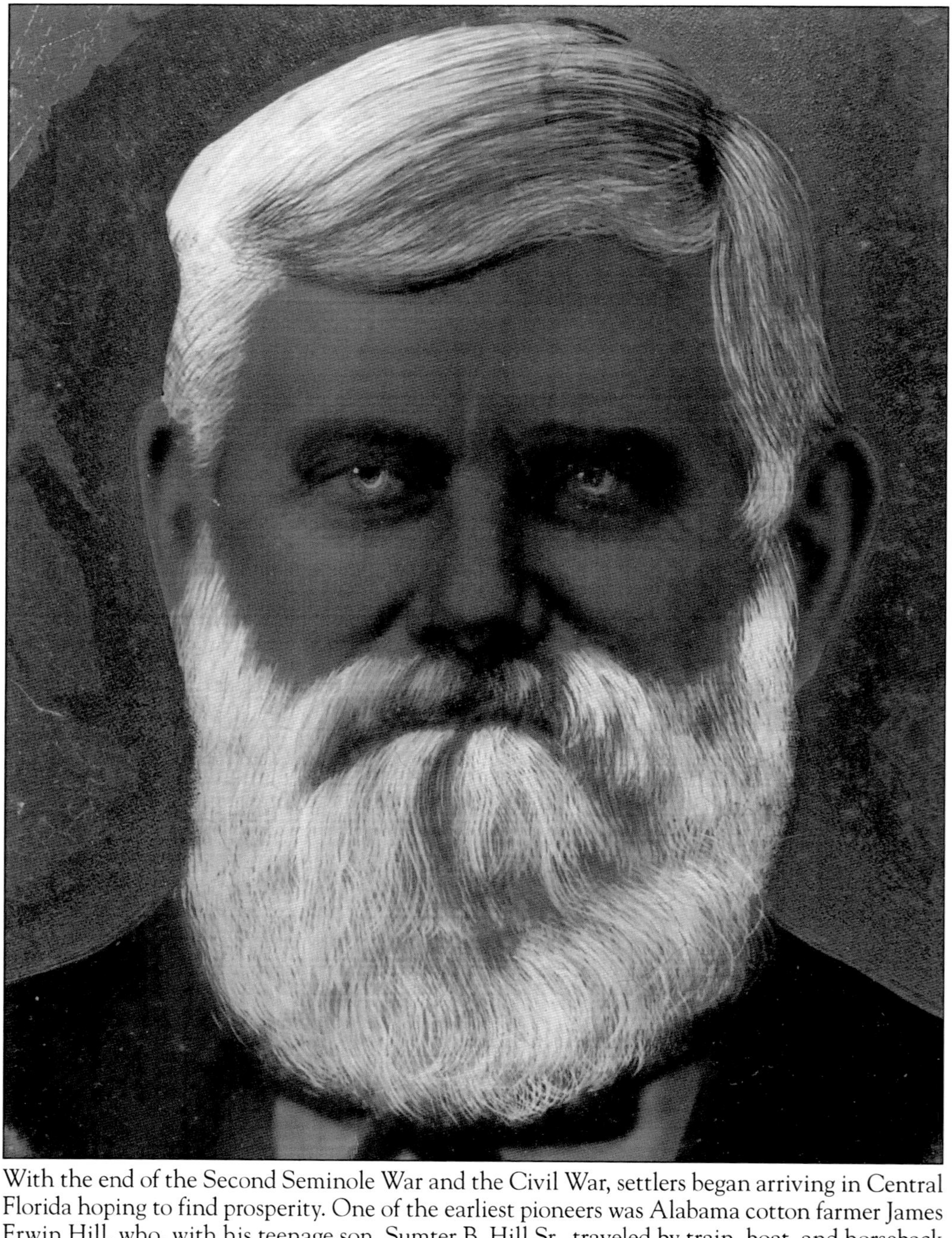

With the end of the Second Seminole War and the Civil War, settlers began arriving in Central Florida hoping to find prosperity. One of the earliest pioneers was Alabama cotton farmer James Erwin Hill, who, with his teenage son, Sumter B. Hill Sr., traveled by train, boat, and horseback to the area. They built a log cabin, and in 1874, they planted a 10-acre citrus grove adjacent to Lake Faith, one of the area's many lakes, using seed from fruit grown in the Kissimmee area. The Hill family established one of the area's first citrus nurseries and replanted after the devastating 1894–1895 freezes. After a trip to Spain, Sumter Hill brought back many varieties of citrus to his groves. The Hill family was involved for a century in citrus production and with local growers' organizations as well as city leadership in Maitland, where both Sumter Hill Sr. and his son J. Harold Hill served as mayor.

This photograph depicts the home of Edwin and Ella Turner, formerly of Yellow Bluff, Florida, who came to Lake Maitland and established one of the first stores in the area. Located on the corner of what is now Maitland and Horatio Avenues, the store carried a variety of general merchandise, including dry goods, groceries, clothing, boots, shoes, and hats. Ella Turner ran a boardinghouse on the second story of the store building.

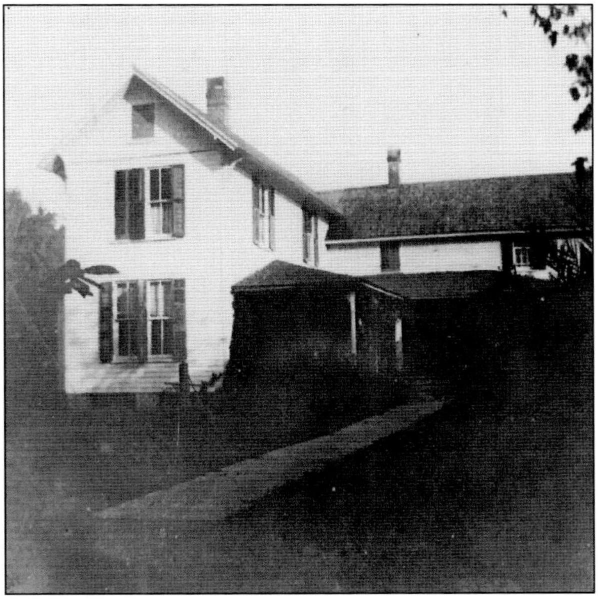

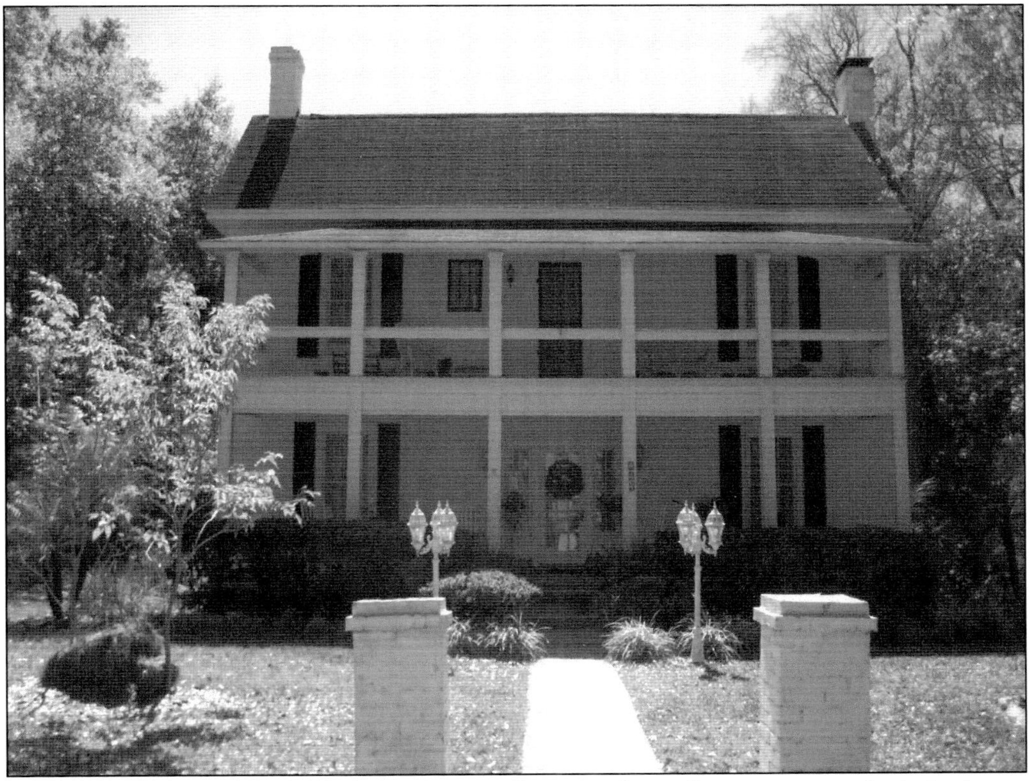

Louis A. Wise, Maitland's second postmaster and owner of a small-town canteen, built this home around 1876, located at 230 West Ventris Avenue. It was sold in 1887 to Dr. Valentine H. Taliaferro, formerly of Atlanta, Georgia. His son, Benjamin Taliaferro, was very active in Maitland social circles and often entertained his friends by singing and playing his banjo. His many business interests in Maitland included a livestock farm north of town and citrus groves on Lake Catherine. The home, a fine example of historic preservation, remains a private residence today.

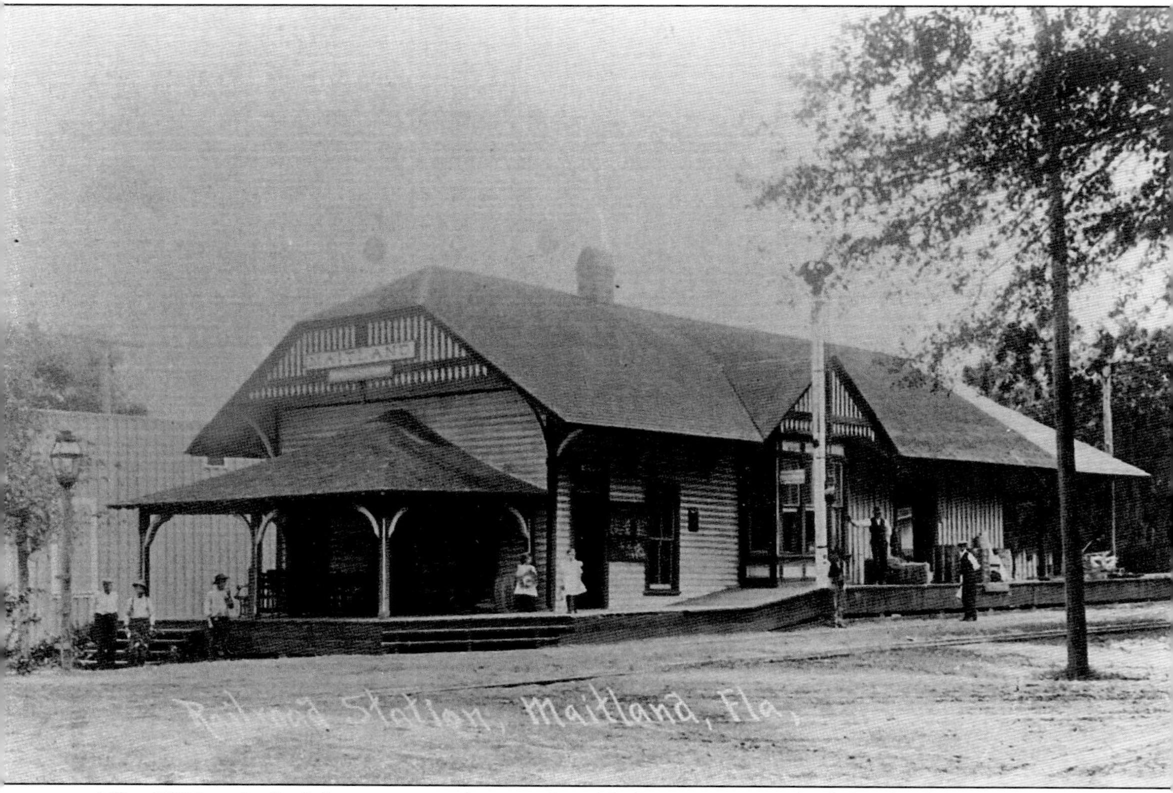

The 1880 arrival of the trains to the area heralded a new era in the life of Lake Maitland. This depot was built a year later for the South Florida Railroad Company, which was founded by three area men and planned to extend from the St. Johns River to Charlotte Harbor on the Gulf of Mexico. On July 1, 1880, the railroad was completed from Sanford to Maitland, and three months later, it connected to Orlando. The engines had extended smokestacks to protect passengers from smoke and cinders. Most importantly, the tracks linked Central Florida to Northern cities, creating markets for area crops and citrus and providing regular mail delivery and tourist transportation. The depot was located on what is now the southeast corner of Maitland and Horatio Avenues.

Two

Founding of the City

In the late 1800s, Lake Maitland grew from a group of settlers into a thriving community and, finally, into an incorporated city. The arrival of the railroad heralded a new era of communication and connection with other areas of the United States. New businesses were formed, including a sawmill, a newspaper, and hotels to house the many visitors who were drawn to the area's natural beauty and mild winters. Many chose to make Lake Maitland their regular winter respite, building homes and often growing citrus and gardens on their properties to enjoy the subtropical climate. With these newcomers, the city, incorporated in 1885, became a cultural and social center. Churches were built, a post office was created, a school was formed, and a public library was founded. Many people flocked to Packwood Hall, located on Maitland Avenue, which served as a commercial and social gathering place for the community. By 1875, only charred remains marked the lakefront site that had once been Fort Maitland, but nearby its name was carried forward in a bustling community that was rising to meet the dawn of a new century.

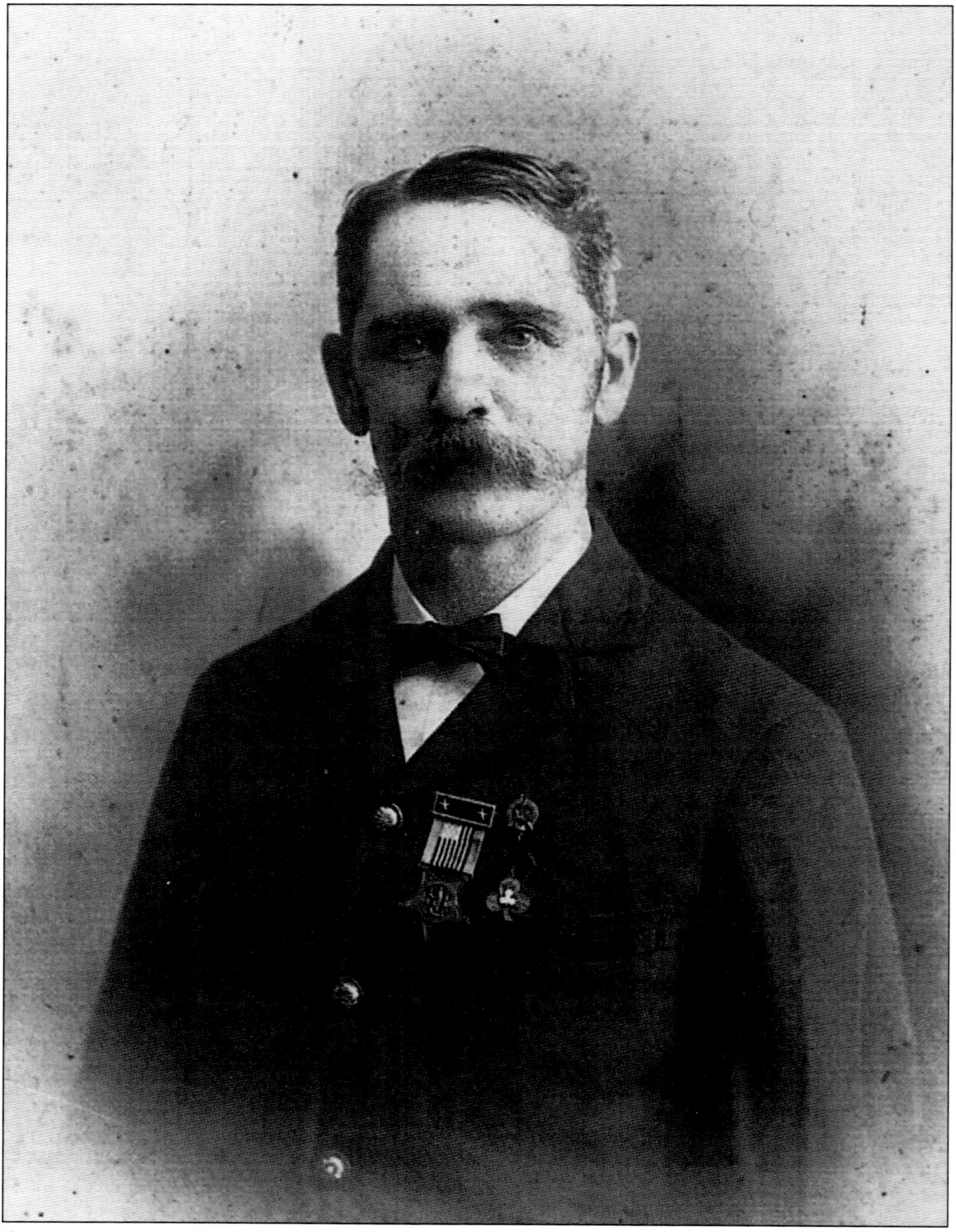

George Horatio Packwood, a New York native, came to Lake Maitland in the early 1870s with his brother, Dr. Richard Packwood. Most recently, they had lived in Louisiana, where they were in the grocery and sugar business after the Civil War. George Packwood quickly became involved in the young community. He built a large house and planted an orange grove on the north side of Lake Sybelia, where he lived for many years. His brother was a physician in the area; and both were involved in helping plant trees to line the city's streets. Three Maitland streets are named for George Packwood: George Street, Horatio Avenue, and Packwood Avenue. Packwood also filed the first plat for the town in September 1881.

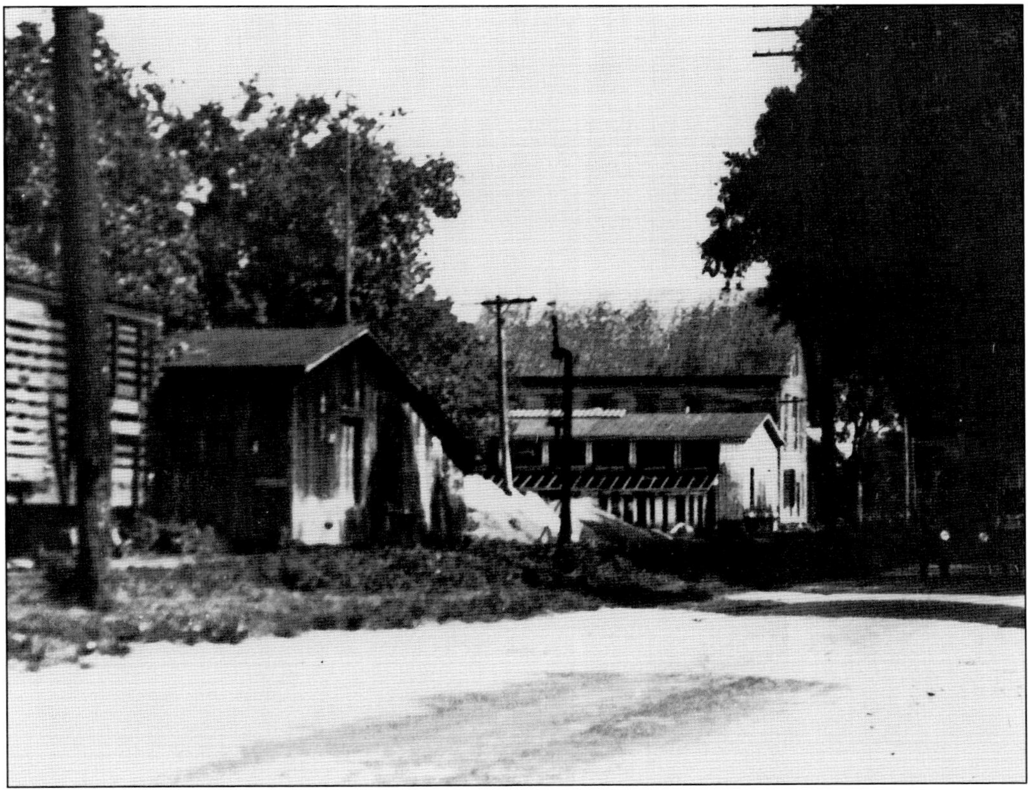

Packwood Hall, originally called the Opera House, was built by George Packwood around 1873 and located along the railroad tracks in the central part of the city. The three-story building was one of the first buildings constructed in Lake Maitland and served as the social center of the community. Its many functions, including its use as a city meeting place, a skating rink, and a theater, made it one of the most important buildings in the city. It was torn down in 1926.

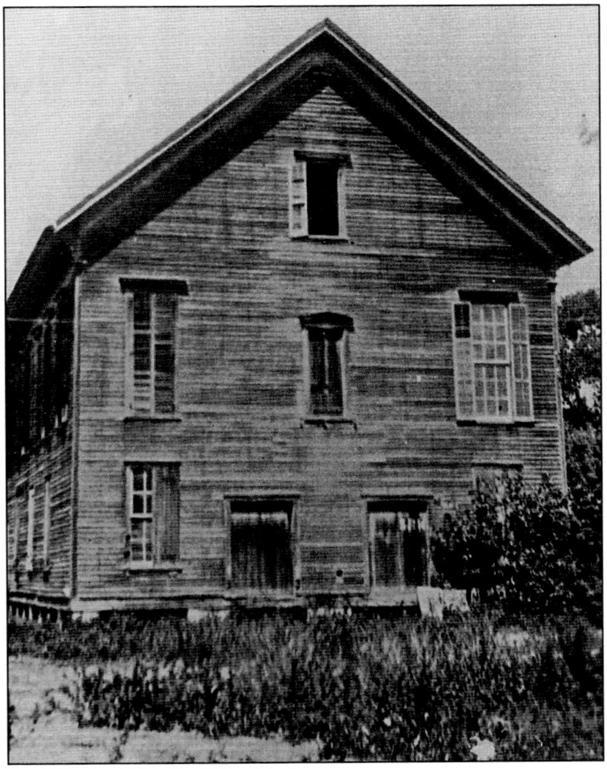

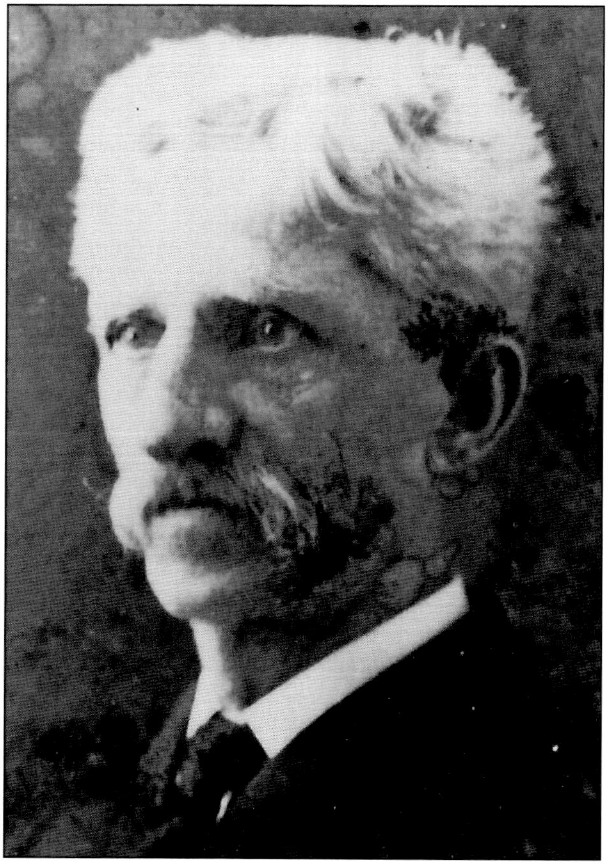

Isaac Vanderpool and his spacious home on the shores of Lake Maitland are shown in these two photographs. Vanderpool, a native of New York City, became interested in Florida during a trip to South America in which he met Henry S. Kedney and Josiah Eaton. In 1870, Vanderpool and Kedney came to Lake Maitland, where Vanderpool bought 160 acres on the lakefront and left Kedney to plant a citrus grove on the property. Six years later, Vanderpool and his new bride, Harriet, moved permanently to Lake Maitland, where he helped lay out the town and built the city's first citrus packinghouse in 1892. Along with Kedney and the Packwood brothers, Vanderpool planted oaks to beautify the city, and he remained an active city promoter during the course of his long life. This photograph of his house, taken around 1890, shows the Vanderpool family enjoying the porch with members of the Kingsley family, who lived next door.

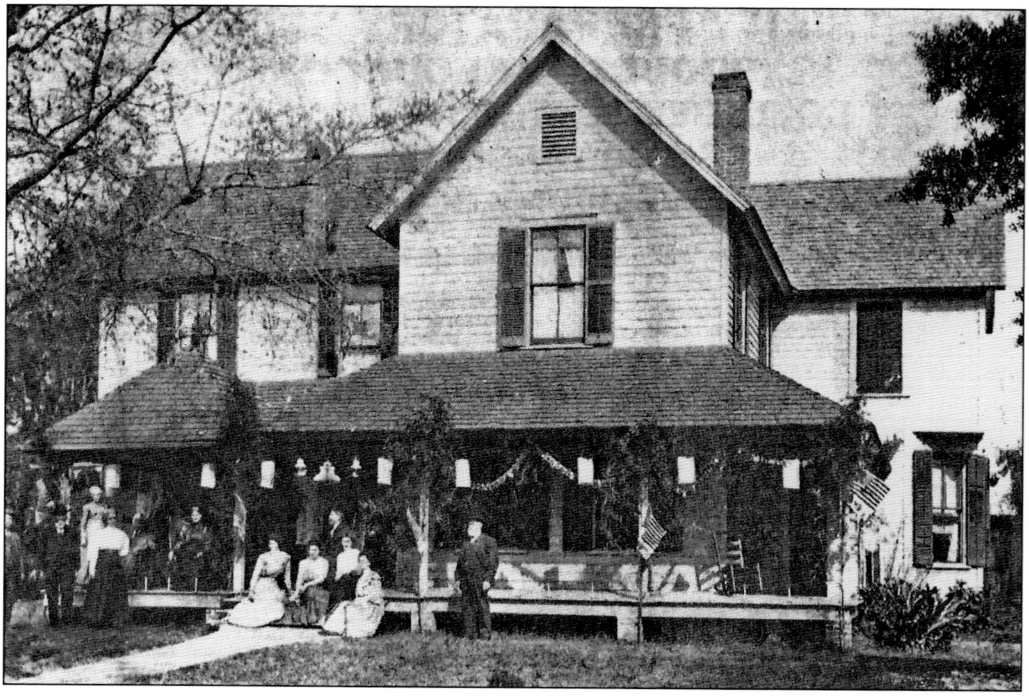

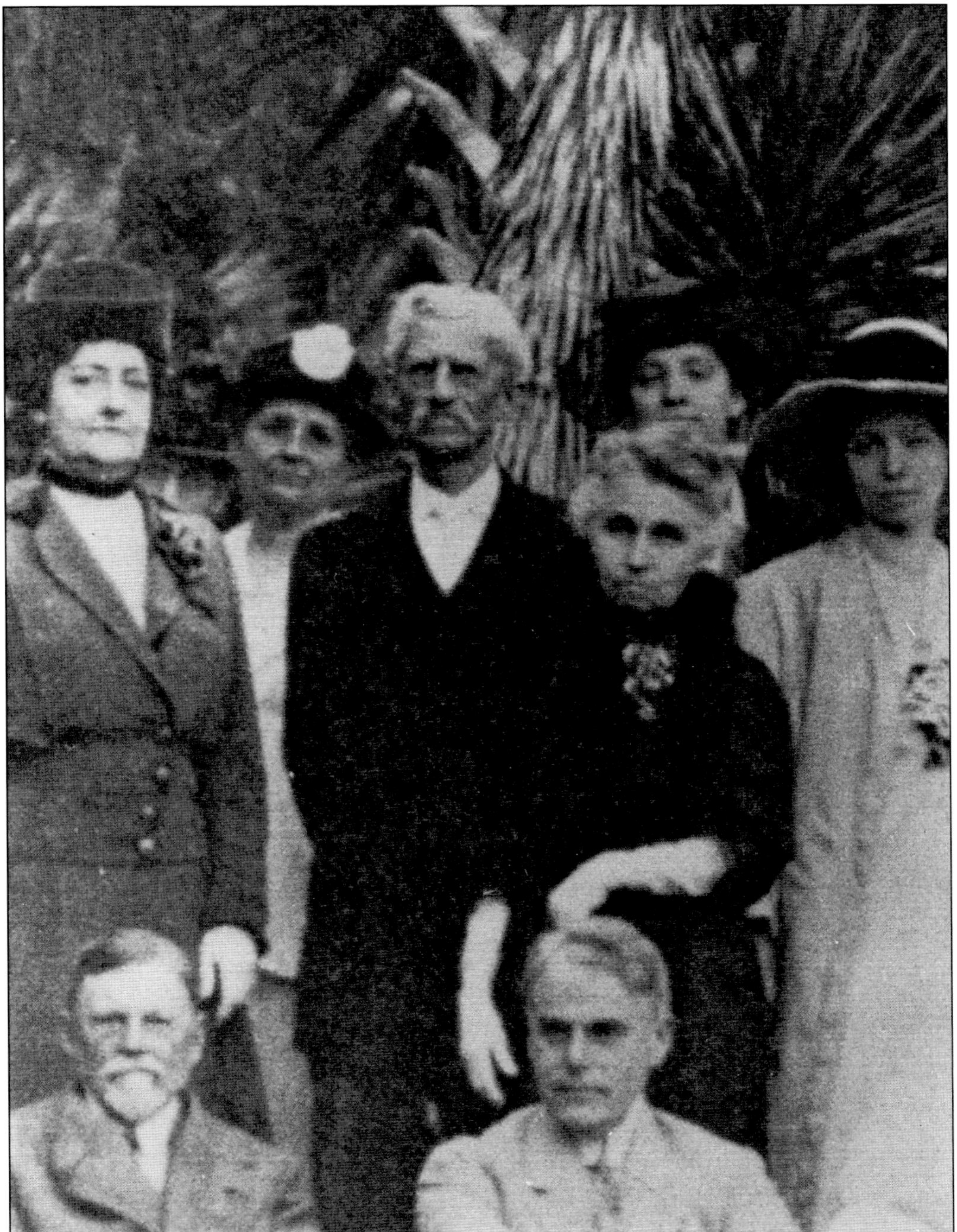

The Vanderpool family was an important pioneer group in the earliest days of Lake Maitland. Isaac and Harriet, shown in the middle of this group, were very involved in civic affairs that included the founding of nearby Eatonville, the start and operation of the Florida Audubon Society, the formation of the Episcopal Church of the Good Shepherd, and helping record much of the city's early history. In 1927, Harriet Vanderpool, who was born in England, authored "Maitland Song," to be sung to the tune of "America the Beautiful," and it was adopted by the chamber of commerce as the city's official song.

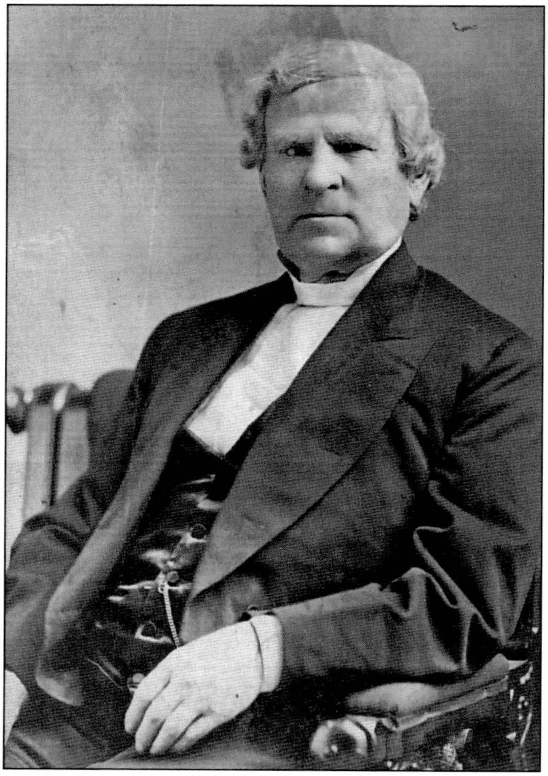

Lewis Lawrence was a New York millionaire who bought 35 acres on the southwest shore of Lake Maitland in 1880. Within three years, he had planted 2,200 orange trees and a 4-acre vegetable garden. An active Republican, abolitionist, and temperance promoter, Lawrence hosted Pres. Chester A. Arthur at his property in 1883. In 1887, Lawrence was one of several Maitland men who helped establish nearby Eatonville, now the oldest incorporated African American city in the United States. Joseph E. Clark, an African American, founded the town on property he bought from Josiah Eaton, a Maitland resident for whom Clark worked. Out of gratitude, Clark named the city for his friend, Eaton. Lawrence bought another 22 acres from Eaton, giving 12 to Clark and 10 acres to the African Methodist Episcopal Church, which was named St. Lawrence Church in his honor. (Courtesy Department of College Archives and Special Collections, Olin Library, Rollins College, Winter Park.)

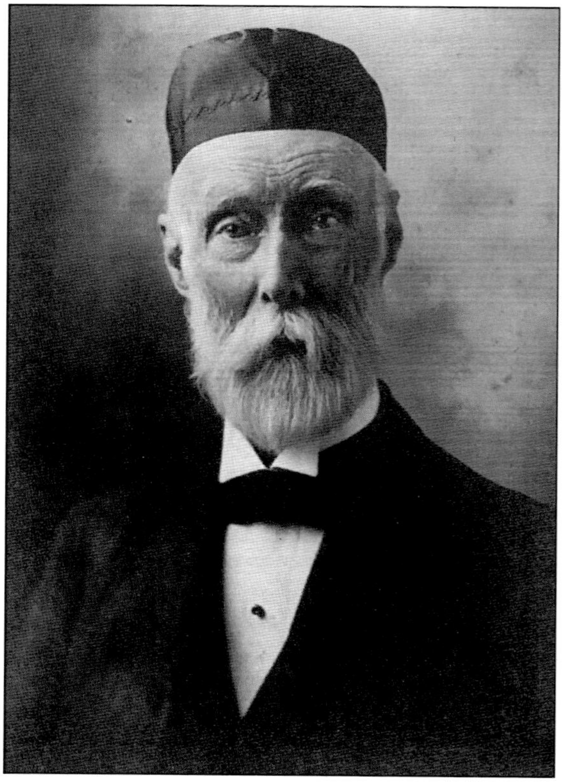

One of the city's early winter residents was Edward Hungerford, a banker from Chester, Connecticut, whose life also intersected with the early days of Eatonville. In 1887, Hungerford's son, Robert, came with him to Lake Maitland. Robert was a physician who befriended a group of young African Americans and exhorted them to get a good education. After providing free medical care to one of these young men, sick with typhoid fever, Robert contracted the disease and died. In 1889, the African American community started the Robert Hungerford School in memory of the doctor—a private boarding and day school for African Americans and the first of its kind in the South. In 1900, Robert's parents deeded 40 acres of land in Eatonville for the school. Edward Hungerford also gave the town of Lake Maitland the property west of Lake Lily that remains a park today.

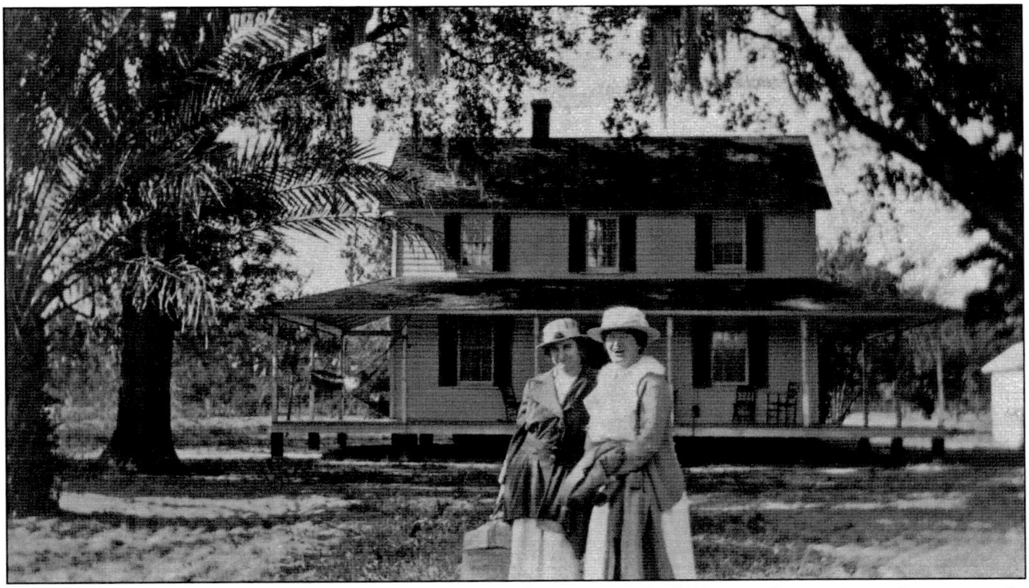

Two smiling women are shown standing before the Hungerford House, located on the west side of Lake Maitland. Built in the late 1870s, it was the home of Edward Hungerford, a Connecticut banker, who came with his family to escape the winter cold. A second photograph shows the residence's shady yard that dipped down to the lake. The house was later owned by the Johnston and Bronson families. The Lake Maitland area, touted for its health benefits and mild climate, drew a number of winter residents every year—a number that increased with the 1880 arrival of the railroad. Prior to that time, visitors wanting to reach Lake Maitland had to arrange travel to Jacksonville, take a steamboat south on the St. Johns River to Sanford, and then ride by horse or ox transport over a dusty, rough military trail.

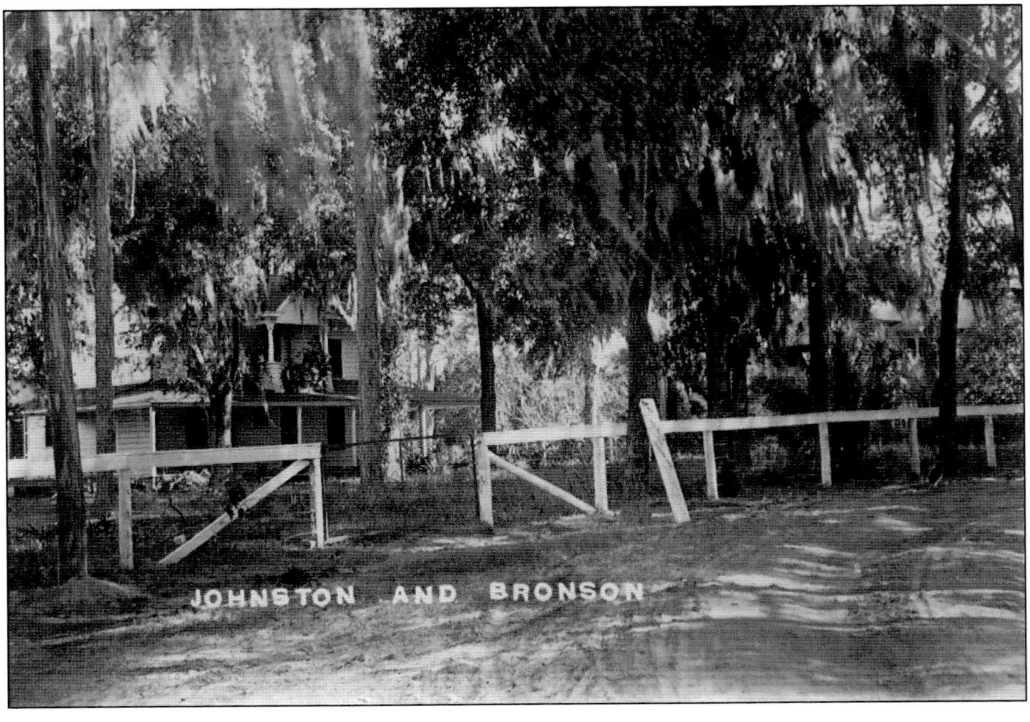

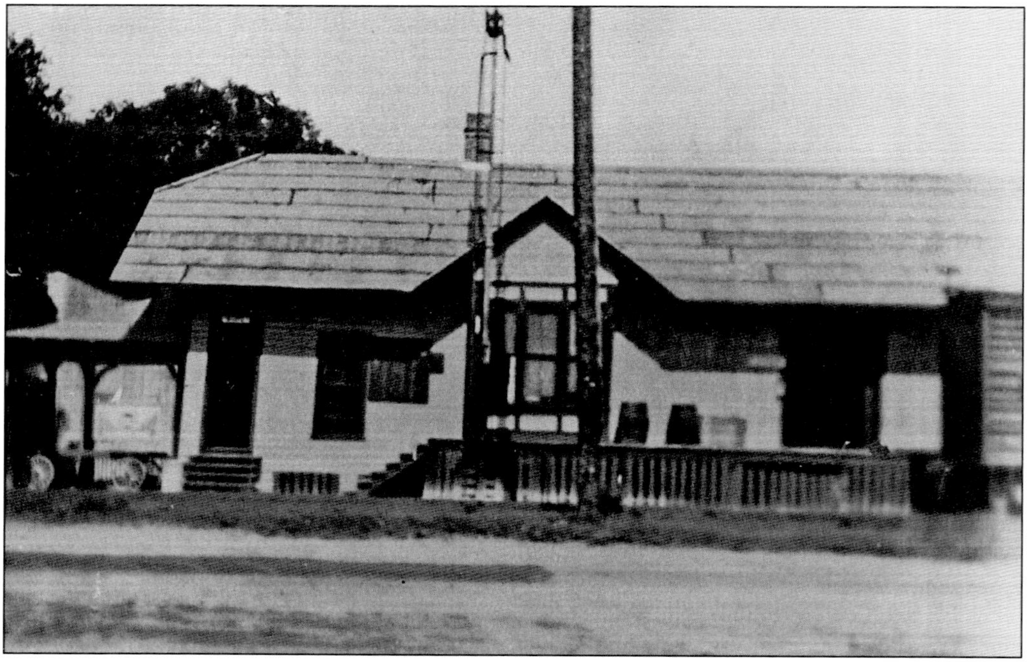

As the city continued to grow, the railroad depot became an important part of life to residents, bringing mail, goods, and visitors and shipping out important products, particularly citrus, to other markets. These two photographs depict the depot, located at what is now the southeast corner of Maitland and Horatio Avenues. It ran north-south along the length of the track and featured a raised loading dock. The Maitland Band celebrates a long-forgotten event in the picture below but serves as a reminder of the depot's lifeblood to the community. Lake Maitland residents often rode the train to Orlando for a day of shopping—a trip that once required an entire day by horse and buggy.

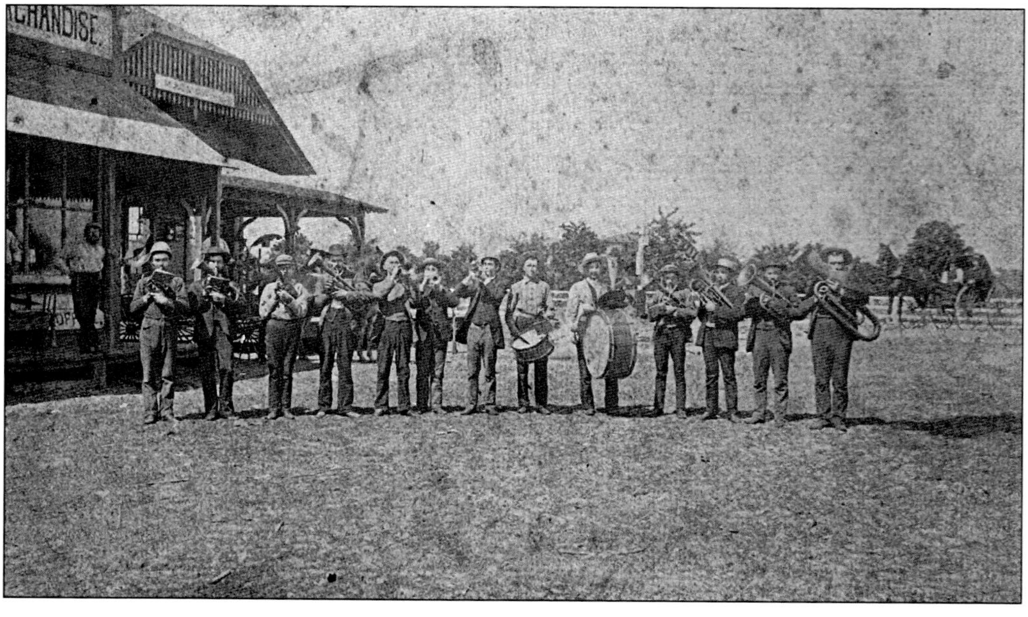

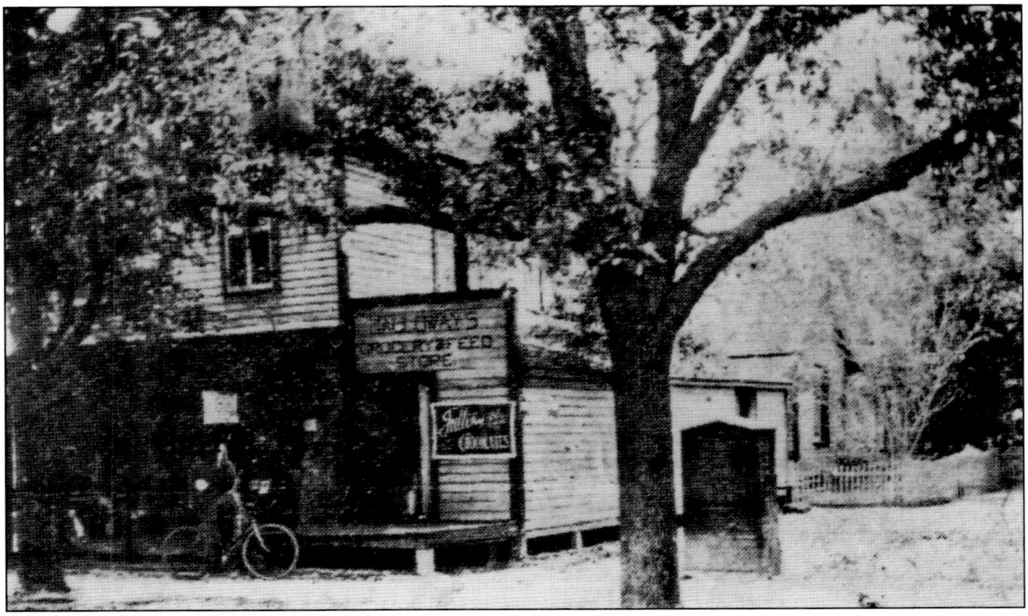

"Galloway's Grocery and Feed Store" proclaims the sign at what was commonly called Galloway's Store, an often frequented market located on the southwest corner of Horatio and Maitland Avenues. The store also served as a gathering place for community members, as shown by the group of men sitting on the porch. Shown from left to right are Braxton Allison Galloway, owner of the store; Maj. John S. Simmons, an early settler; and his son, Pat Simmons, who is seated on the steps. Two other men are unidentified. In 1910, Galloway's son, Carl Hill Galloway, would start the first telephone service in the city in order to connect the store to its customers.

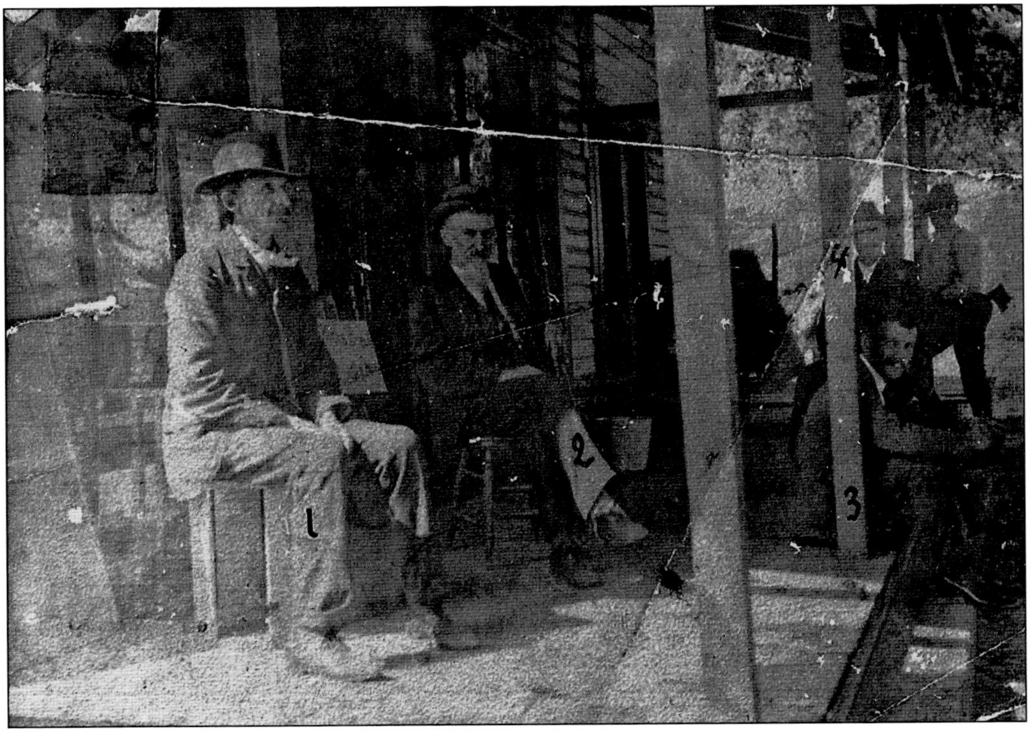

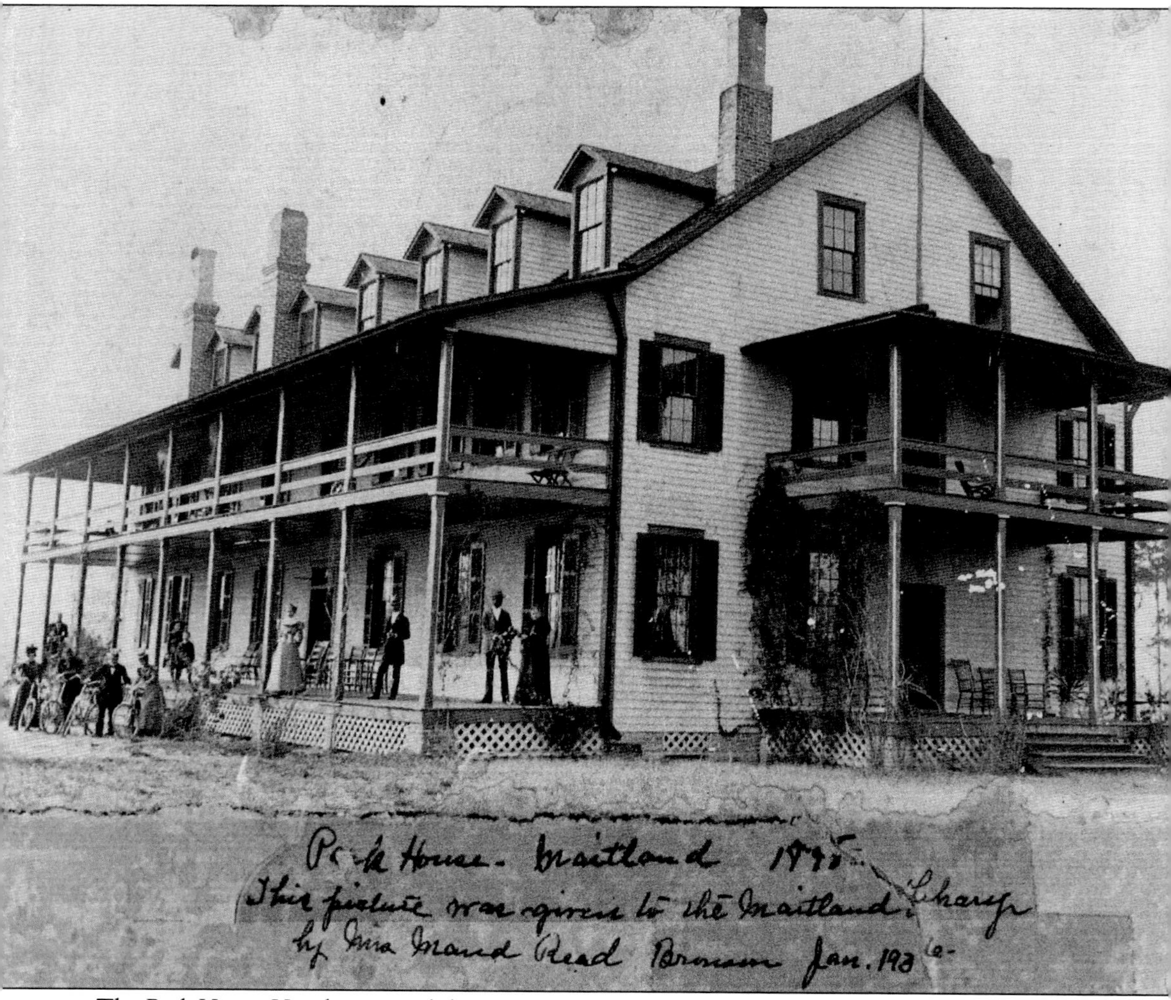

The Park House Hotel, renamed the Maitland Inn in 1902, was built by Philadelphia businessman James Wilcox, who owned much land south of Maitland and also built St. Mary of the Nativity Catholic Church on Lake Eulalia. Most hotel visitors arrived by train, disembarking on special platforms at the city's railroad depot to wait for transportation to local hotels. This photograph from 1895 shows residents enjoying the balmy winter climate on the spacious porch of the hotel, which hosted a number of prominent guests in the area.

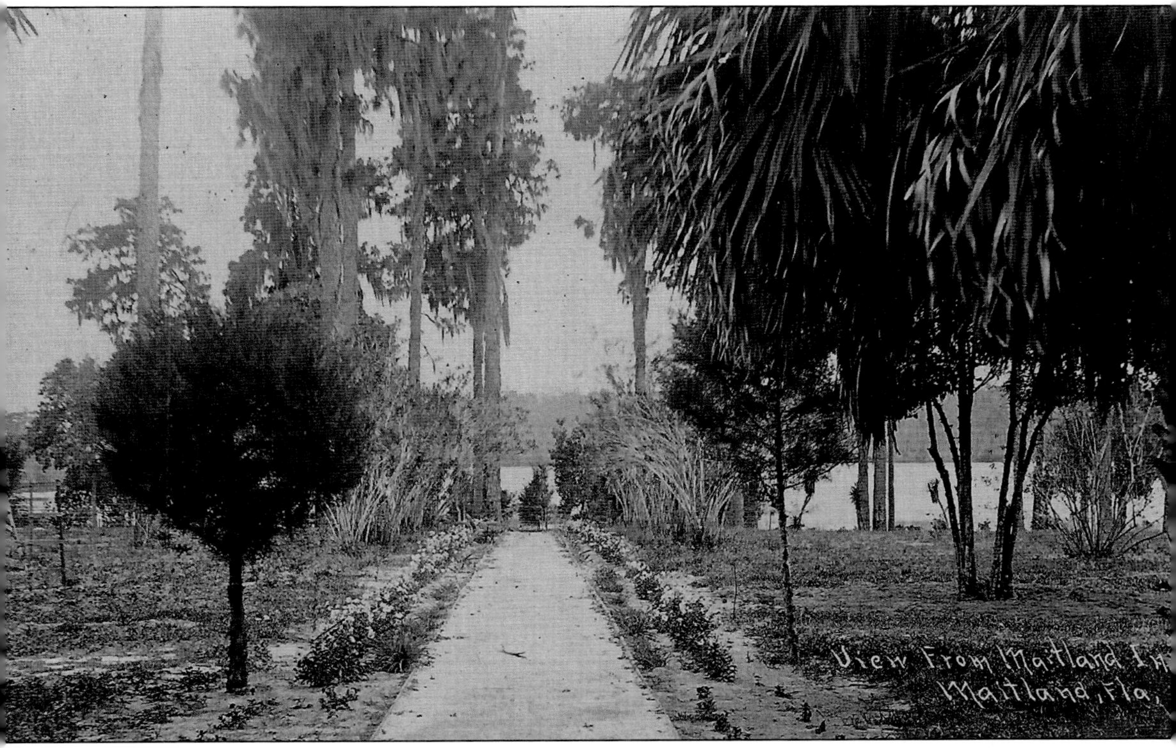

This view is from the rear of the Park House Hotel, showing the hotel's long path to Park Lake and its carefully cultivated grounds. Winter visitors often came for the health benefits touted by area leaders and to oversee their investments in citrus groves that thrived in the local environment. Residents took great pride in their homes, often surrounding them with elaborate gardens, including palm trees and stately cypress that appealed to visitors escaping snow and freezing temperatures in the North. The building was destroyed by fire in 1916.

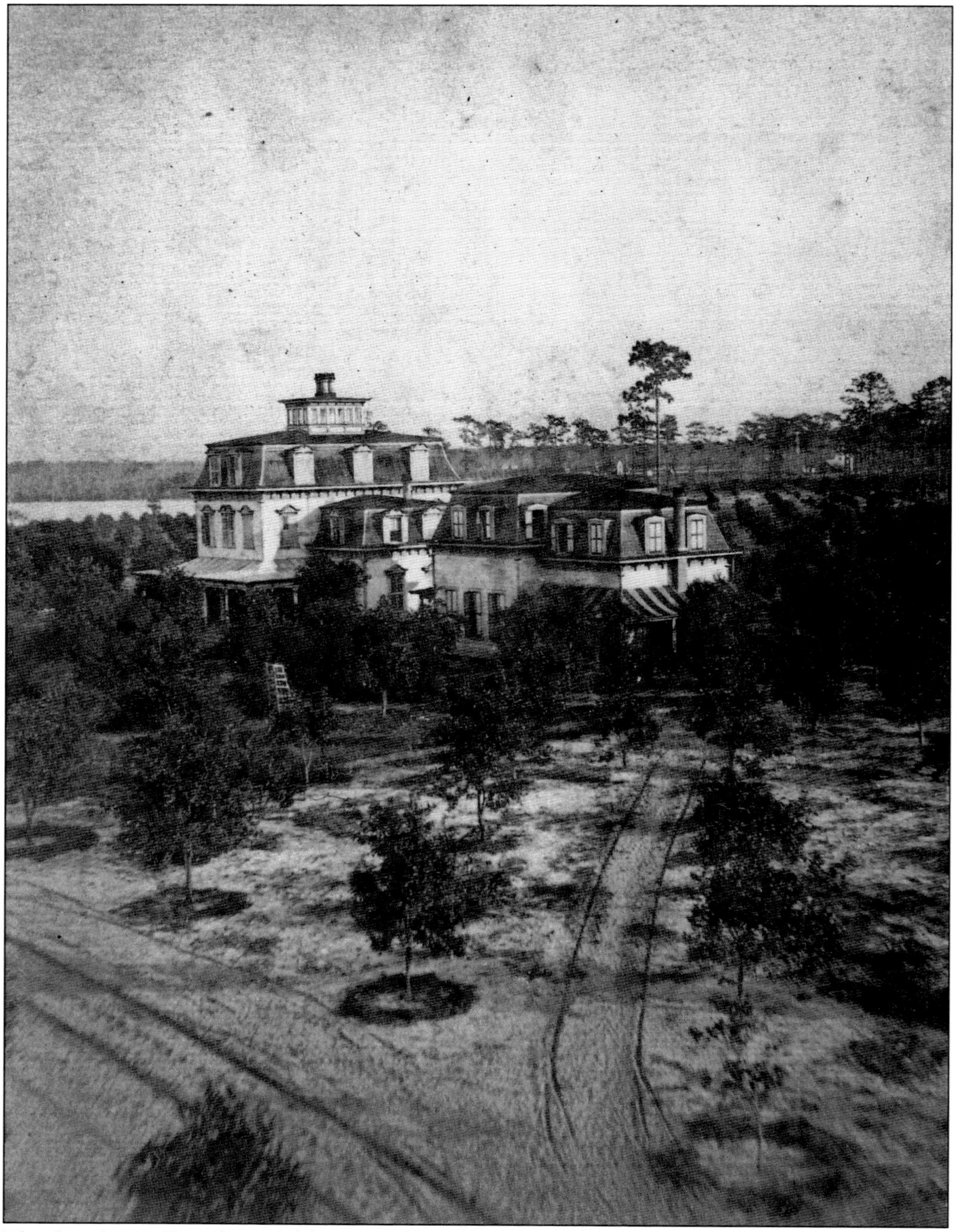

This handsome French-roofed home and hotel, known as the Bigelow House, was built by John Bigelow of Concord, Massachusetts, who bought property on the south shore of Lake Maitland in 1875. One of the features of the building was a rooftop cupola, which offered a view of Lake Maitland and much of the surrounding area. The hotel, located in a grove of 8,800 citrus trees, also had extensive gardens. At the train's Bigelow Station, visitors were met by horse and buggy and transported to the hotel. On June 26, 1881, Bigelow was struck and killed by lightning while closing the cupola windows during a storm. The hotel passed to several owners and later was demolished.

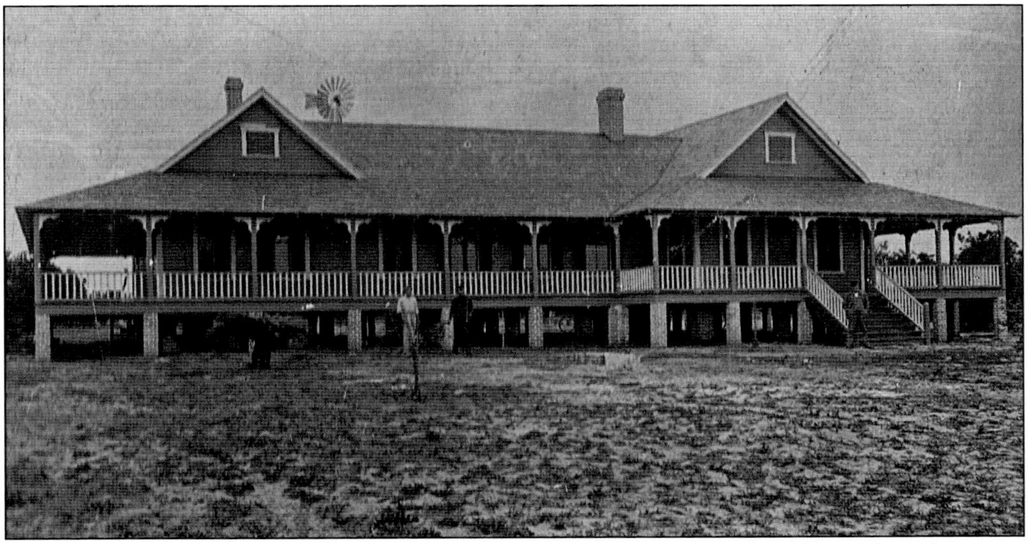

Lake Maitland's early residents often brought a little bit of "home" with them when designing some of the area's earliest residences. William Willett, born in England, wanted his home on 56 acres on the north shore of Lake Maitland to resemble an English seaside resort. Known as Feathered Oaks, the wooden home was built in 1896 and featured five living rooms, a kitchen, and bathrooms as well as water, gas, and other modern conveniences. The Willett home also held pool tables, roulette wheels, and a large gun case. Skeet shoots were frequently held on the grounds, as the photograph below from March 19, 1906, shows. Here a large group readies for shooting, including William B. Jackson (center), an early Maitland resident who served several years as mayor. The family owned one of the area's best producing citrus groves until they were hit by freezes. They were replanted, and William Burwell Willett, Maitland's mayor from 1913 to 1914, continued to own the house until 1940. It was torn down in the 1960s to make way for a housing development.

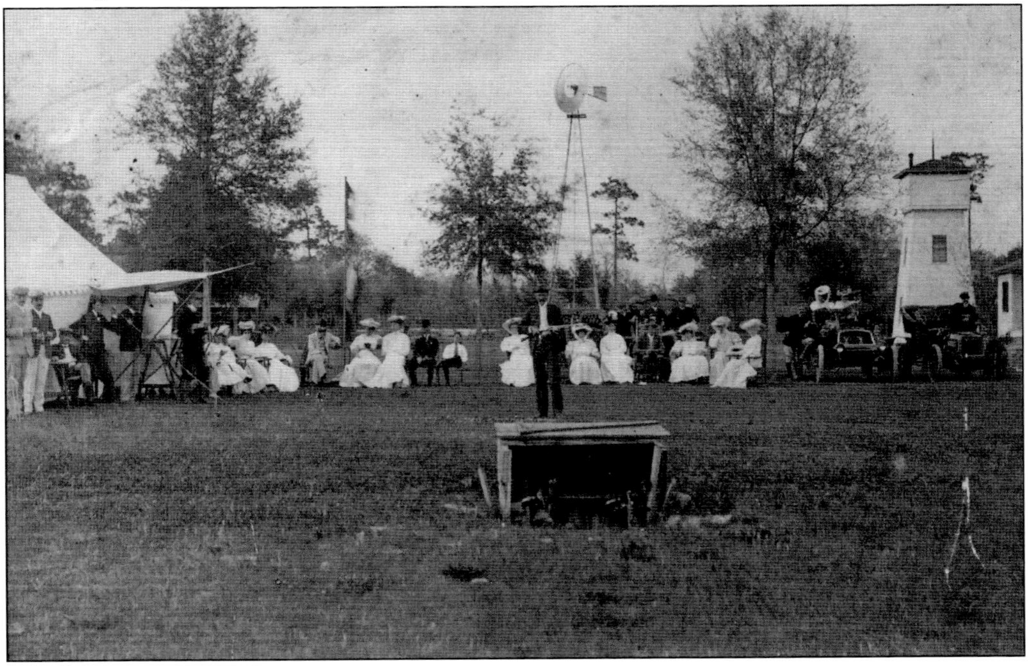

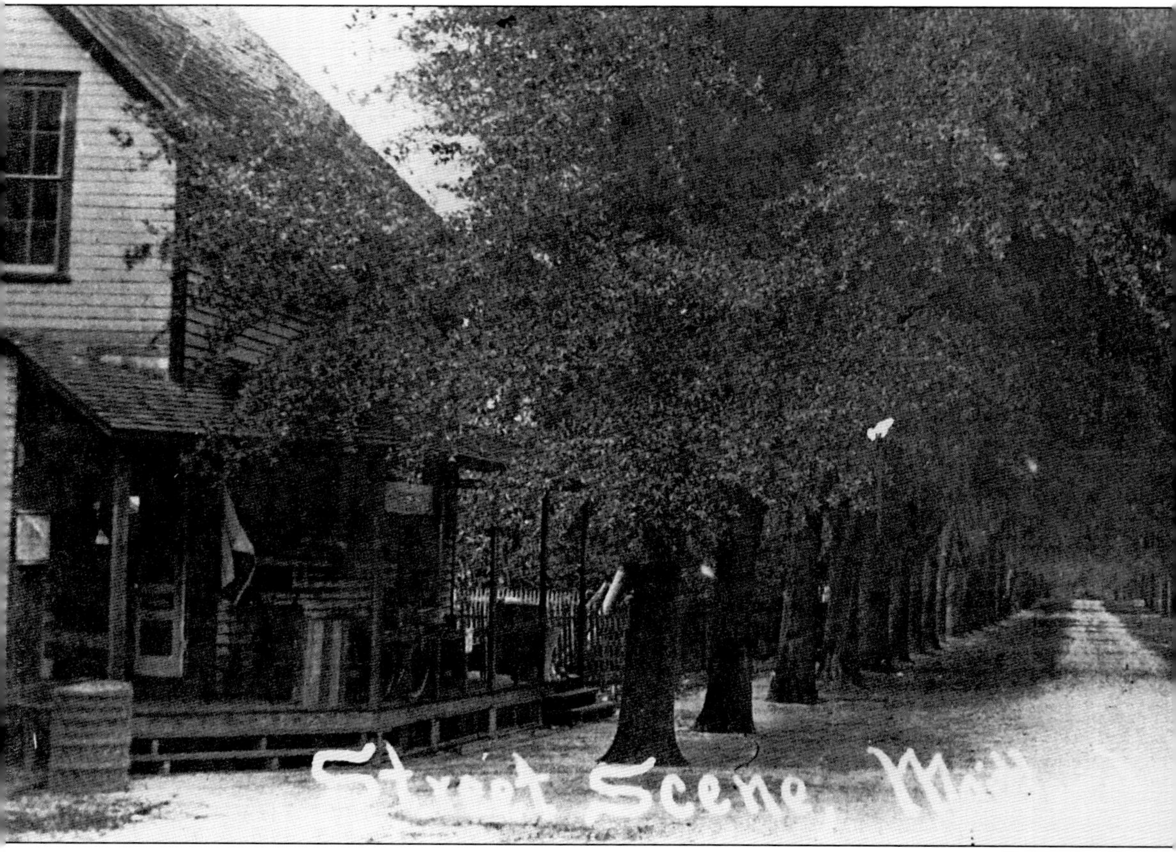

These two photographs, when combined, offer a wider view of Horatio Avenue looking east at the crossing of Maitland Avenue in approximately 1885. The store to the left with a water barrel in front is Edwin Turner's General Store. His wife, Ella, ran a boardinghouse in the quarters above the store. The trees lining the street were planted along the dirt road by early pioneers. A c. 1900 magazine article lauded the city's "handsome water oaks" that bordered the streets and described the community and its clear lake waters as "picturesque." The article also praised city leaders for keeping "all the undergrowth away from the shores, which gently incline to the water's edge."

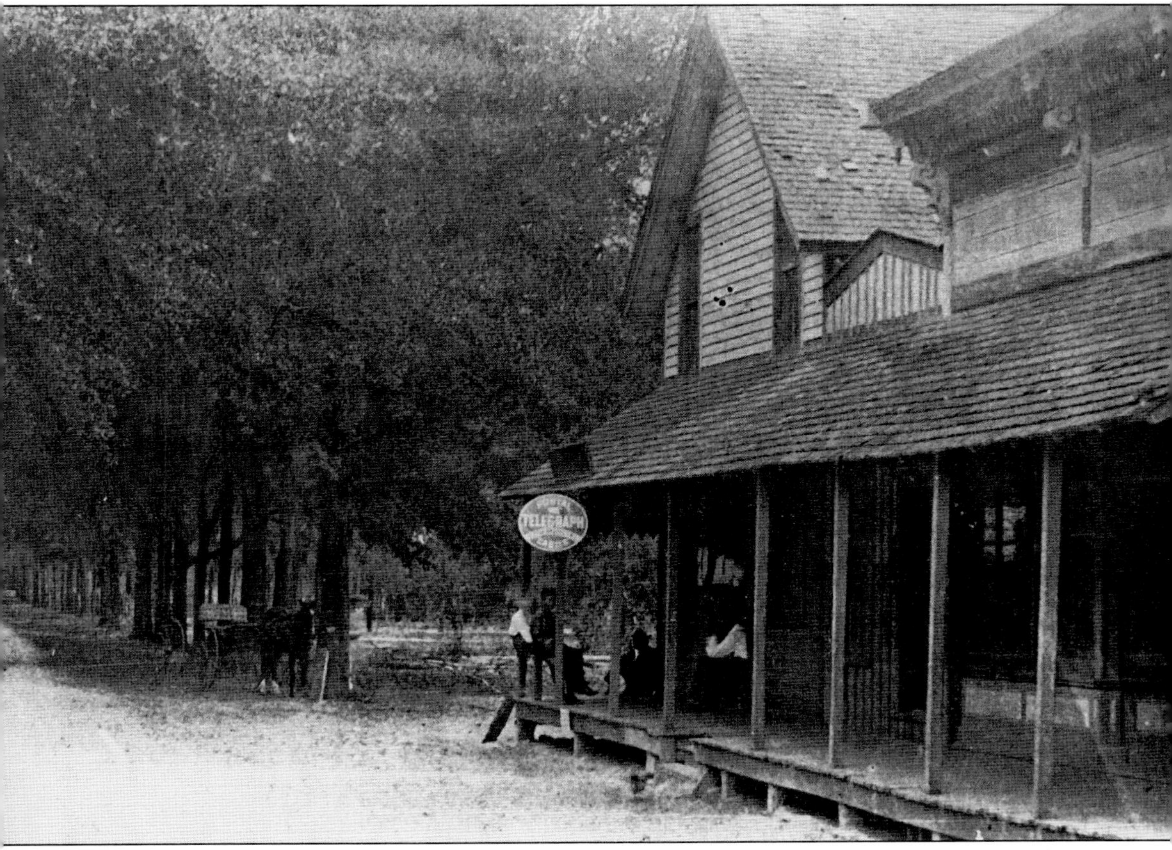

On the right side of the street, a horse and buggy wait patiently while a group of men gather on the front porch of a general store built by Confederate veteran Nicholas Bayard and later owned by Harriet Vanderpool. It was the first store building erected in the city. Note the sign advertising cable, telegraph, and postal services. Such communication services were vital to early residents, serving as links to commerce and to friends and relatives left behind in other parts of the country. To the far right is a general store built and operated by George T. Stith and William B. Jackson.

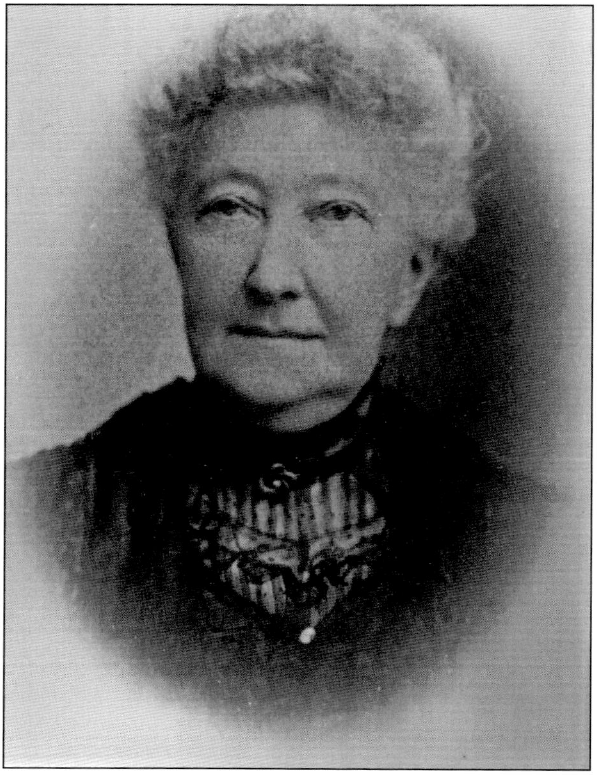

Sarah and William Waterhouse were two of the earliest residents in Maitland, and their presence is still felt in the community. The Waterhouses moved from Greenport, Long Island, New York, in 1882. A Union soldier during the Civil War who had been incarcerated at the infamous prison at Andersonville, Georgia, William brought his carpentry and construction skills to the area, building many of its finest early homes. He also carried the papers to Tallahassee for Maitland's incorporation in 1885 and served as alderman on the first city council, a post he held for 36 years with a few terms as its chair.

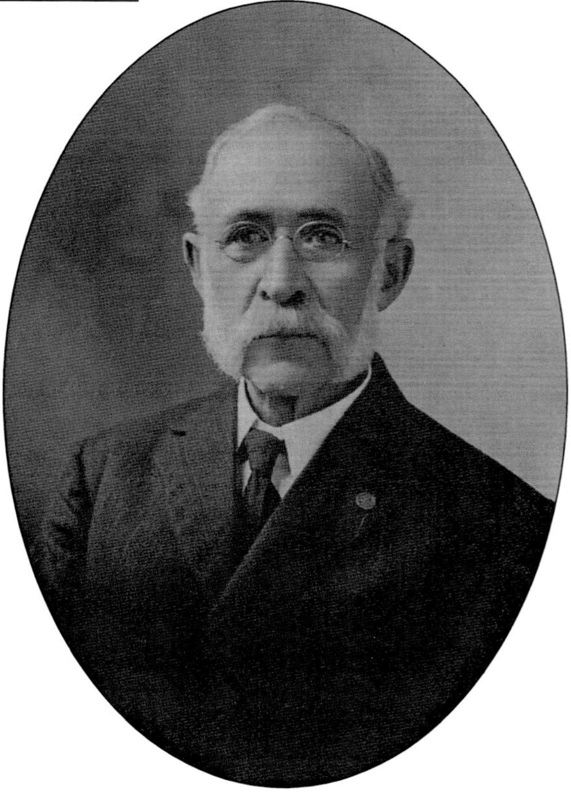

In 1883, Sarah and William Waterhouse built this two-story wooden vernacular-style home on the south shore of Lake Lily. Along with their children, Stella and Charles, they lived in the home for many years. As this photograph shows, Charles, an architect, celebrated his 1896 wedding with a reception at the home. The house remained occupied by Waterhouse descendants until 1989, when it was sold to the City of Maitland. The house was carefully restored and furnished with period furniture and currently is operated as a museum by the Maitland Historical Society. Now known as the Historic Waterhouse Residence, the building is listed on the National Register of Historic Places.

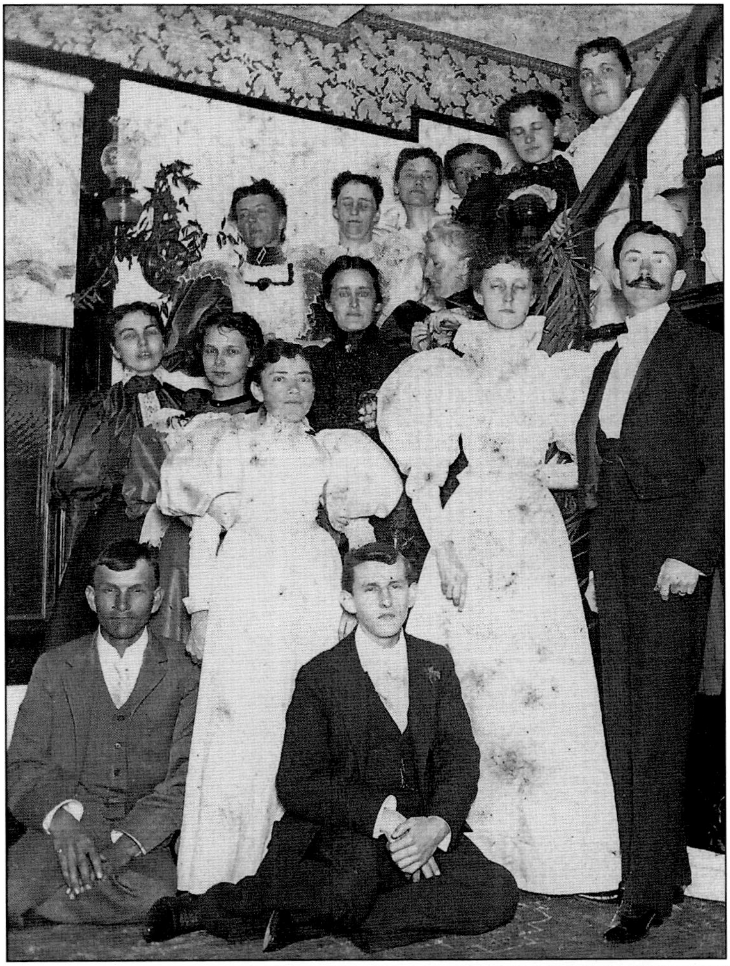

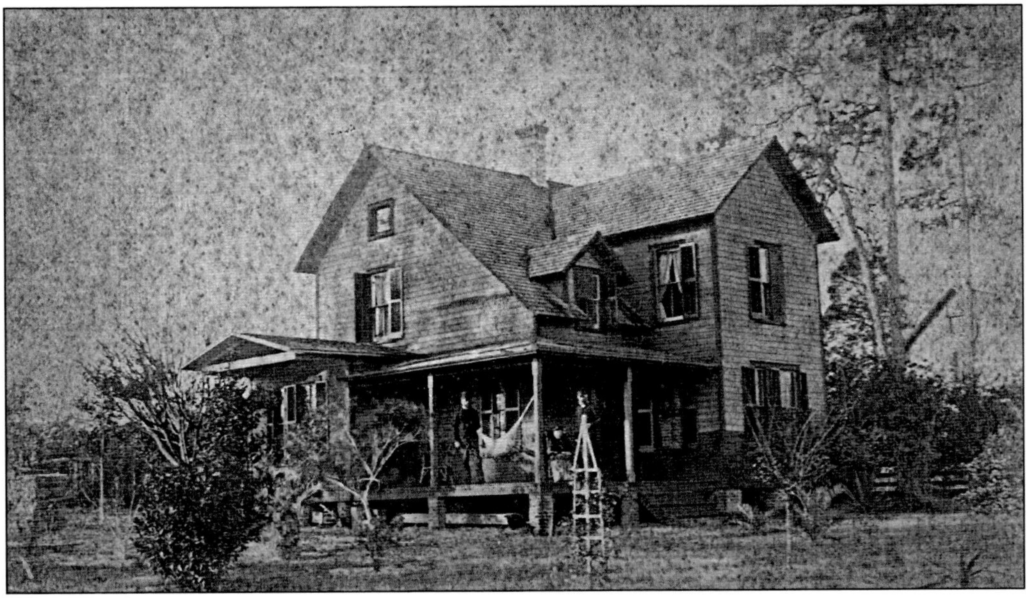

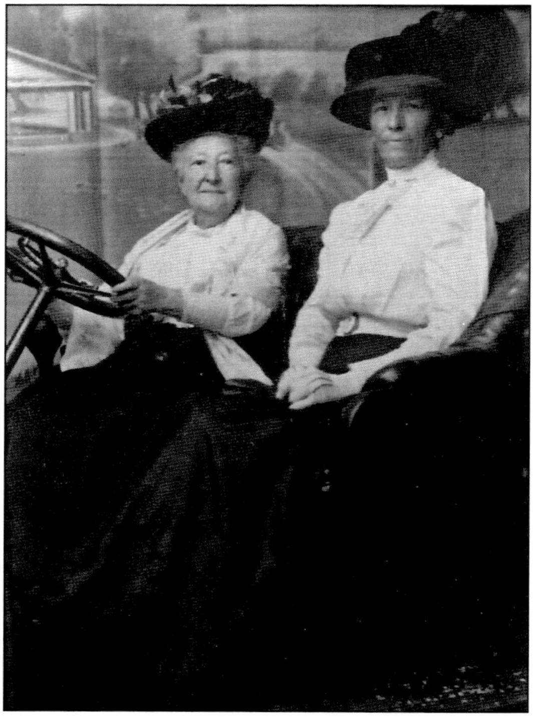

Here Sarah Waterhouse (left) and her good friend Ellen Lancey, wife of author and historian Maj. Sidney Herbert Lancey, pose for a portrait inside what was then a very modern car. The car is real, but the background is a painted backdrop. Years later, Waterhouse's daughter Stella would remember first traveling by train from Sanford to Maitland—transportation that would be made easier in coming years with the advent of the automobile and subsequent road construction and paving.

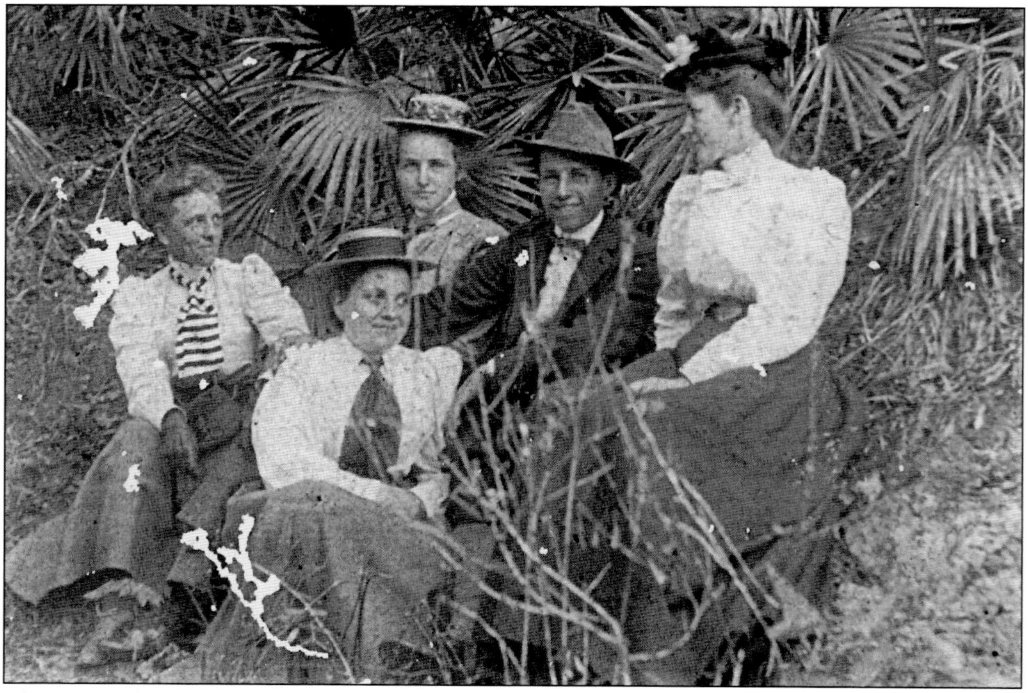

The many pleasures of life in the area included outings to popular outdoor spots. In this March 1899 photograph, a group that includes children from some of the city's founding families poses during a stop on their bicycle trip to Hoosier Springs, now known as Sanlando Springs. Shown from left to right are Caroline Kingsley, Stella Waterhouse, Paula Dommerich, Charles Vanderpool, and Nell Crane, a winter visitor with the Kingsley family.

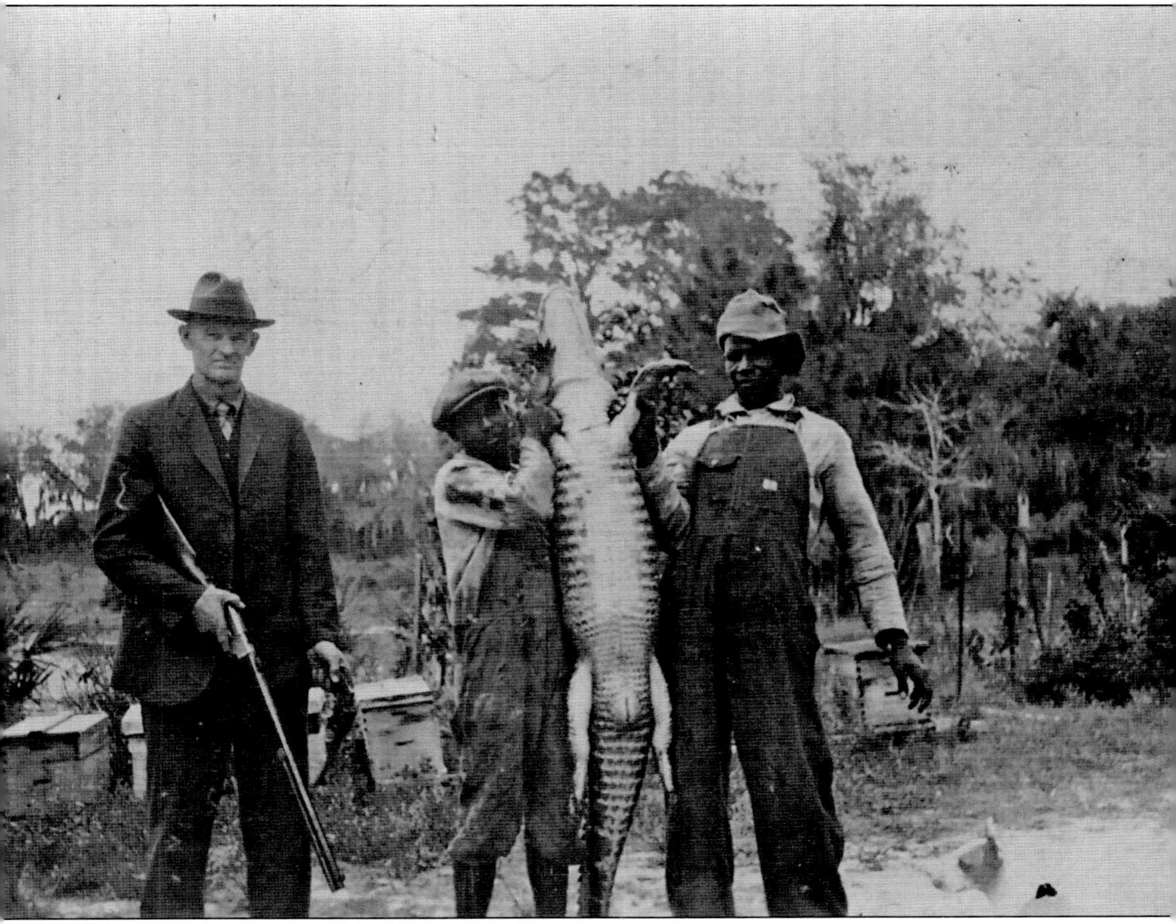

One of the surest signs for visitors that they had reached the subtropical climes of Lake Maitland was the residency of alligators in the area's swamps and eight lakes. An 1893 newspaper article reported that alligators were so desirable to Northern visitors that the reptiles were intentionally placed in Lake Lily, the city's central lake, and were fed daily so they could be seen by excited observers. Alligators were hunted by local residents and prized for their meat, hides, and teeth. As this group of unidentified men shows, area alligators could reach 6 feet or greater. The first laws to protect the state's reptiles were enacted in 1916, and by the middle of the century, they were considered an endangered species. Today their numbers have recovered enough for the state to allow very limited hunting.

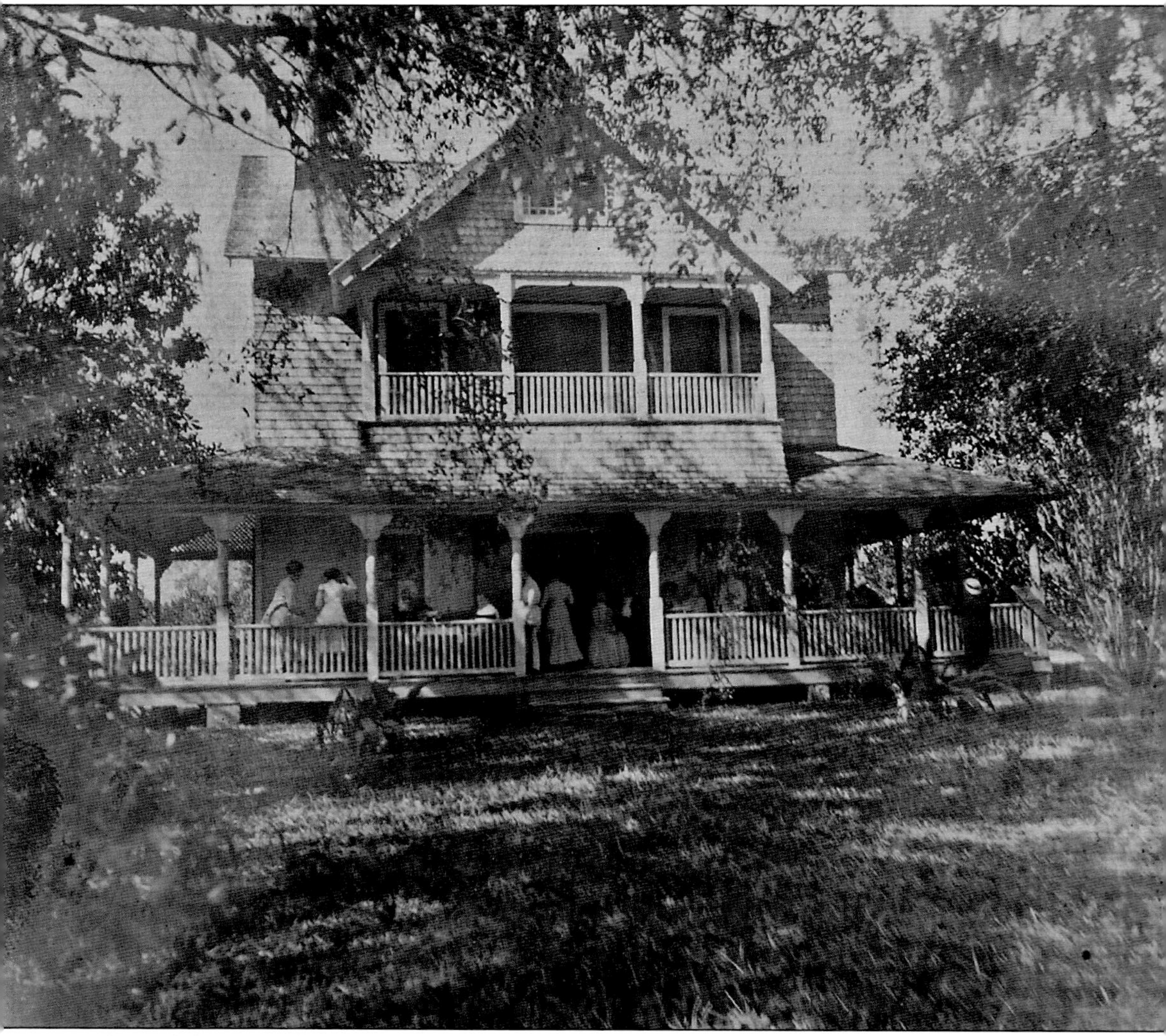

One of the many large homes built along the shores of Lake Maitland was Under Oaks, the home of the Kingsley family. It was built in 1882 by Dr. Abigence Kingsley of Elizabeth, New Jersey, and used as a winter home for his family for decades. The wooden home, built by William Waterhouse, is typical of the frame vernacular style, built to take advantage of the Florida climate with spacious balconies and porches on which people could gather to enjoy the weather. Its lawn, which extended to the north shore of the large lake, allowed breezes to reach the home, which was elevated from the ground to allow better circulation. It was owned by the Kingsley family until 1941 and has remained a private residence.

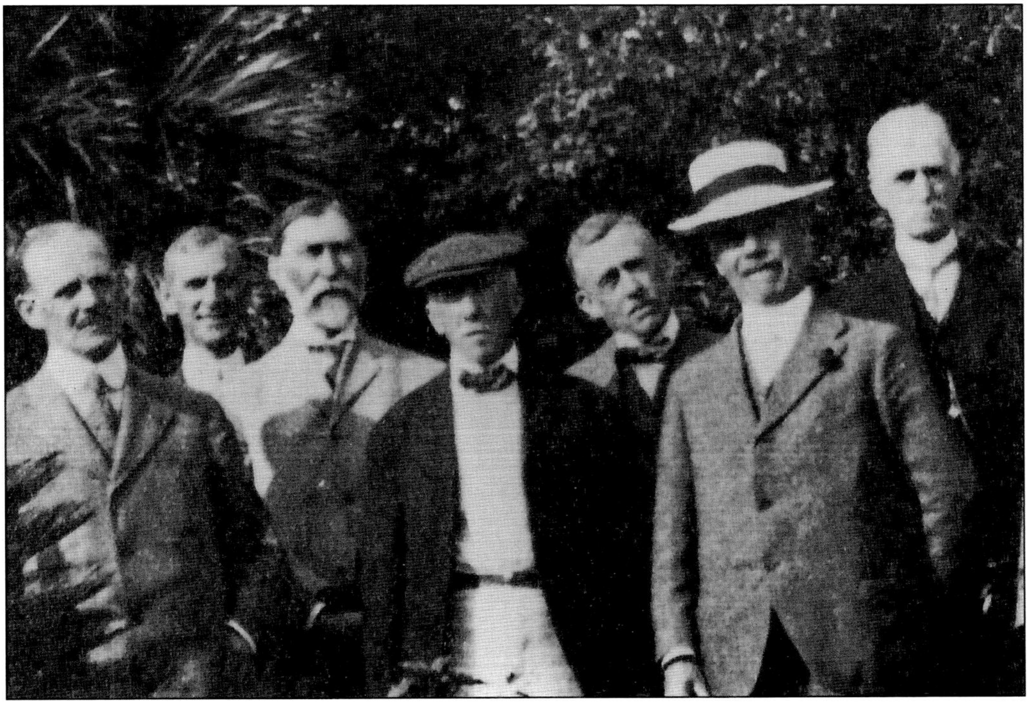

The Kingsley home, Under Oaks, was not just a beautiful home but also was the setting for one of the community's most popular events—a spring picnic on the lawn hosted by the Kingsley women. There the family and their guests would celebrate the end of their winter stay with a gathering for up to 100 people, marking the close of the city's winter social season. These photographs show a multi-generational group gathered in the yard near the back porch of the home, enjoying their time with friends and anticipating the coming of warmer months.

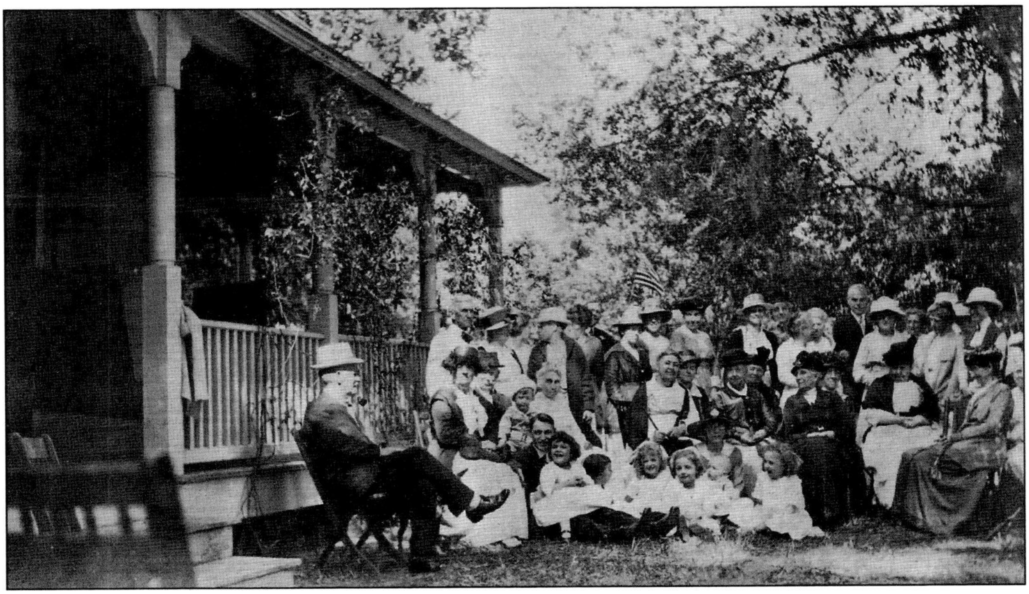

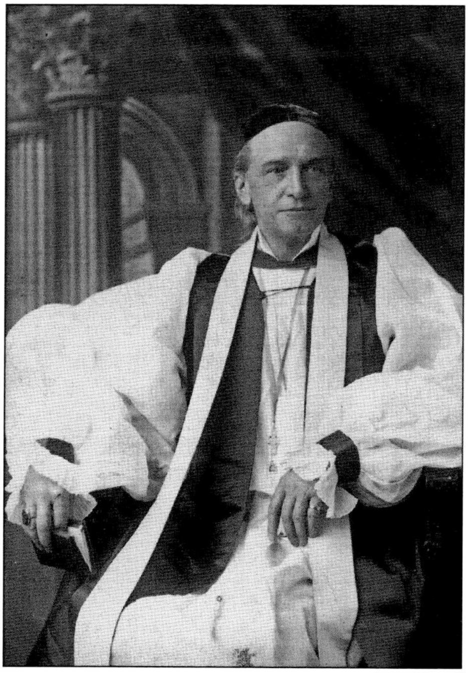

The Right Reverend Henry B. Whipple, Episcopal bishop of Minnesota, was a Maitland winter resident who had a long and honored career as an advocate for reforms in U.S. relations with the Native Americans. He corresponded with 11 presidents, even interceding for the lives of the Dakotas with Abraham Lincoln, and his work is widely considered to have preserved the people and culture of the Dakota and Chippewa Tribes, who called him Straight Tongue because he kept his word.

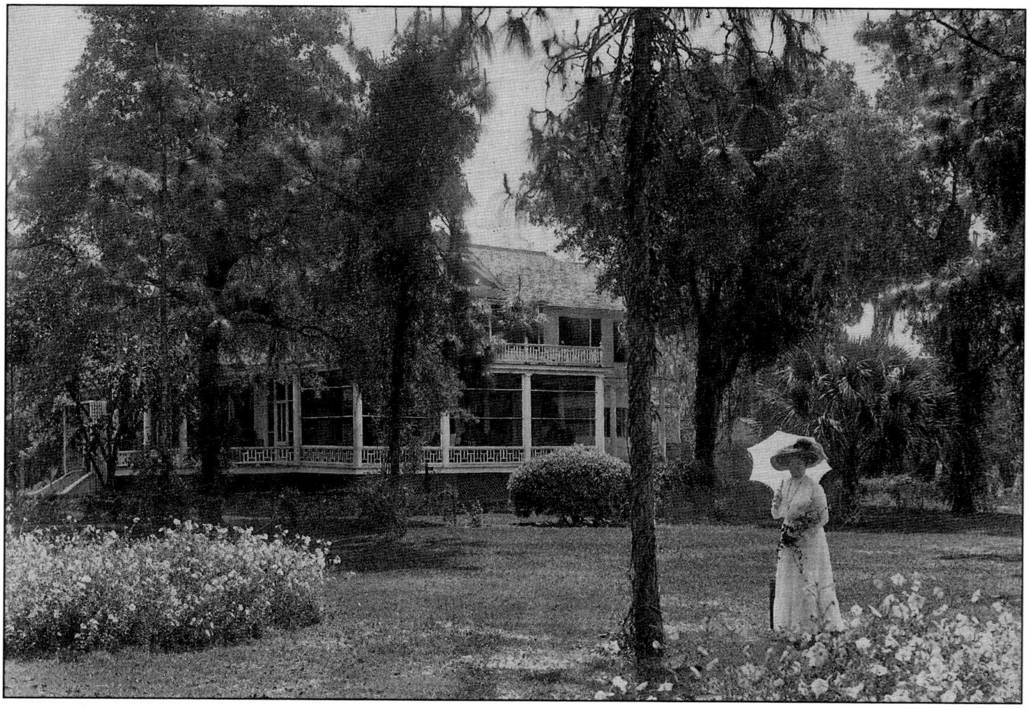

Evangeline Whipple, second wife of the bishop, stands in front of the Whipple home, known as Casa Mia, and its beautiful grounds, located on Lake Street. Whipple started visiting the area in the 1870s and built the house, used as the couple's winter residence. In 1879, Whipple began conducting Episcopal services at a parlor in his home and later donated land across the street as the site for the Church of the Good Shepherd. Whipple officiated at the church until his death in 1901.

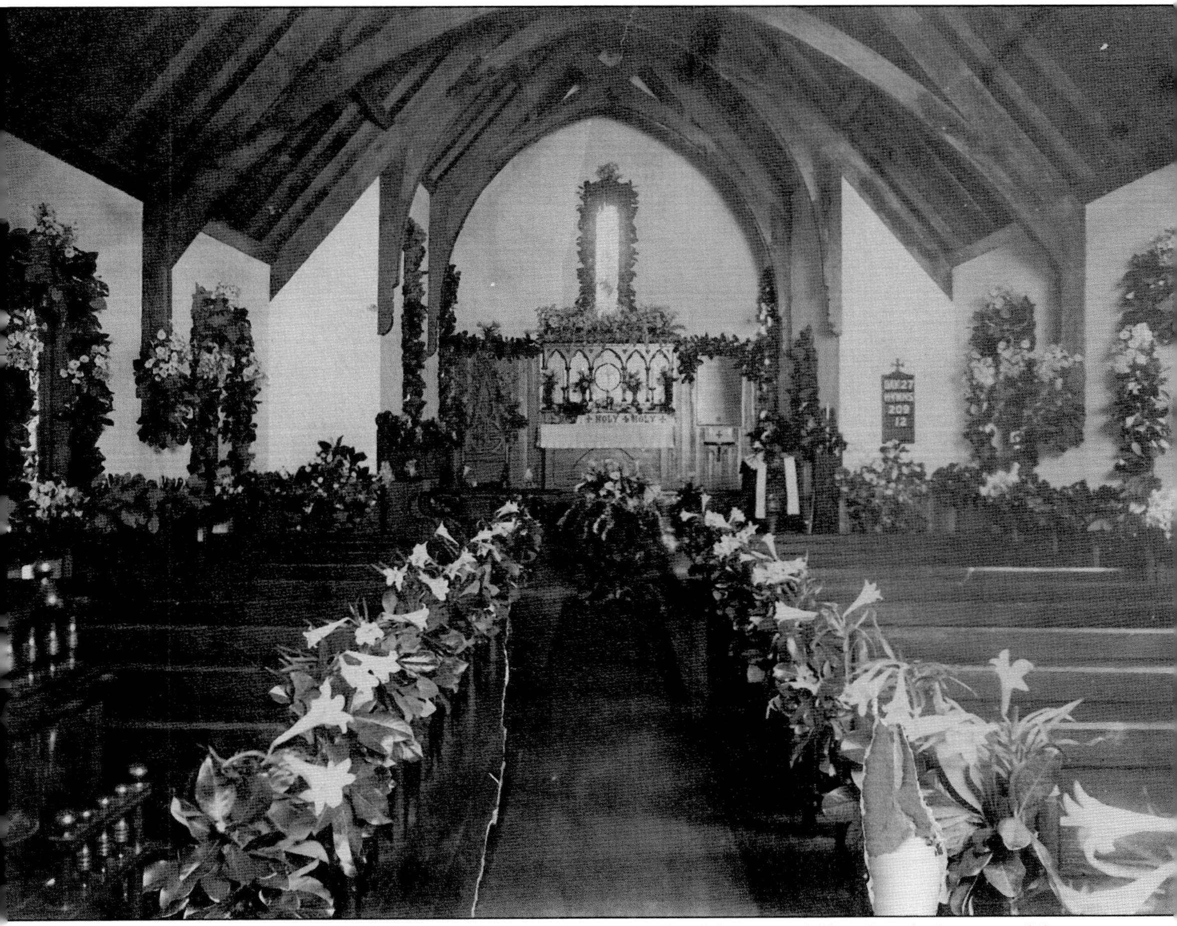

This photograph is of the interior of the Episcopal Church of the Good Shepherd, decorated for a service around 1890. The oldest church in Maitland, located on Lake Avenue, was completed in 1883 and dedicated to the memory of Whipple's recently deceased son and daughter. Its stained-glass windows are memorials to many area pioneers. The city had several other churches, but Good Shepherd remains the city's oldest church building.

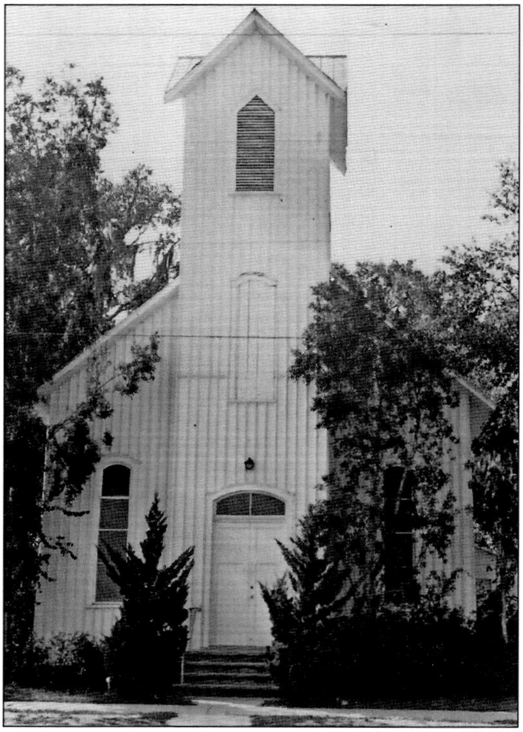

The First Presbyterian Church of Maitland, pictured here, was organized in 1882 by 10 early settlers, and the pine building, considered an example of "pioneer ecclesiastical architecture," was erected a year later under the direction of the Rev. W. G. F. Wallace. It was built by David Morrison, who also constructed the communion table, and the pews were built by William Waterhouse, another early Maitland resident. Special guests through the years included Pres. Chester A. Arthur and Rose Cleveland, sister of Pres. Grover Cleveland and a frequent area winter resident. The building was razed in 1967 and replaced with a modern structure that stands today on U.S. Highway 17-92.

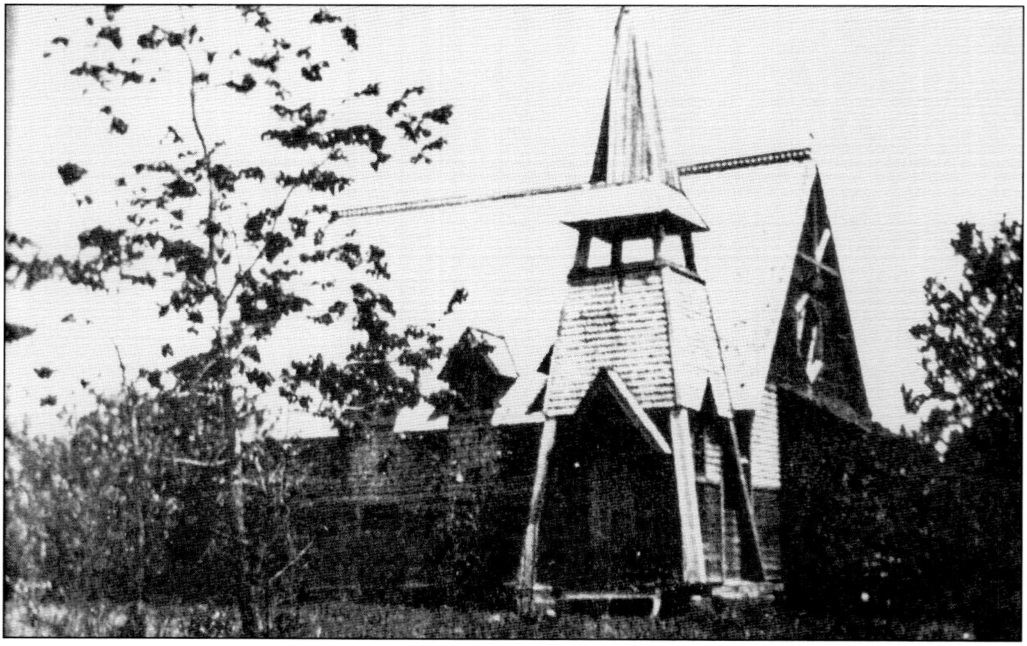

St. Mary of the Nativity Church was a wooden 100-seat Roman Catholic church built by James Wilcox, owner of the Park House Hotel, in 1881 on Lake Eulalia on what is now Lake Avenue. It was the first Catholic church built within the Diocese of Orlando, and it was deeded to the Right Reverend John Moore, bishop of Florida. Fr. Michael McFaul was pastor until 1887, when the church's congregation was combined with another in Orlando and the Maitland property was sold.

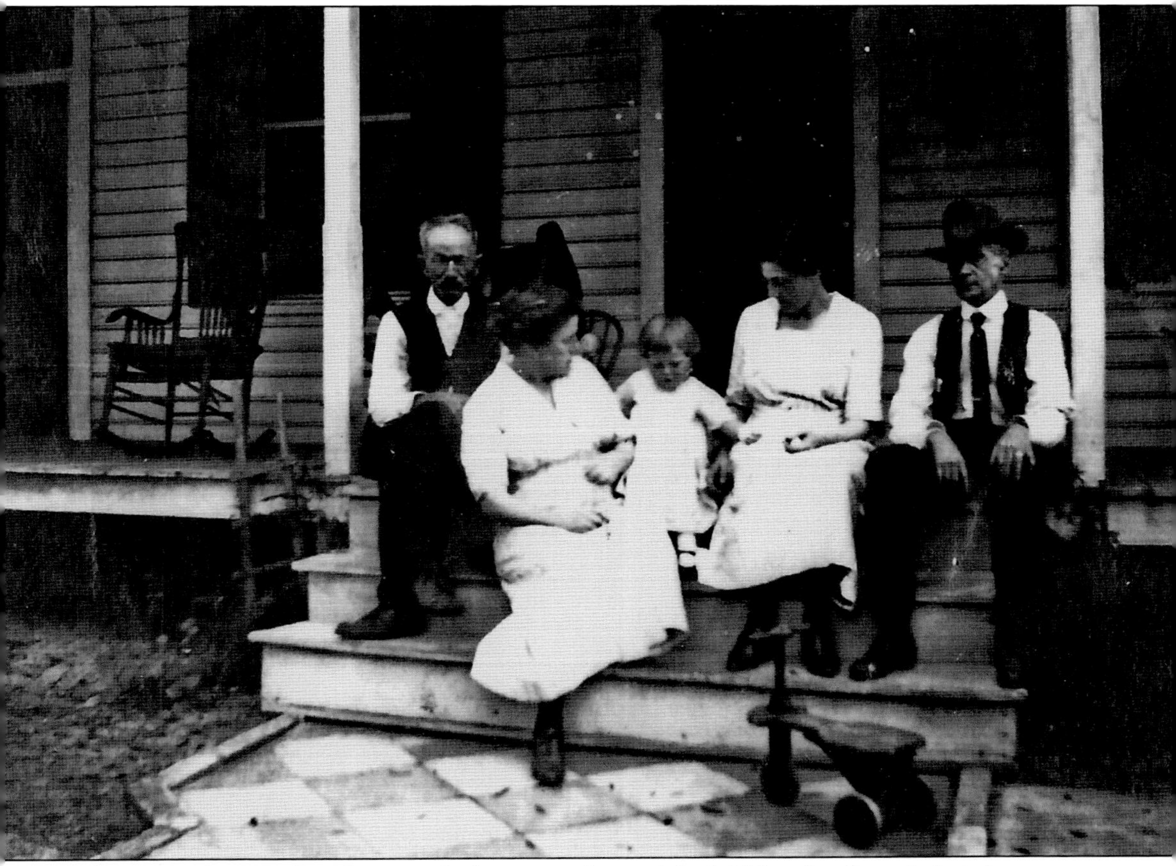

Taken around 1920, this photograph shows members of the McNair family and their house on George Street. Seated on the porch from left to right are Charles B. McNair, Margaret McNair, their daughter Isabelle McNair, and Helen Poor. The man on the far right is unidentified but may be Pat McNair, another member of the family. Charles McNair married Margaret Simmons, daughter of early Maitland pioneer John S. Simmons, and he served as an elder of the First Presbyterian Church for many years.

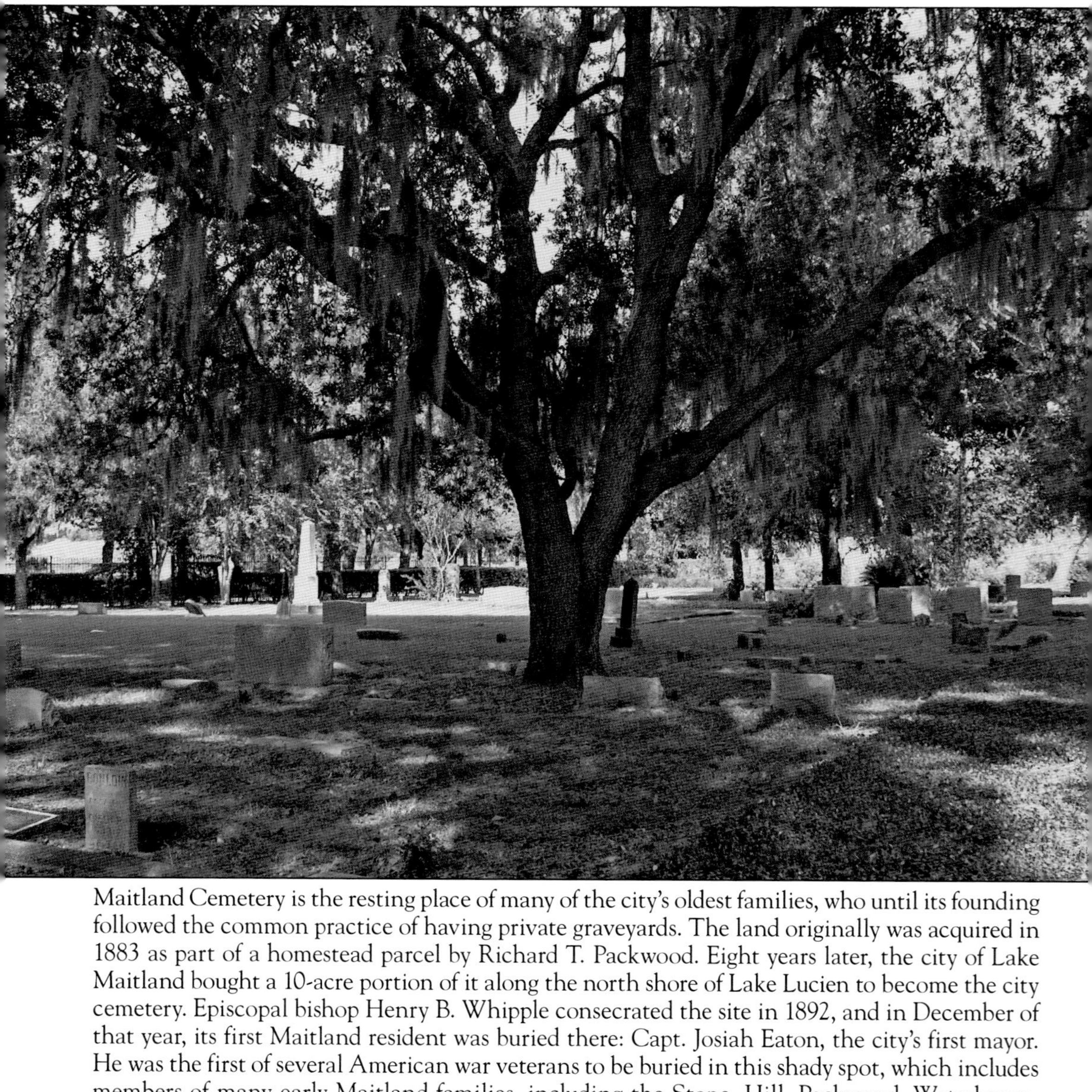

Maitland Cemetery is the resting place of many of the city's oldest families, who until its founding followed the common practice of having private graveyards. The land originally was acquired in 1883 as part of a homestead parcel by Richard T. Packwood. Eight years later, the city of Lake Maitland bought a 10-acre portion of it along the north shore of Lake Lucien to become the city cemetery. Episcopal bishop Henry B. Whipple consecrated the site in 1892, and in December of that year, its first Maitland resident was buried there: Capt. Josiah Eaton, the city's first mayor. He was the first of several American war veterans to be buried in this shady spot, which includes members of many early Maitland families, including the Stone, Hill, Packwood, Waterhouse, Simmons, and Vanderpool families. In 1996, a group of concerned citizens formed a committee to restore the cemetery, which had fallen into disrepair, and it was rededicated later that year.

Three

THE CITY GROWS UP

By the early decades of the 20th century, Lake Maitland had become a modern city bolstered by new businesses, agriculture, and visits from tourists eager to partake of its natural beauty and recreation. Although the citrus industry was badly damaged by back-to-back freezes in 1894–1895, growers replanted the "liquid gold" and continued to produce oranges and grapefruit for Northern markets. The city also became a place for many "firsts" in the community. In 1900, Clara and Louis Dommerich hosted a group of concerned citizens who agreed to found the Florida Audubon Society—an organization dedicated to saving the state's birds that would have a big impact on the state. Ten years later, Carl Hill Galloway installed the town's first switchboard at his father's store. Soon after, he helped bring an electric light system to the city. Other signs of change included new residential subdivisions that were platted and built and the coming of the first grouted, brick road in Florida, called the Dixie Highway, which connected the city to other Central Florida communities and heralded the new popularity of the automobile.

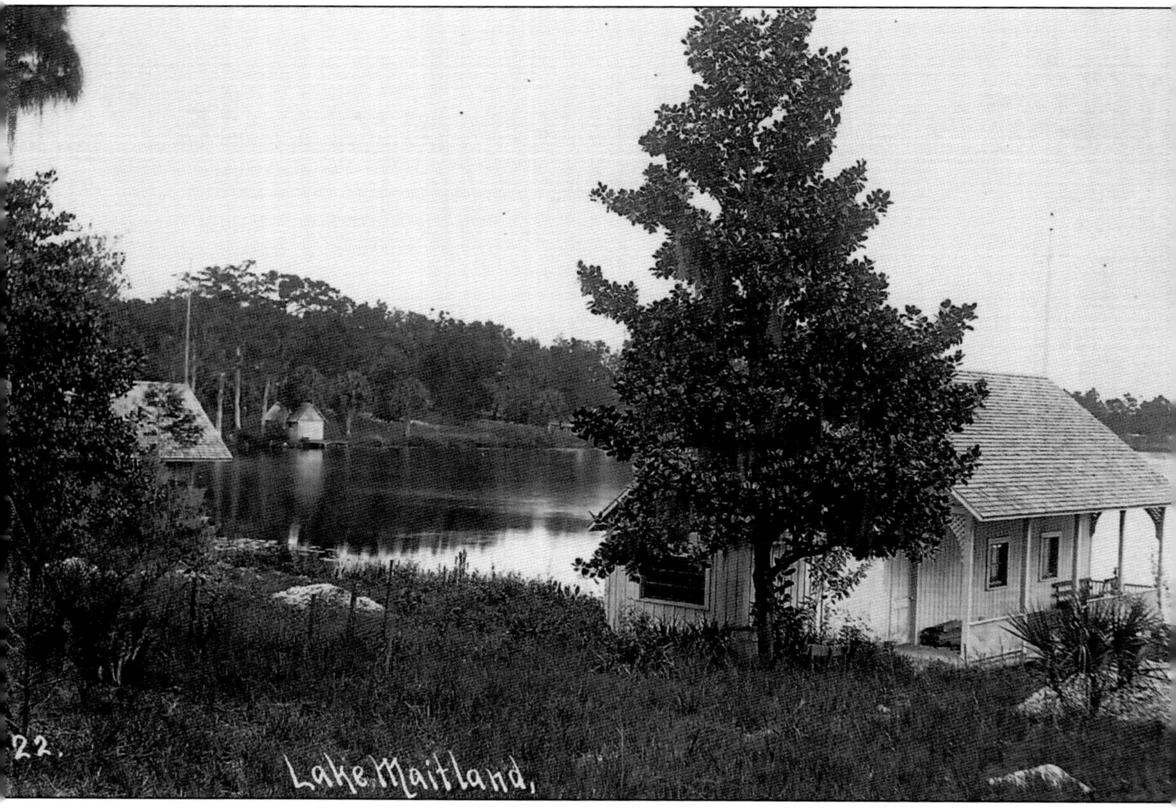

Lake Maitland was the largest lake in the city and its shores were home to many of its grandest houses and estates. As this photograph shows, most lakefront homes had boathouses that allowed for easy access to the lake and provided storage during months when they were not in use. This view is of the Hall and Bronson boathouses, located on the western shore of the lake—near the site of the original Fort Maitland.

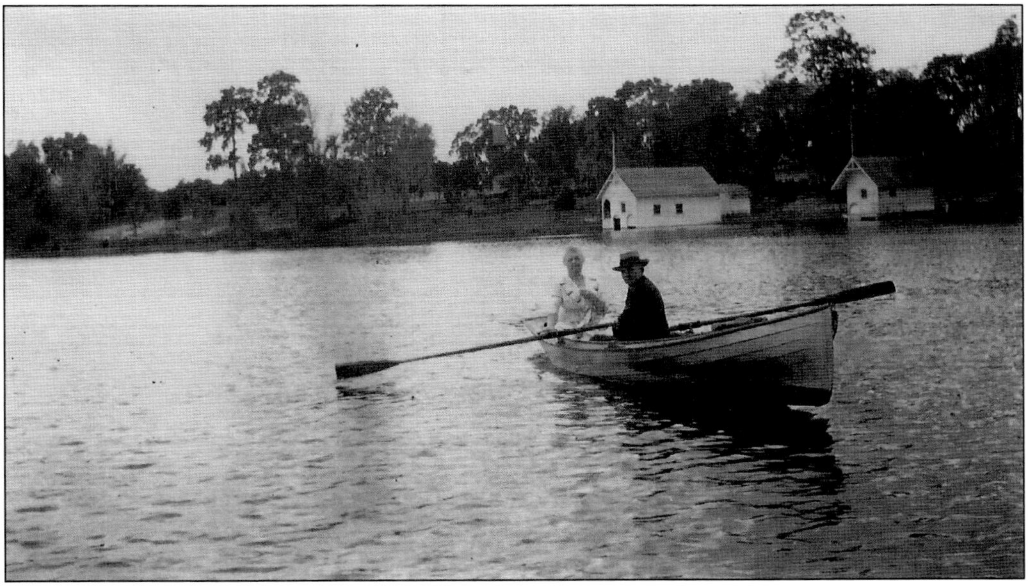

Sunshine, a balmy climate, and the many outdoor activities afforded by its natural features made Lake Maitland and its nearby community a natural draw for people from other areas. Above, Edward and Jane Hall enjoy a leisurely paddle on the lake near their family boathouse on the western shore of the large lake. Below, members of the Hall family enjoy a day out on the lake's clear waters. Today their wooden boats and oars have been replaced by fast-moving motorized vessels and fishing boats—enjoying the recreational pleasures the lake provides.

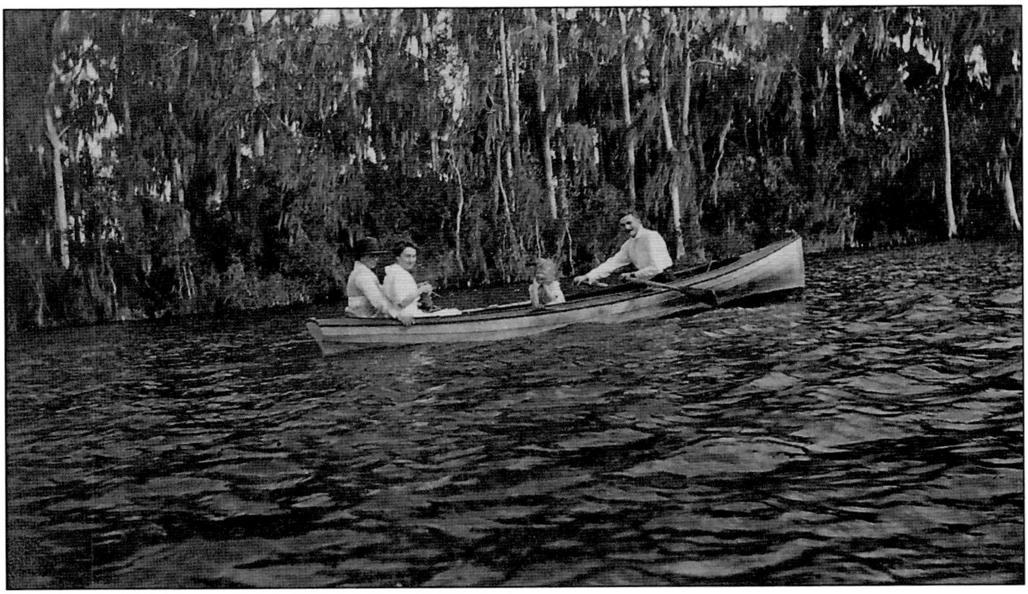

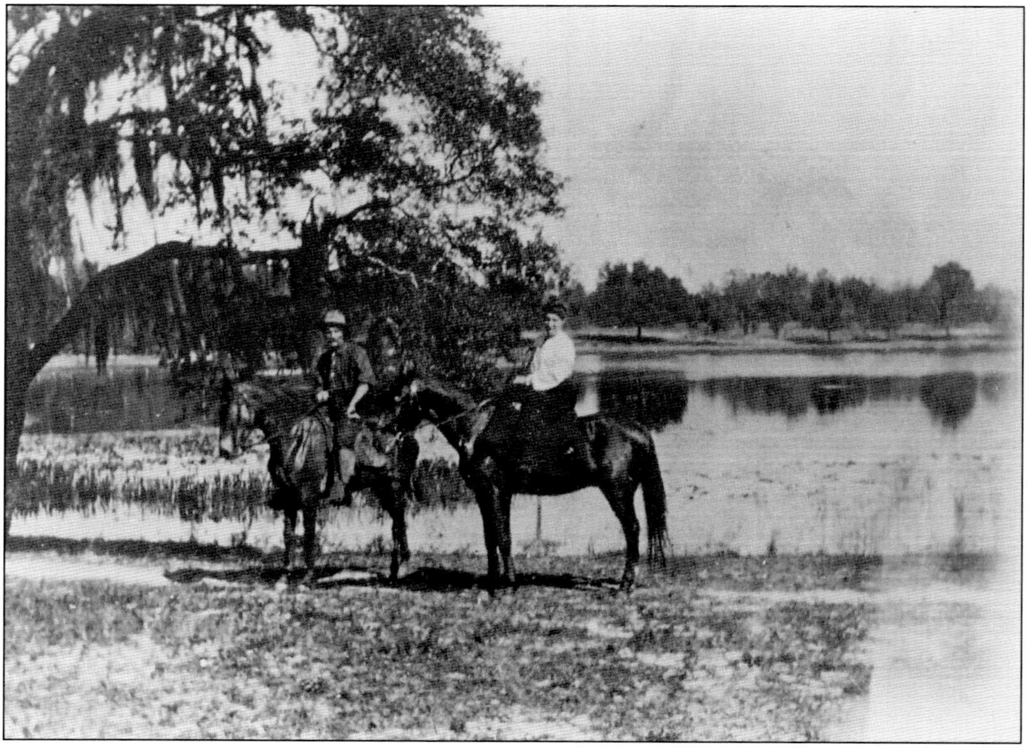

The city's many lakes were a centerpiece of its natural beauty, enjoyed by visitors and residents alike. Lake Lily, located near the downtown core, continued to attract people to its calming waters. Above, Pat Simmons (left) and Ruth Rosa are shown riding their horses to the lake's shore, a common sight in that era. Below, members of two of the area's earliest families enjoy a stroll and the lake's breezes. Pictured are, from left to right, Stella Waterhouse, Sarah Waterhouse, Lillie Waterhouse, William Waterhouse, George Strong, and Clarissa Strong. The Waterhouse family lived in a two-story home located near the lake's shore.

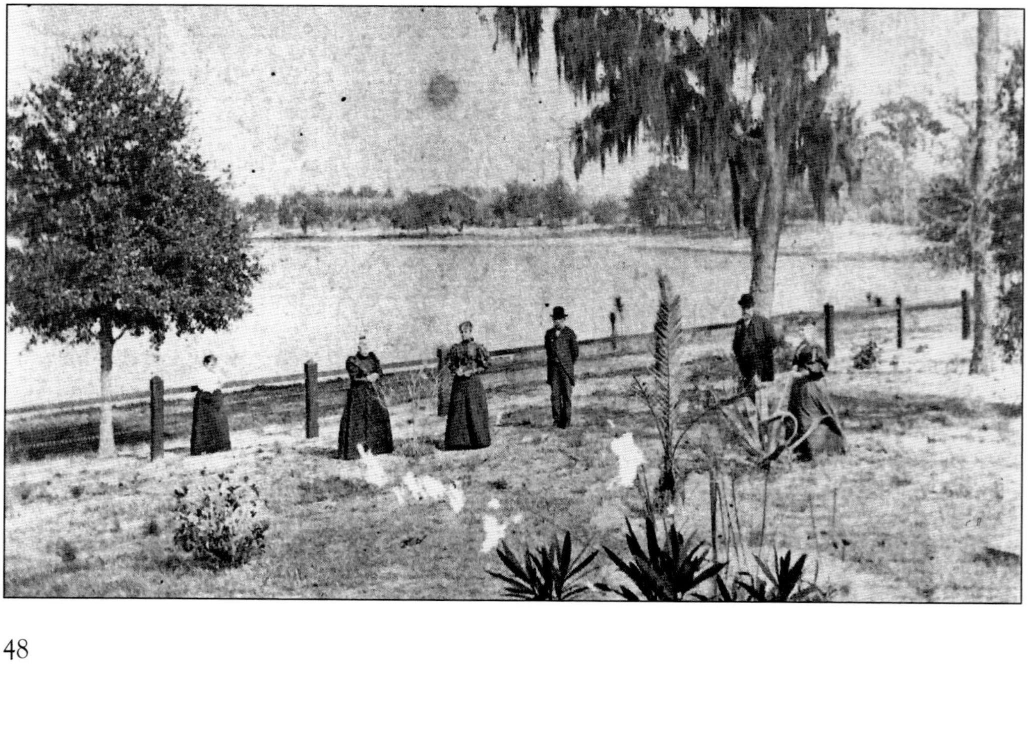

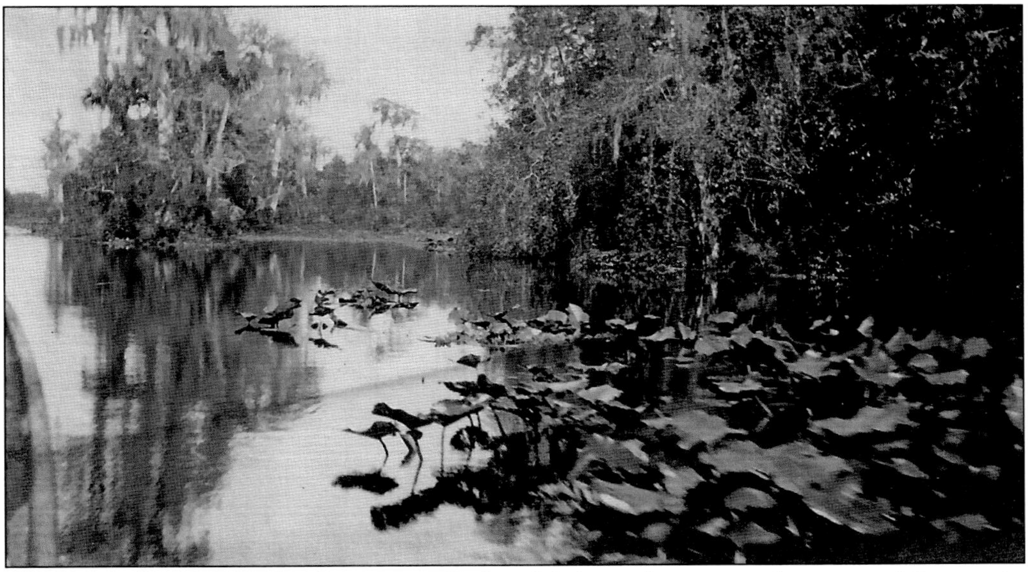

Although the Lake Maitland area is studded with lakes, other outstanding natural features in the area regularly drew the city's residents. The Wekiva River, a waterway fed in part by the aquamarine boil of Wekiwa Springs, was a prime destination for visitors who wanted to enjoy its crystalline waters and nearby wildlife. Located 12 miles north of the city, the river, its spring, and a hotel drew many tourists in the late 1800s and early 1900s. Today the river is one of the most protected in the state, and the springs are part of the state park system.

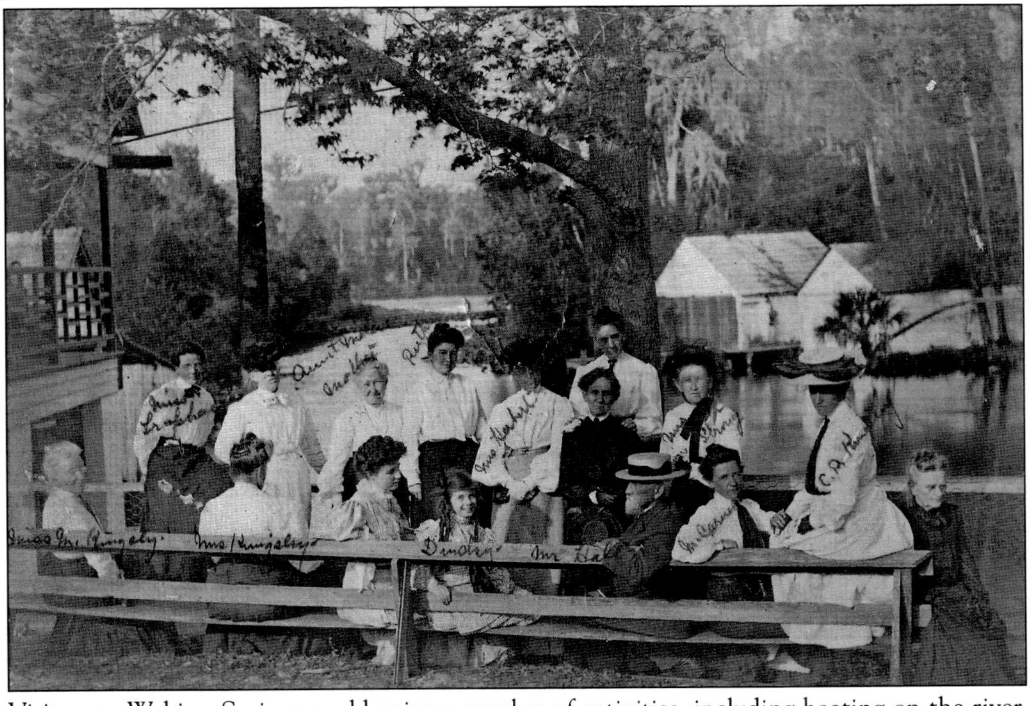

Visitors to Wekiwa Springs could enjoy a number of activities, including boating on the river, fishing, and swimming. In this photograph, a group of 16 city residents enjoys an outing at the river and springs, including Sarah Waterhouse, Ruth Rosa, Charles Hall, and several members of the Kingsley family.

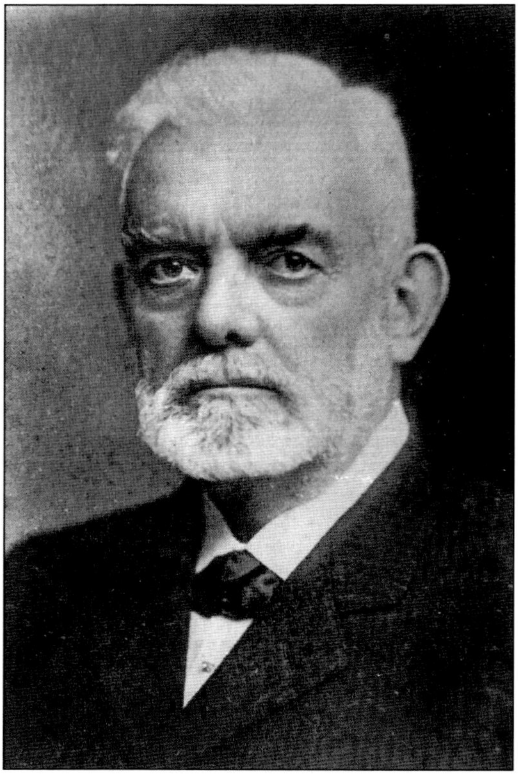

One of the area's leading philanthropists was Louis Dommerich, a wealthy New York textile merchant who had been born in Germany. He wintered with his family in Lake Maitland at his grand 400-acre estate on the shores of Lake Minnehaha. Even though they were only part-time residents, Louis and his second wife, Clara, also born in Germany, were notable benefactors to the area. Louis contributed to Rollins College in nearby Winter Park and served as a college trustee. Clara Dommerich was equally important to the local community, donating 360 books to help create the Maitland Public Library, which her family supported for many years.

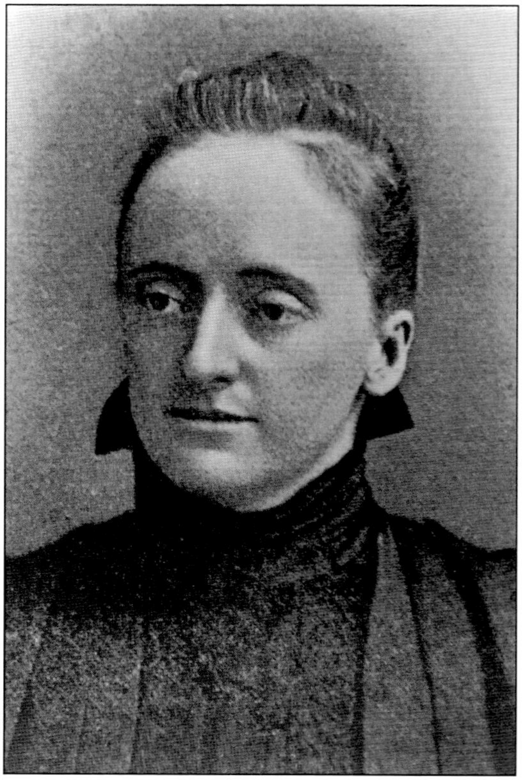

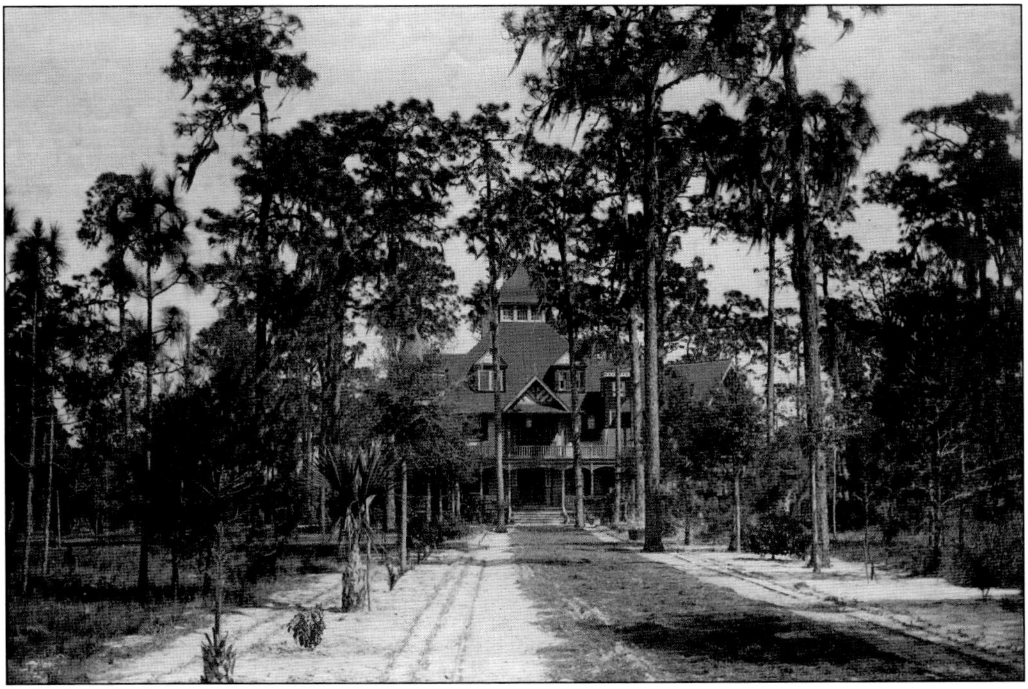

The Dommerich estate was one of the most elegant homes in Lake Maitland. A drive down a tree-lined sandy road took visitors to the three-story 30-room estate, called Hiawatha Grove, built by the family in 1890. The house edged Lake Minnehaha, featured porches, turrets, and gables, and was surrounded by 130 acres of landscaped grounds. In later years, his daughter Paula recalled how Louis Dommerich daily would put birdseed out at feeding stations on his porch and whistle to attract the many birds in the area, including cardinals and juncos. A bird sanctuary was established on the property. (Above courtesy Rollins College.)

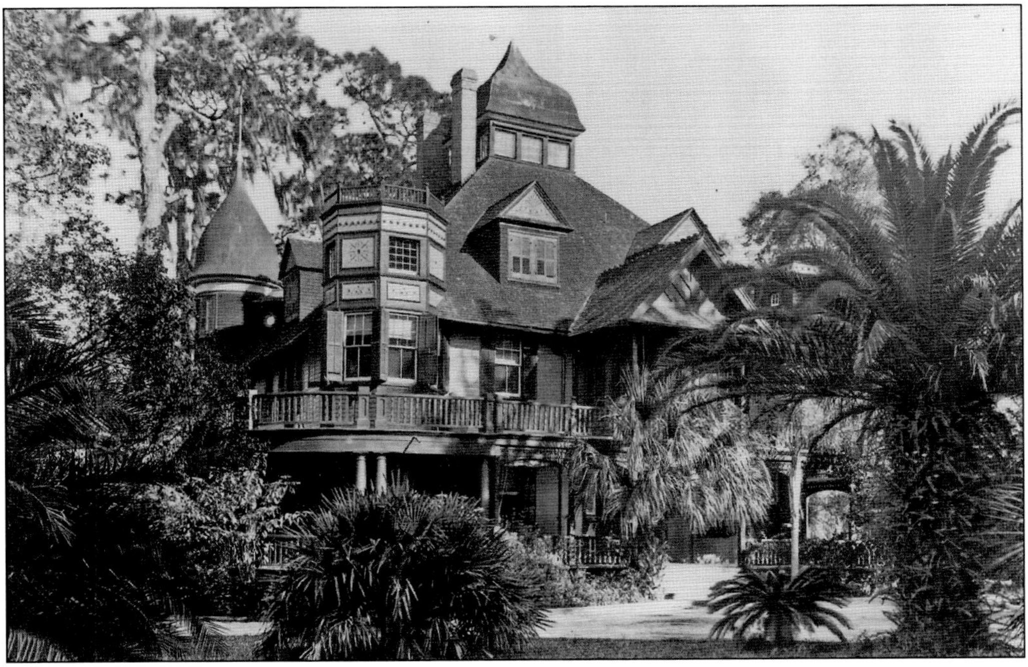

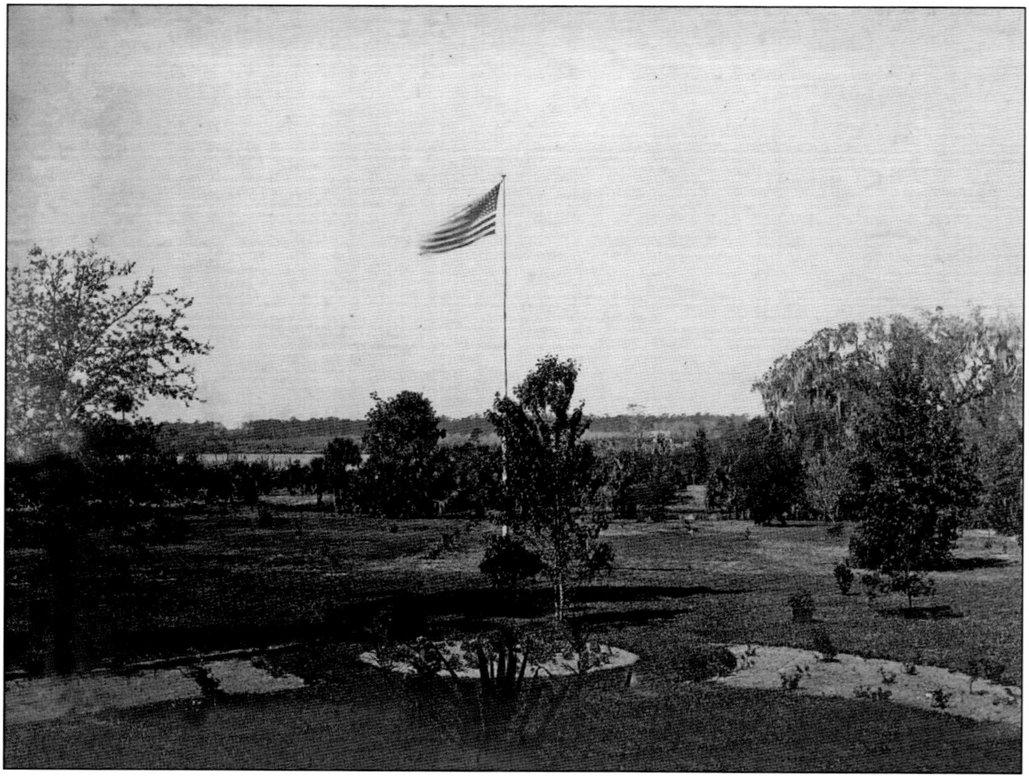

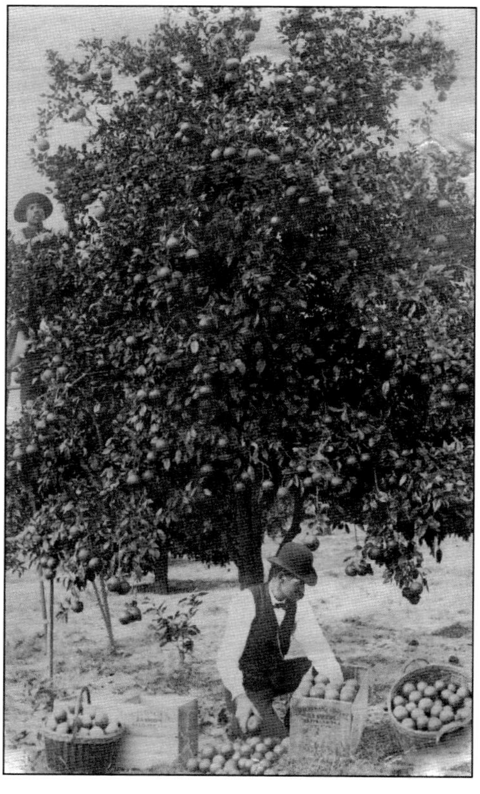

The front lawn of Hiawatha Grove, shown in this photograph from March 21, 1896, featured a man-made pond and flagpole and sloped down to Lake Minnehaha, where the family had a large boathouse. The Dommerichs, who reveled in the beauty of nature, constructed 8 miles of boardwalk trails that wound through the extensive property and afforded its many visitors long, luxurious walks. The estate was sold for a record $420,000 in 1954 to developers, who demolished the house and created subdivisions that bear the Dommerich name. (Courtesy Rollins College.)

The Dommerich estate also included 72 acres of citrus trees, from which the home's name, Hiawatha Grove, is derived. The Dommerichs bought the estate's property and its groves from Bolling R. Swoope, shown here in the foreground of this photograph. Swoope, for whom a Maitland street is named, came to the area from Virginia in 1874 and purchased land already planted in citrus trees. In addition to their groves, the Dommerich estate featured a packinghouse where fruit was prepared for shipment to commercial markets. (Courtesy Rollins College.)

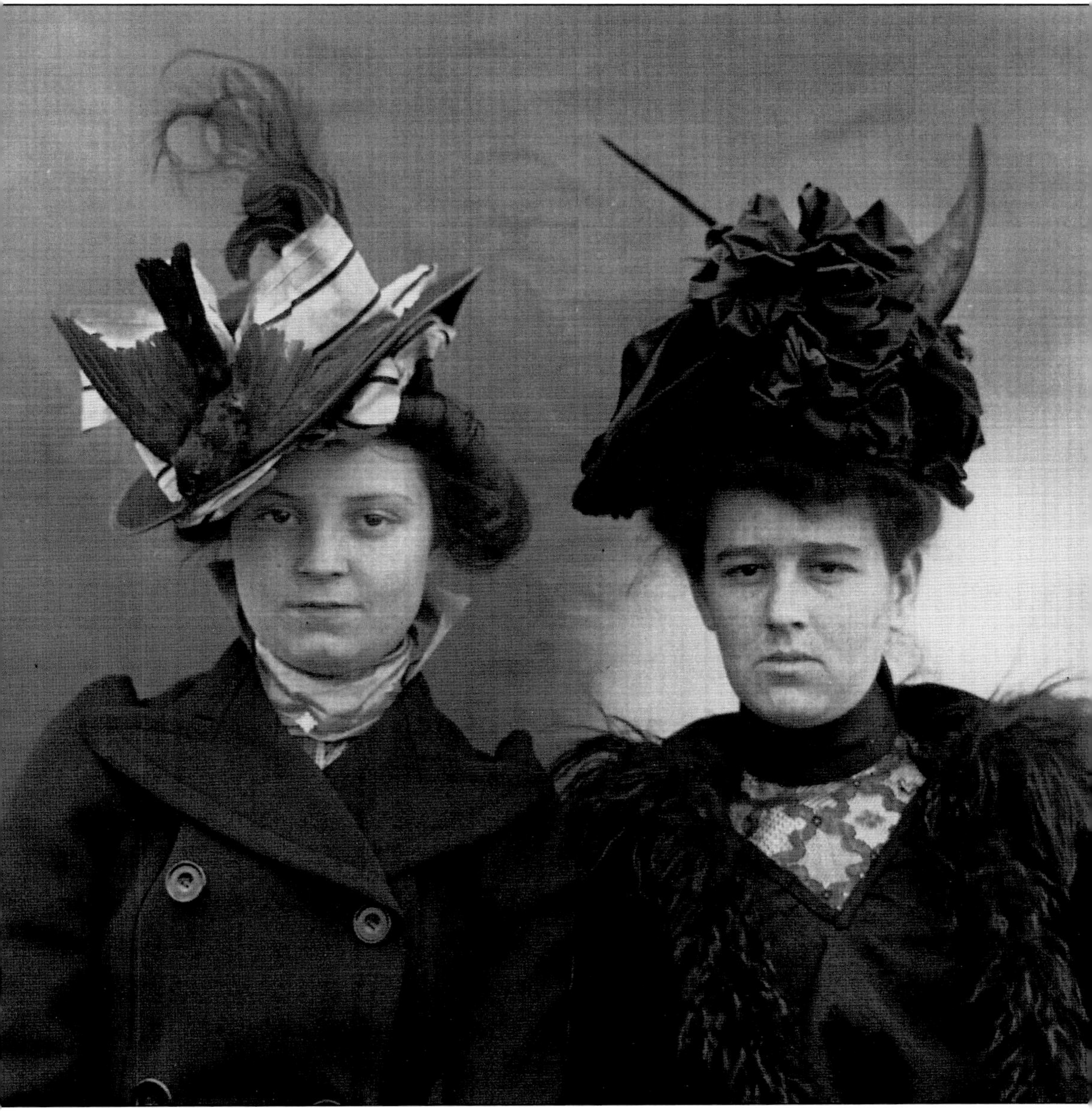

In March 1900, at the behest of Clara Dommerich, a group of 15 influential residents gathered at the Dommerich estate to found the Florida Audubon Society. For many years, Dommerich and others across the United States had been alarmed about the wholesale slaughter of the state's birds, whose bodies and feathers were used to adorn women's hats, a fashionable style of the period shown in this photograph. The birds, particularly wading birds that sported luxurious plumage during nesting season, were killed by the millions to supply the national and international millinery trade. The Florida Audubon Society worked tirelessly to secure laws to stop the plume trade and protect the state's birds. (Courtesy Sloane Gallery Collection.)

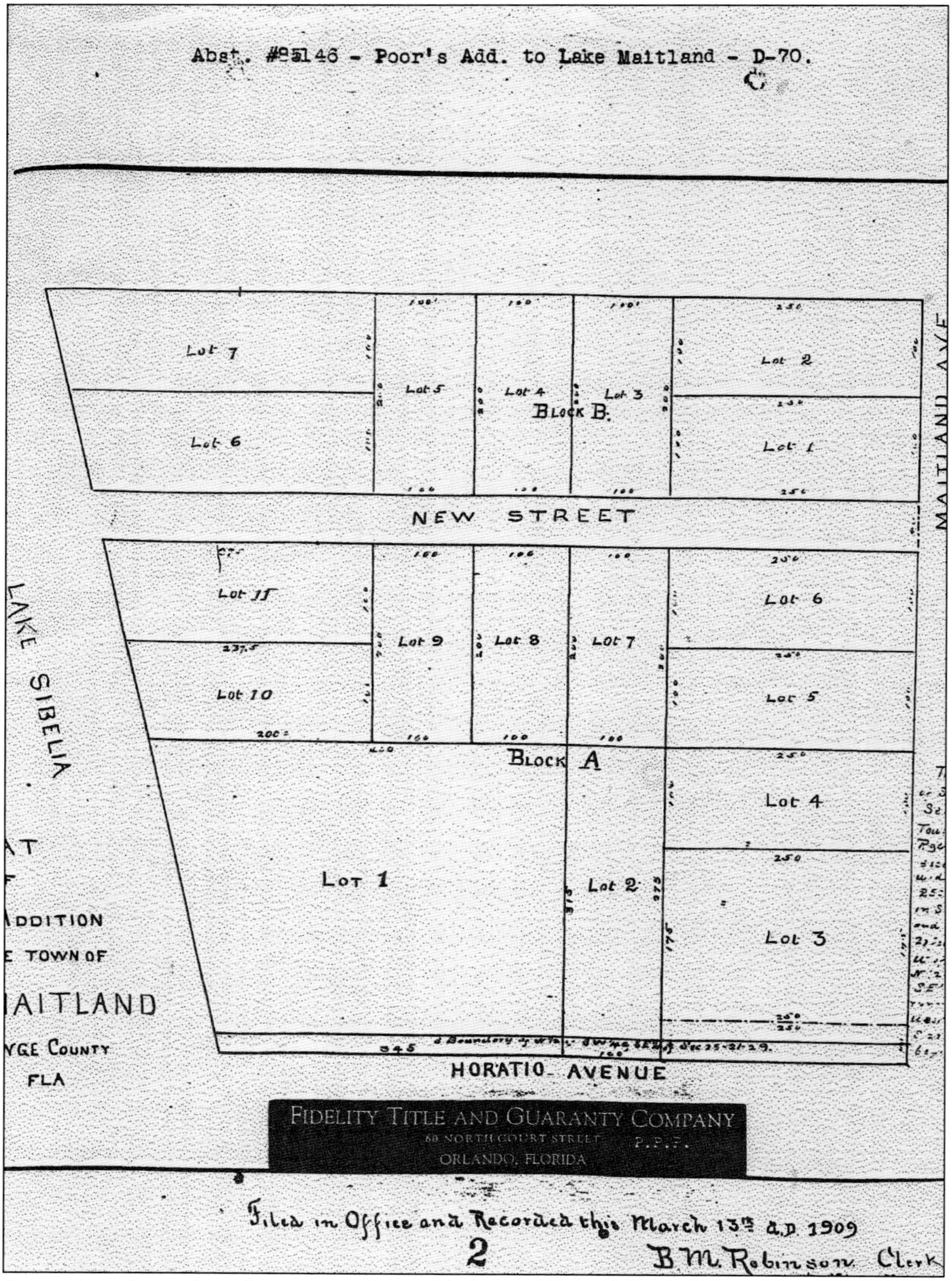

A sure sign of growth in the area was the establishment of six subdivisions between 1901 and 1915. Among those in which buildings still exist were Poor's Addition, in 1909, whose plans are pictured here, and Coffin's subdivision, platted in 1914. It was bounded by Horatio and Maitland Avenues and Lake Sybelia Drive. The advent of World War I and a mild recession brought most construction to a standstill in the area—something that would change dramatically two decades later.

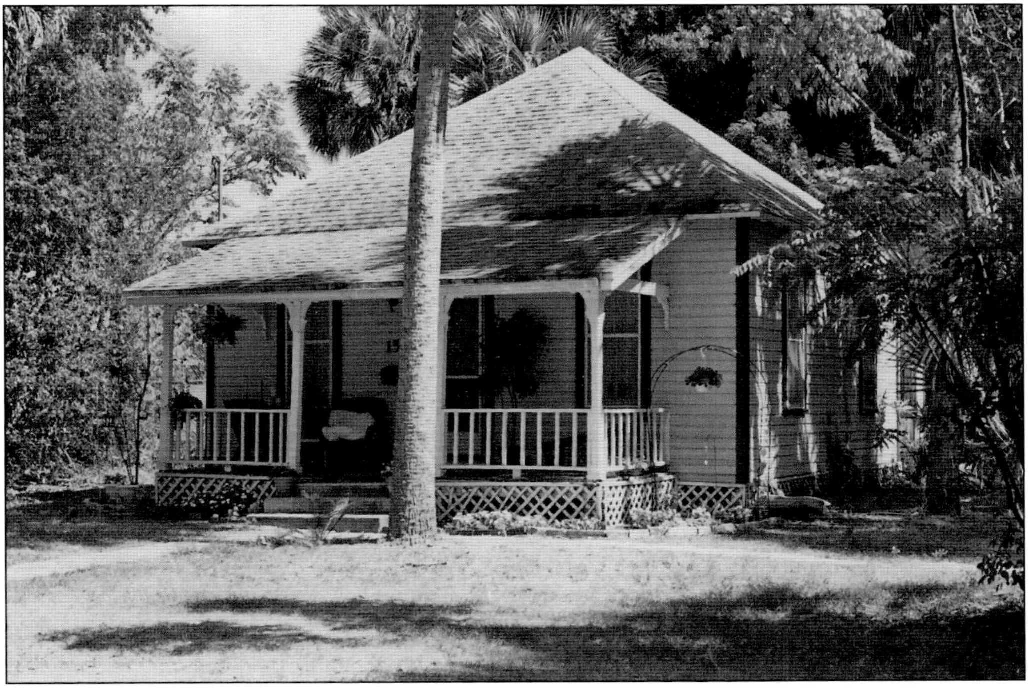

Maria "Mary" Wahl, who had immigrated with her family to the United States from Germany in 1896, bought this house, located on lots 5 and 6 of Poor's Addition. Located at 150 West George Avenue, the house was built in the frame vernacular style and now is a private residence, as shown in this modern photograph. Wahl's son Willie worked at the Maitland railroad depot.

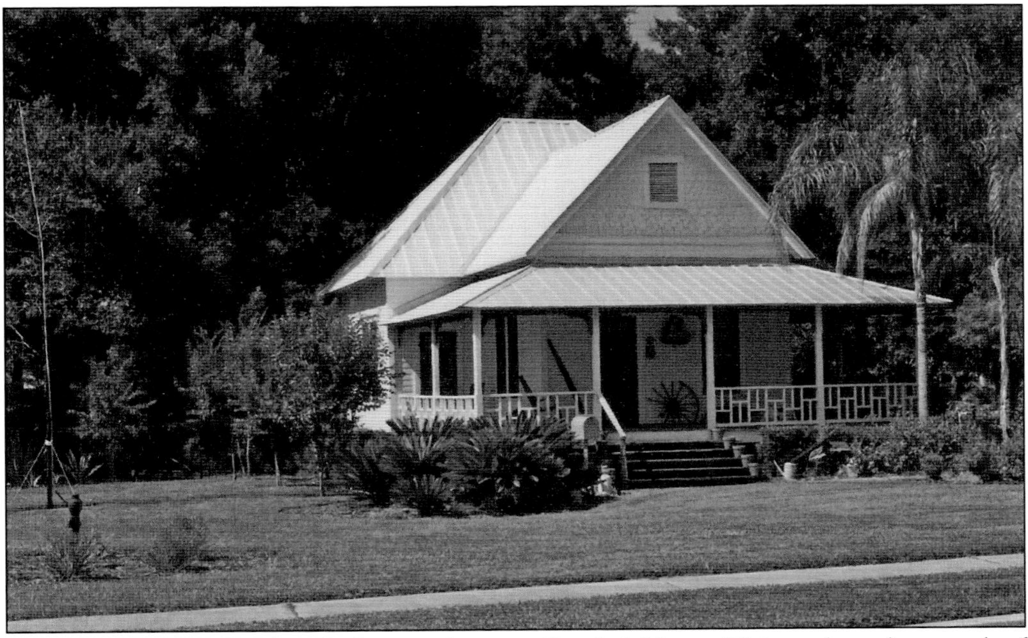

Joseph B. Poor found a place for his own home in Poor's Addition. This modern photograph of the two-bedroom house at 251 West Horatio Avenue was his personal residence, built in 1909 in the same style as the Wahl house. Its kitchen originally was detached from the wooden house, and the metal roof and elevated floor were typical of period Florida architecture.

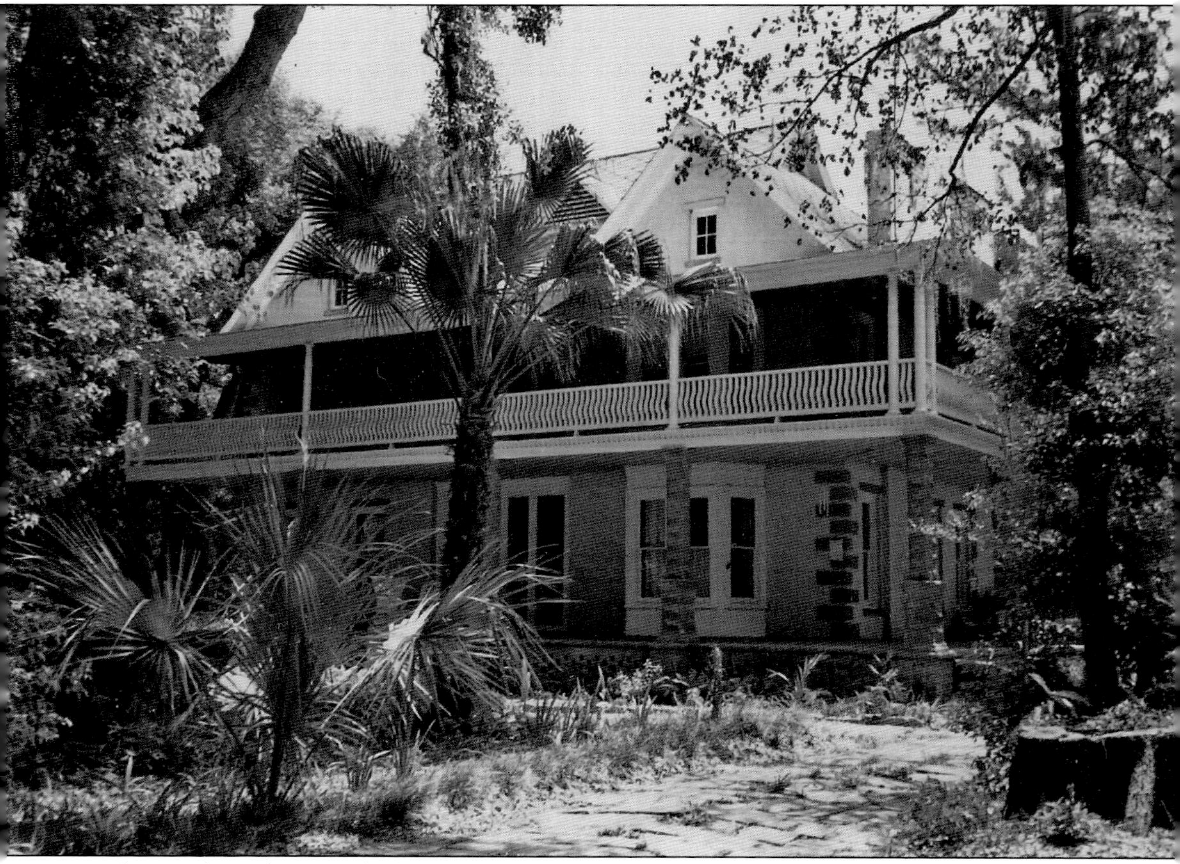

This modern photograph shows Greenwood Lodge, a 1906 home built by Sumter Brock Hill. It was constructed at the site of what had been the Greenwood Lodge and Home School, built by Brig. Gen. Alfred Iverson, a Confederate veteran. Iverson's wife, Adela, an educator and musician, and Ellen Howe Judson operated a seminary at the site for a number of years. A later owner included Alice Lloyd Key Potter, the granddaughter of Francis Scott Key, author of the U.S. national anthem. The current home, located at 104 Stone Hill Drive, features upper and lower verandas and fireplaces in many rooms and was built to take full advantage of Florida weather. While the exterior of the house is brick, its wooden interior was crafted from longleaf pine. It remains a private residence.

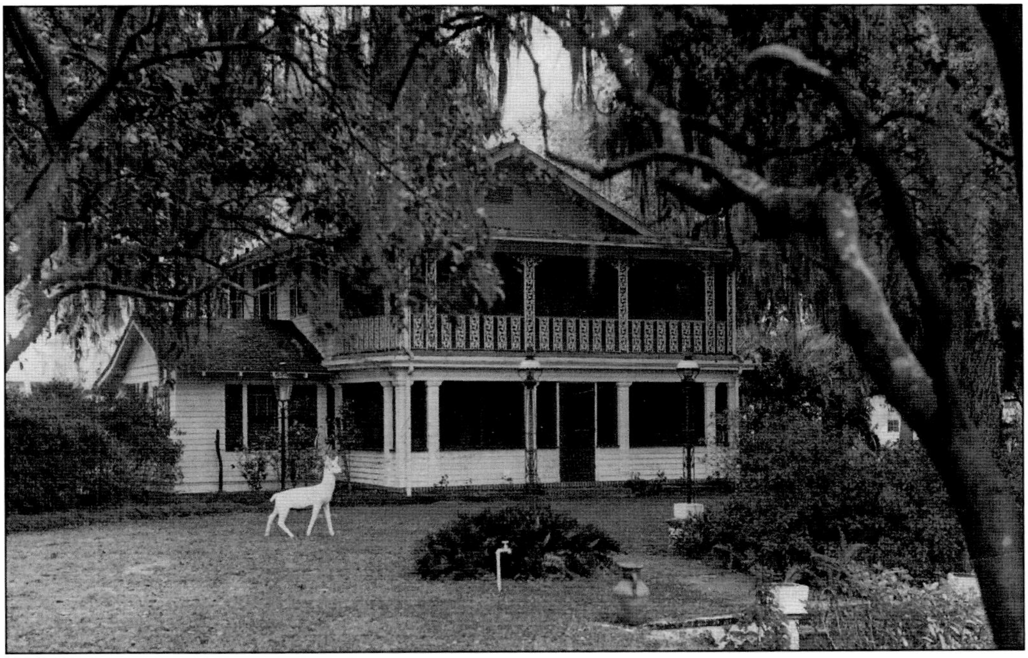

This two-story wooden home was built in 1915 and owned by Thomas Henkel in the 1920s, earning it the name Henkel House. It sat at the corner of Magnolia Road and U.S. Highway 17-92, an intersection known through the years as Henkel's Corner. The heavily treed property featured a creek on the north side of the property called Maitland Run. The building remained a residence until 1973, when it was sold and revamped into a restaurant. The building is now gone, and the property is currently home to an independent movie theater, Enzian Theater.

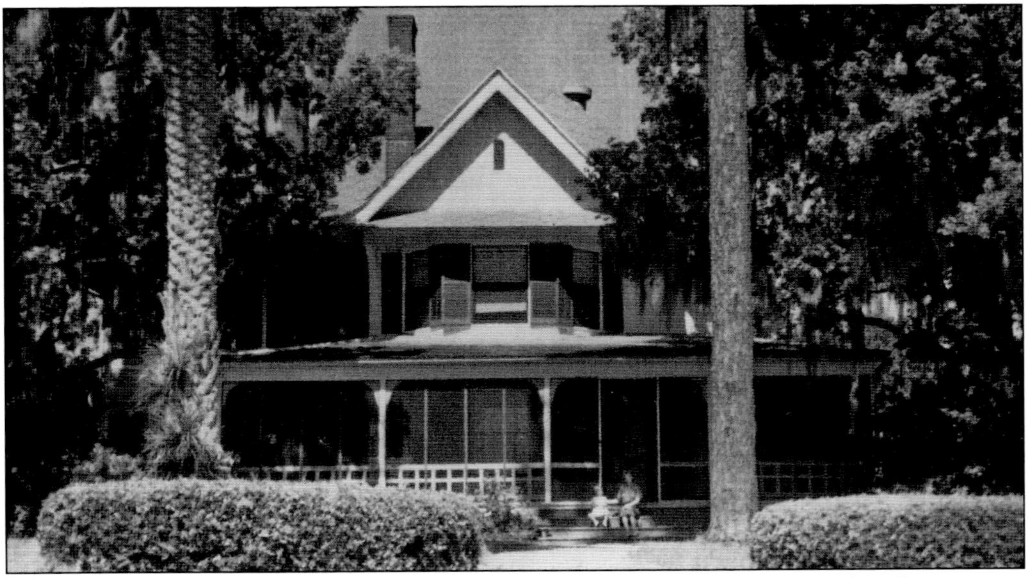

After the 1915 death of Minnesota businessman Cyrus Thurston, who wintered in this spacious Queen Anne–style home, it was named Glencoe Groves by its new owner, Chicago businessman James Hirsch, a former Chicago alderman who often was seen in a chauffeured Cadillac. Although the residence passed through many hands during the years and now operates as a bed-and-breakfast, the building on Lake Avenue is known in Maitland as the Thurston House.

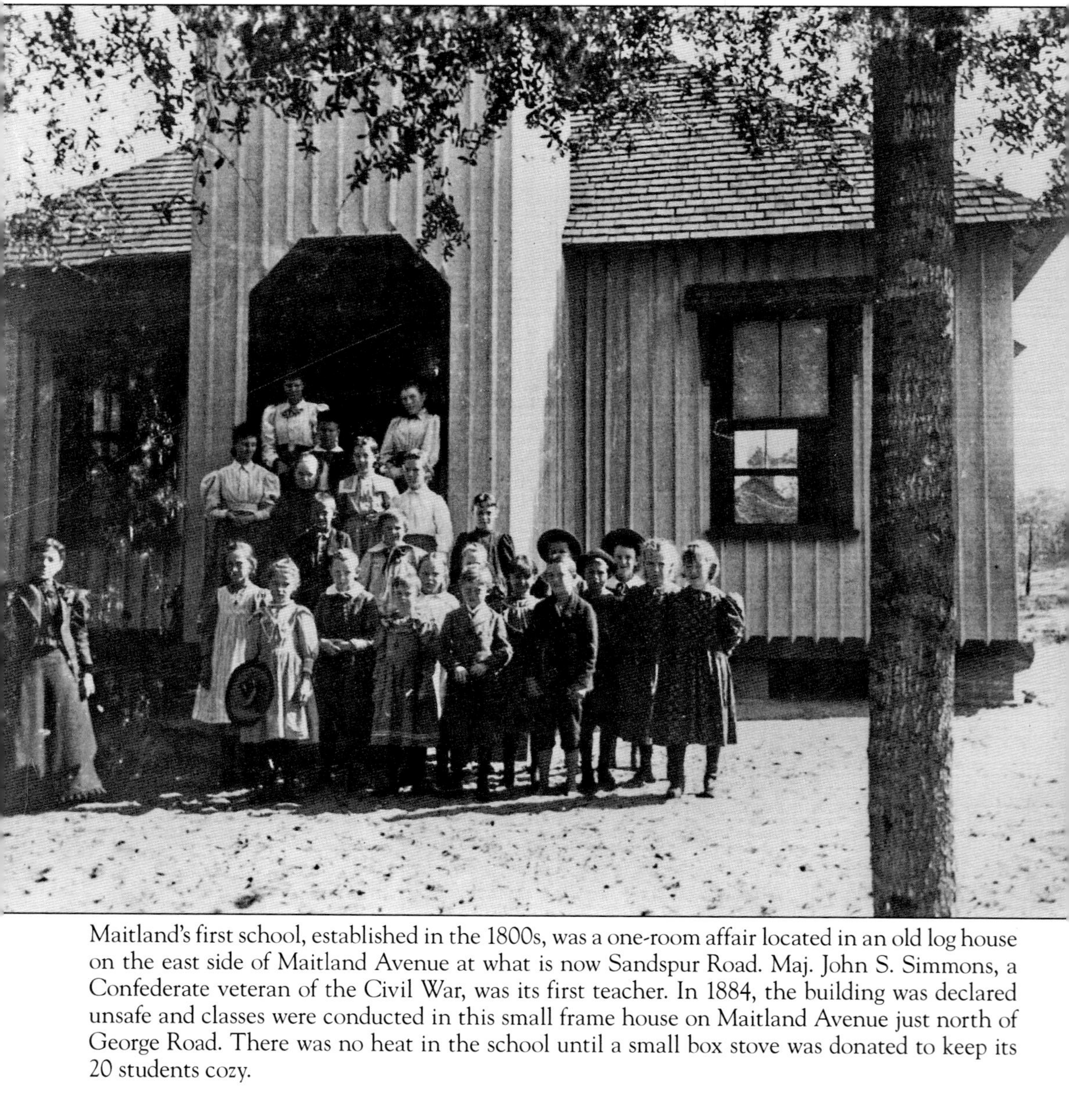

Maitland's first school, established in the 1800s, was a one-room affair located in an old log house on the east side of Maitland Avenue at what is now Sandspur Road. Maj. John S. Simmons, a Confederate veteran of the Civil War, was its first teacher. In 1884, the building was declared unsafe and classes were conducted in this small frame house on Maitland Avenue just north of George Road. There was no heat in the school until a small box stove was donated to keep its 20 students cozy.

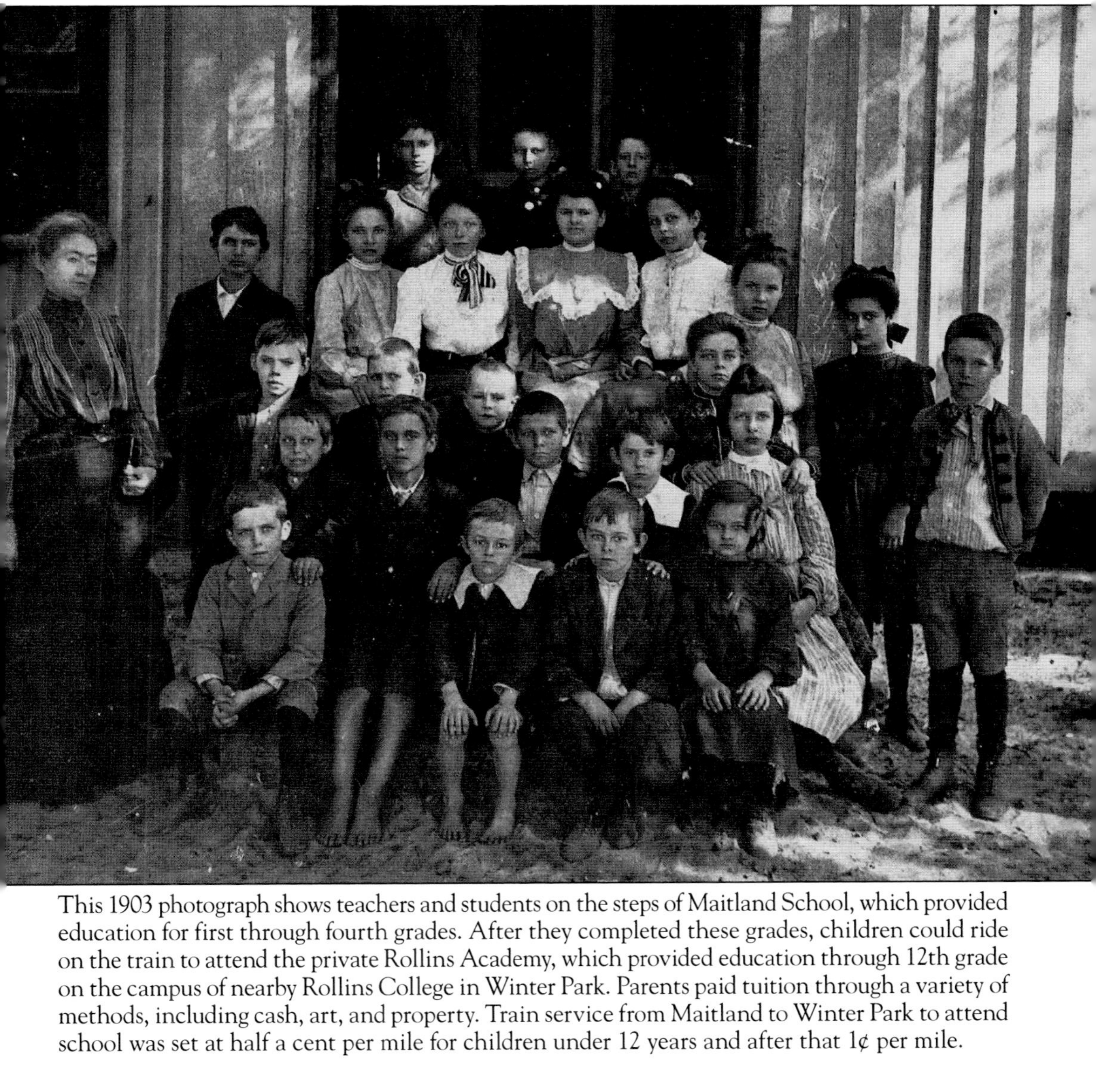

This 1903 photograph shows teachers and students on the steps of Maitland School, which provided education for first through fourth grades. After they completed these grades, children could ride on the train to attend the private Rollins Academy, which provided education through 12th grade on the campus of nearby Rollins College in Winter Park. Parents paid tuition through a variety of methods, including cash, art, and property. Train service from Maitland to Winter Park to attend school was set at half a cent per mile for children under 12 years and after that 1¢ per mile.

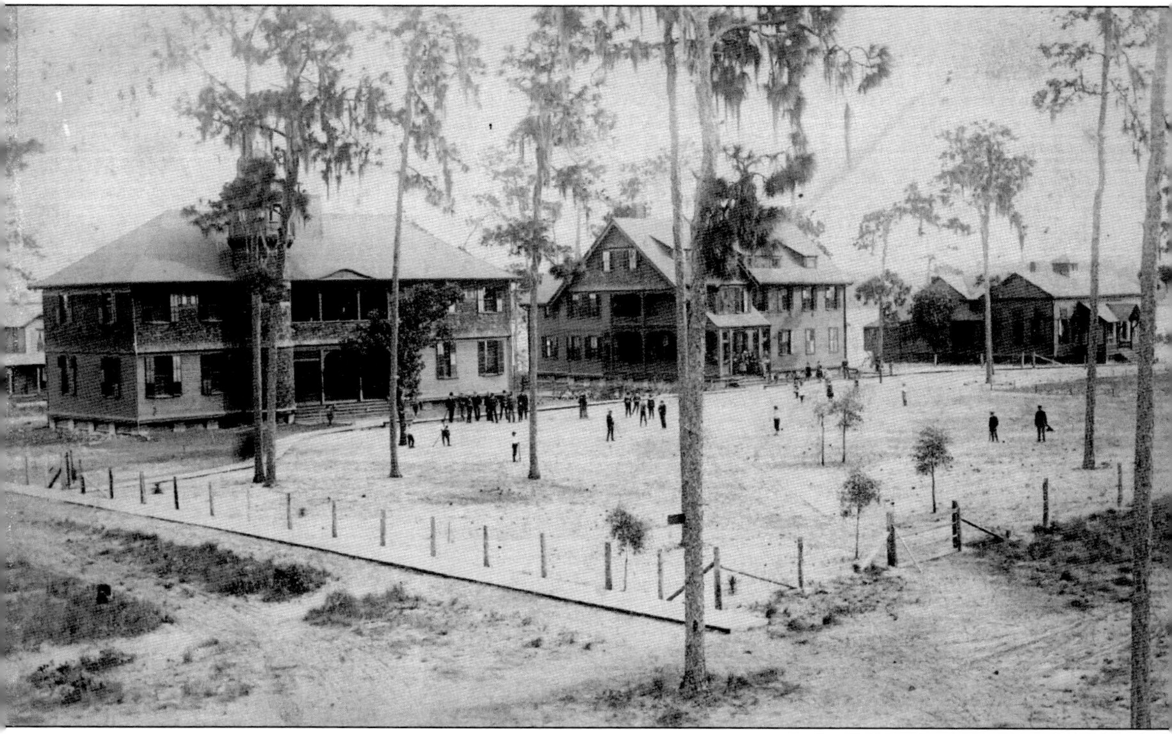

Founded in 1885 in nearby Winter Park, Florida, Rollins College had important ties to the Maitland community and others in the Central Florida area. The coeducational liberal arts school, the oldest recognized college in Florida, also featured Rollins Academy, where many Maitland children were educated from grades 5 to 12 and then continued their education at the college. This image of Rollins, made about 1888, is one of the earliest taken of the campus and features what were then the college's main buildings: from left to right, Knowles Hall, Pinehurst Cottage, and the Dining Hall. Note the fence around the edge of the campus—legend has it that it was built to keep out grazing cows. The lakefront college's surroundings are more urban now, and enrollment in 2009 totaled 3,259 in the school's programs. (Courtesy Rollins College.)

Helen (left) and Alice Waterhouse were two students who attended the Rollins Academy and then Rollins College. The granddaughters of William and Sarah Waterhouse, the twins, pictured here at the academy in 1914, withdrew from the college before graduating after their father, Charles, an architect, was sent to France to superintend building of YMCA huts there. Their mother, Lillian, then living in New Jersey, wanted the girls closer to home, so they transferred in 1922 to business school in Passaic, New Jersey.

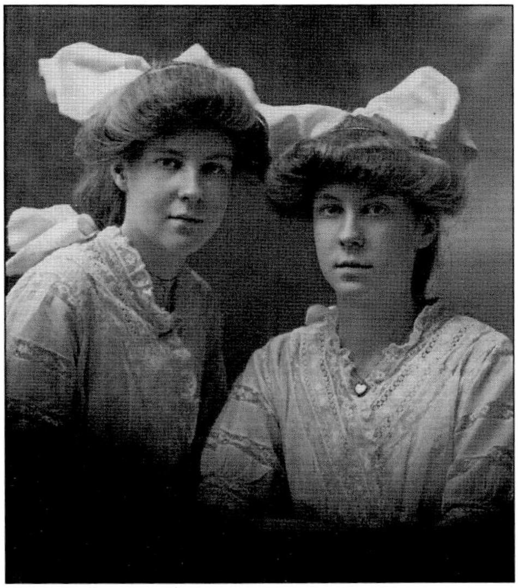

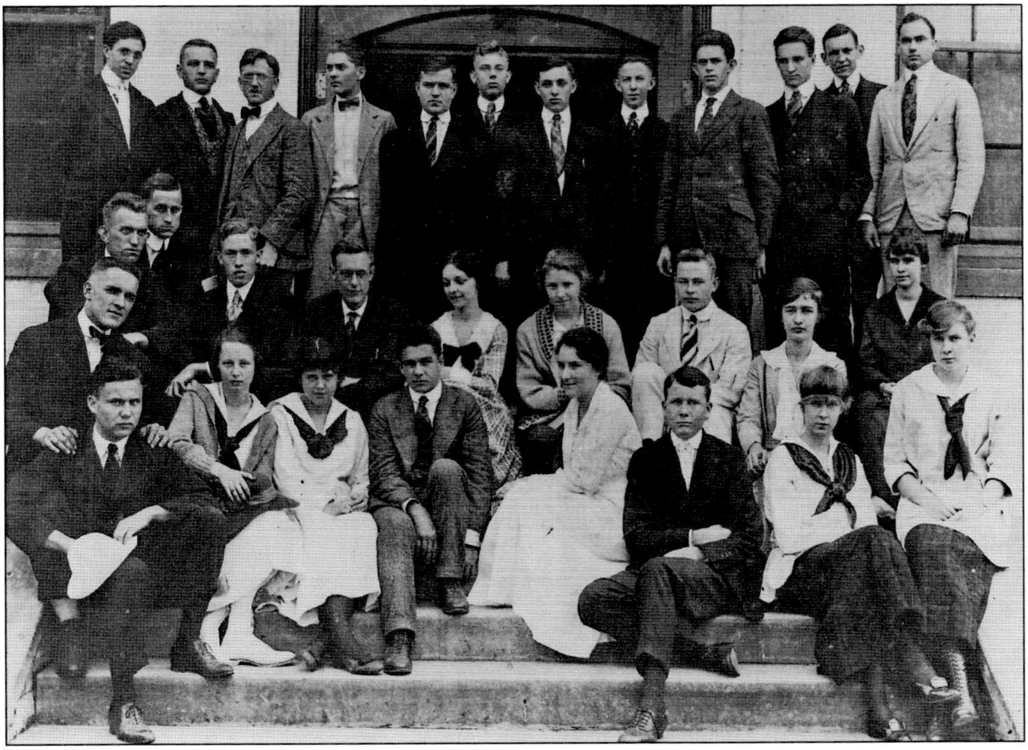

Look closely at the bottom right to find Helen and Alice Waterhouse in this group photograph from their days at Rollins College around 1919–1920. Included are, from left to right, (first row) Warren Ingram, Isabel Foley Whaler, Vivian Barbour Howison, Leonard Fletcher, Kitty Gates, Ephraim Conway, Alice Waterhouse, and Helen Waterhouse; (second row) Bob Greene, Benjamin C. Shaw, Raymond W. Greene, Stanley Mansfield, Prof. Eric Palmer, Sarah Yancey, Elizabeth Russell, J. Harold Hill, Harriette Mansfield, and Sadie Sawyer Pellerio; (third row) James I. Noxon, Albert Randolph Lake, Robert Hutchinson, Charles M. Stilwell, Robert Dancy, William Giddings, Robert Stone, Harold C. Tilden, Frederic Harris Ward, Forrest B. Stone, Maynard Froemke, and coach Thomas E. Royal.

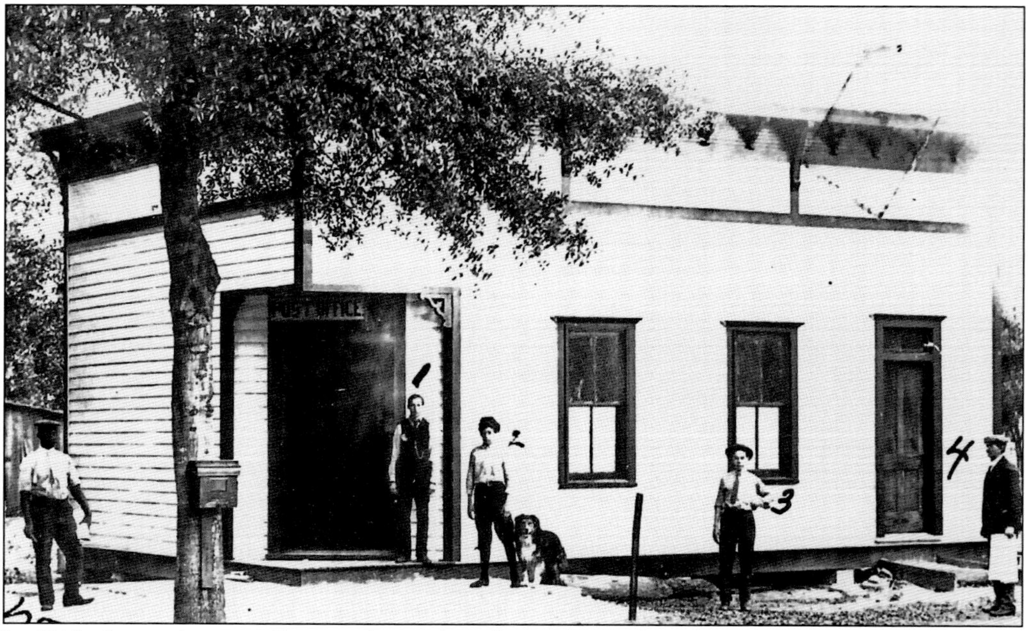

In 1911, the city's post office was located in this one-story building at the northwest corner of Horatio and Maitland Avenues, across the street from the railroad depot. The community's first post office was established for what was then called Lake Maitland in 1872 and was operated out of the home of Christopher Columbus Beasley, an early settler who was appointed postmaster. He served 25 families, of which only 13 lived within 2 miles of the office. The post office later operated out of George Stith's general store on Horatio Avenue. In 1901, the post office designation was shortened to "Maitland."

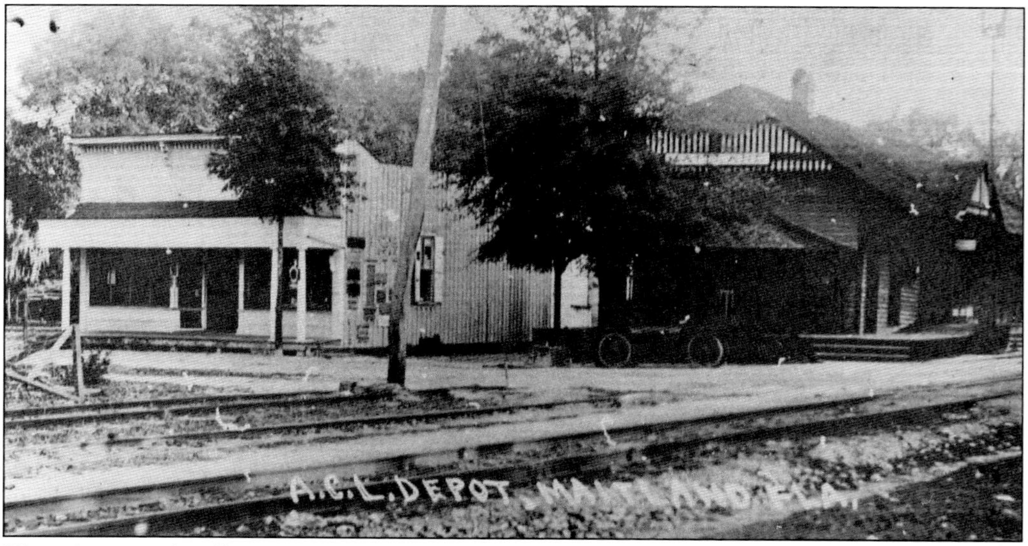

This photograph offers a 1915 view of the Maitland depot and the adjacent Hill's Store. The depot for many years was the center of city transportation and commerce. Four stores were built near the depot and its tracks to take advantage of the many people who regularly traveled there for train and telegraph business. The store, built in 1885 by George T. Stith, was sold to Sumter B. Hill around 1900 and in 1921 was sold to James Brown. Four years later, Brown built a new store on the southeast corner of Horatio Avenue and Independence Lane.

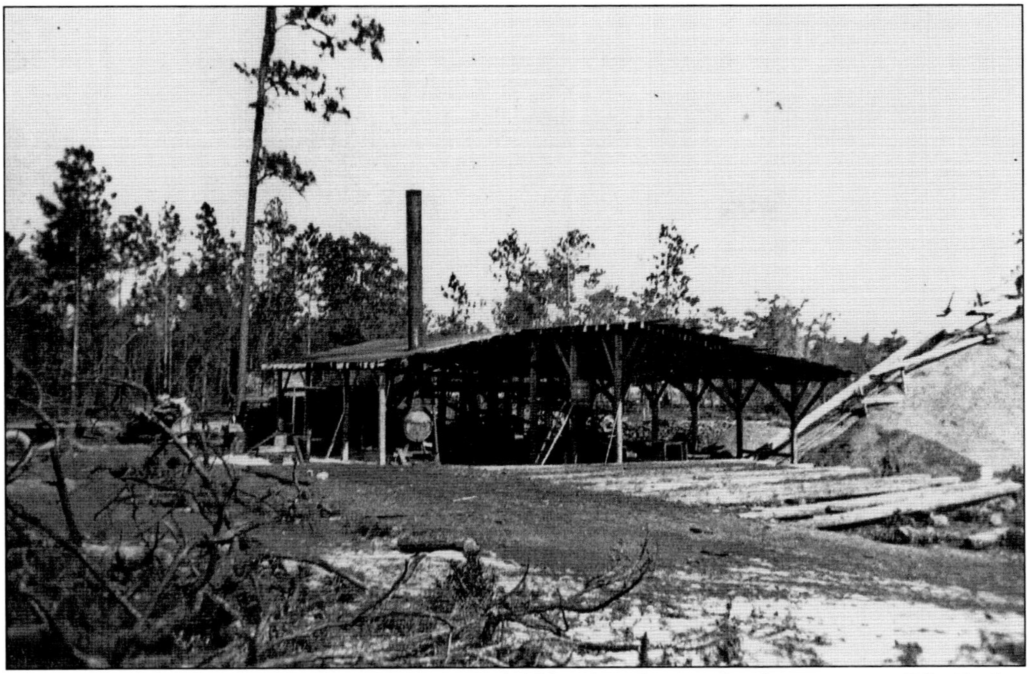

The area's rich pine forests provided important lifeblood in the Maitland community. The Parker Lumber sawmill, shown in this *c.* 1921 photograph, was located at the north end of Marion Way, about 100 yards east of Maitland Avenue. The sawmill specialized in rough-cut lumber harvested in Central Florida. By 1934, the company was also selling other building products and manufacturing different kinds of building materials. The last sawmill and manufacturing occurred in 1960, and the company became a retail lumber and building supply house.

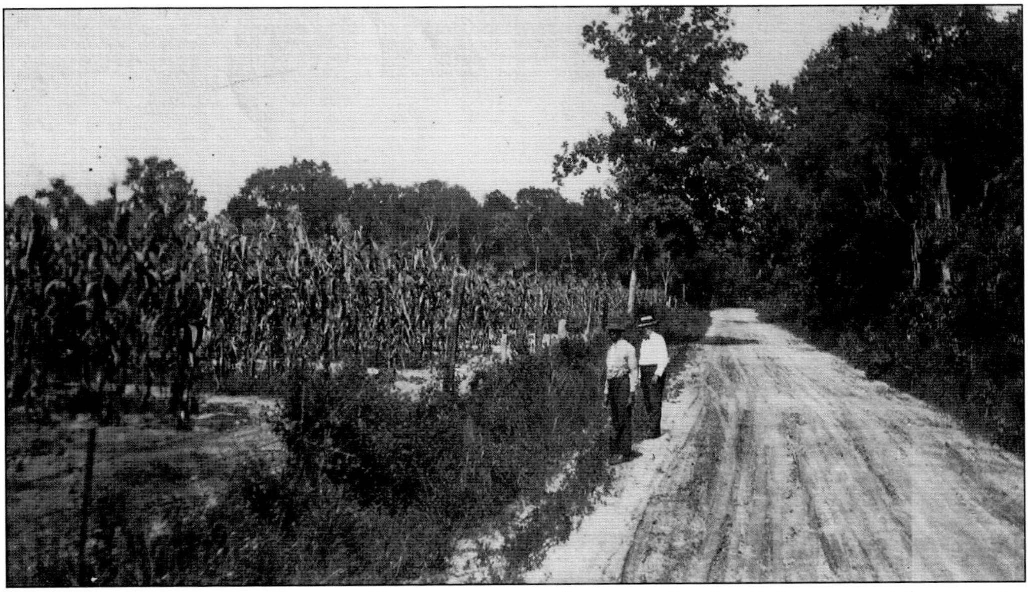

Although the community was rapidly growing, agriculture remained a vital commercial enterprise in the area. Only a short trip from downtown, residents would find citrus groves and vegetable fields. This photograph shows Ed Hall (right) and an unidentified visitor at Hall's garden near his Eagle Grove located on Adams Road near Horatio Avenue.

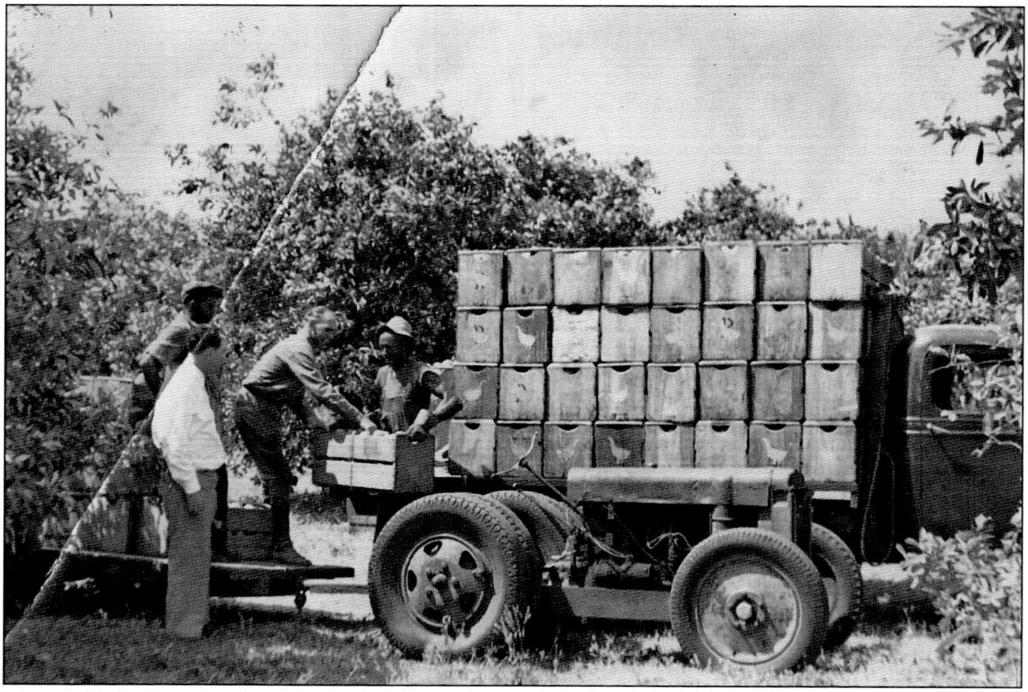

Many of Lake Maitland's earliest settlers sought their fortunes in the citrus business, planting many acres of groves throughout the region. The area was hit hard by freezes in December 1894 and February 1895. The growers who remained in the area replanted and waited for the new trees to produce fruit. These photographs show pickers harvesting citrus from a nearby field and packing them into crates. The crates were taken to one of several area packinghouses, including the Pilgrim Packing House, shown here in 1915. Fresh fruit was processed and repacked for Northern markets, using local rail lines for shipments. Pilgrim Packing House was destroyed by fire in 1926.

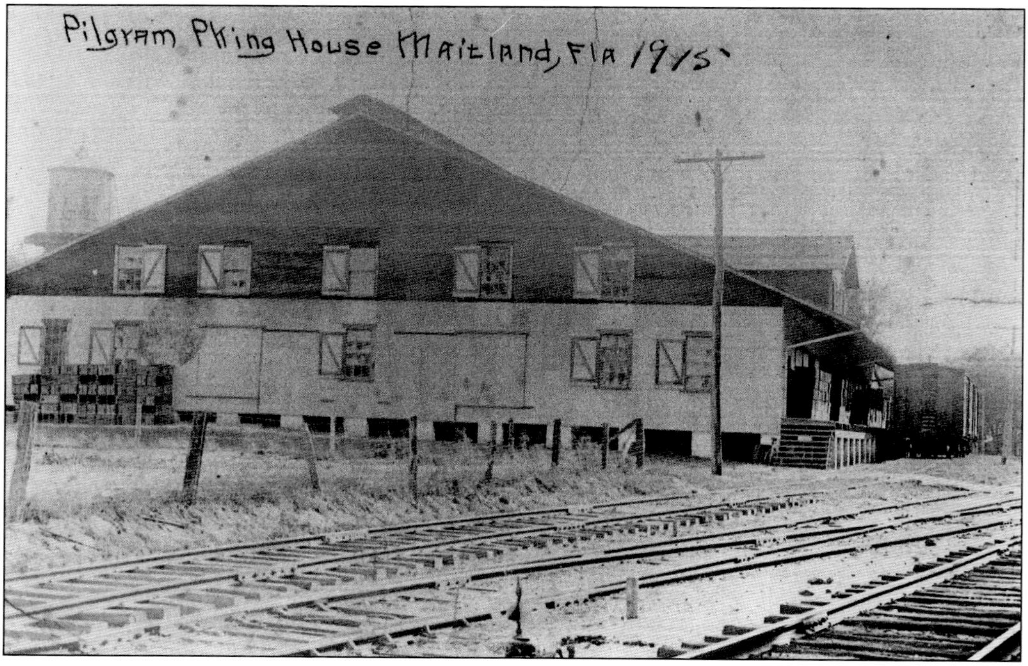

Four

A New Era

With the arrival of the 1920s, the city of Lake Maitland joined in the Florida boom—for business, tourism, and new residents. Although the city's name didn't officially shorten to "Maitland" until 1959, that was its unofficial name. Housing began to spring up in what were once agricultural areas, and new businesses came to town to serve the growing population. Growth slowed during the Great Depression, but a new light shone on the city with the arrival of noted artist and architect Jules Andre Smith, who visited the area in the 1930s and established a residential research studio to encourage artists to experiment in their work. Its Aztec-Mayan style gave the city a unique flavor and remains a cultural center for the community. Nothing, however, would change the city as much as the post–World War II economic bonanza that swept through Florida, bringing massive population growth and a new style of living—suburbia. Maryland's Martin Marietta Corporation's decision to open a new division in the Orlando area to participate in the rising space industry forever changed the city. Citrus groves and wooded areas rapidly were transformed into housing tracts and shopping centers, some bearing names of the city's pioneers, but Maitland's new growing population did not forsake its founders' tradition of excellence, benevolence, and civic involvement.

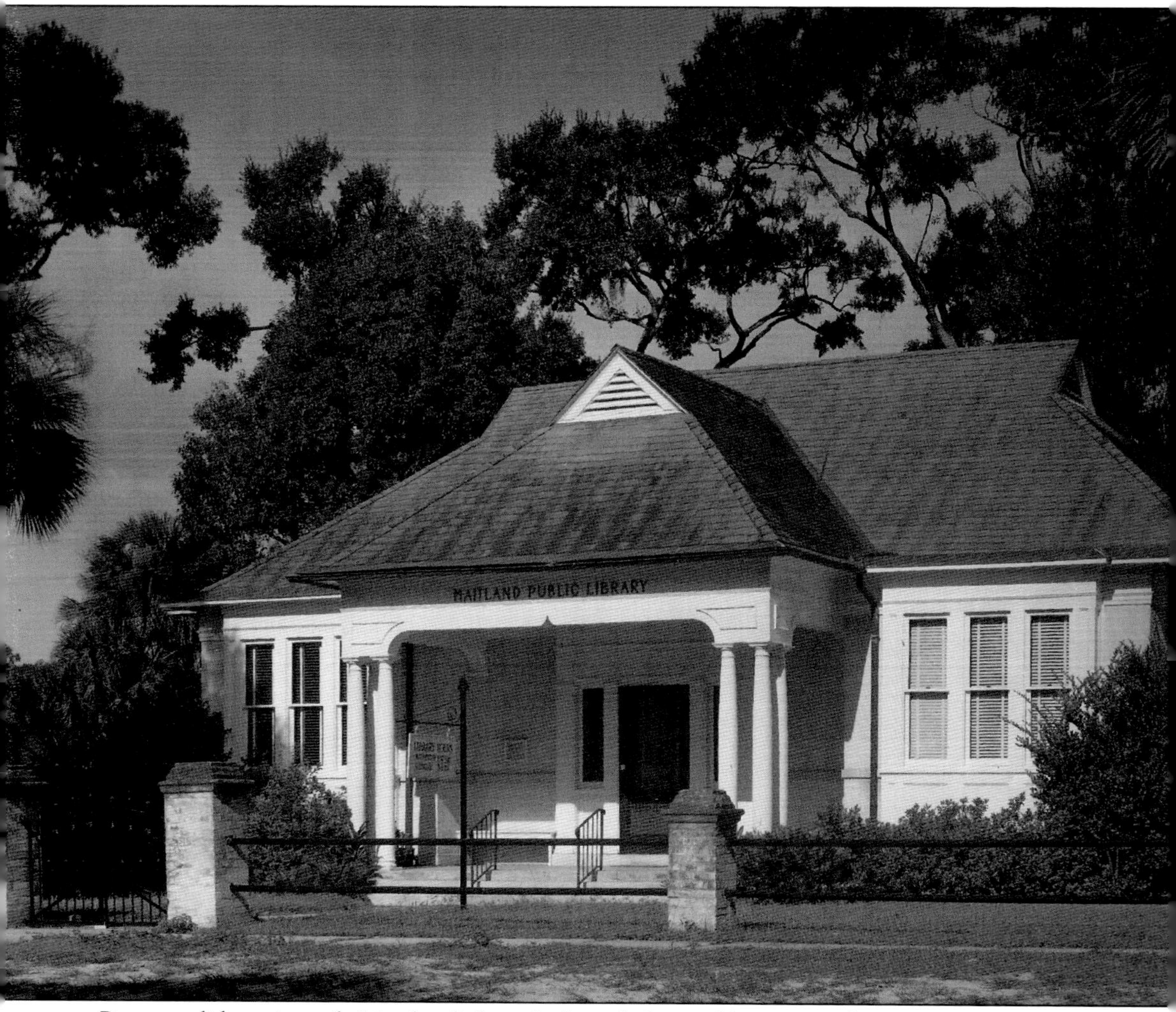

Progress did not impede Maitland's love for knowledge and learning. The Maitland Library long has been an important part of the city's life and learning. It was founded in 1896 with a gift of 360 books from Clara Dommerich, whose family was a strong supporter of the library, and was located in a local teacher's living room. The library later moved to a Horatio Avenue store until the current building was erected at 501 South Maitland Avenue. The original section of the building was designed by architect Charles B. Waterhouse and built in 1907. Several additions were made in the last century to help it meet the needs of the growing community. Today the library has more than 85,000 items in its collections and provides a wide range of services from computer classes to children's activities.

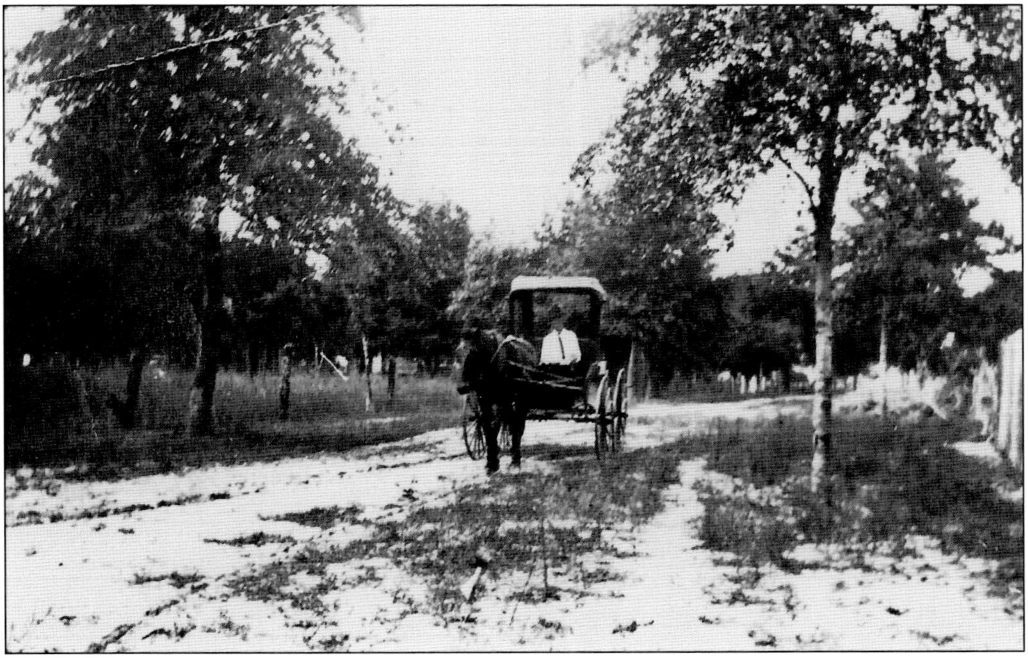

These photographs show John Pinder, an early Maitland resident, in two different scenes that reveal the city's different faces. Above, Pinder, who working in an area citrus packinghouse, is shown riding with his horse-drawn buggy in 1912 on then-unpaved George Avenue. The scene looks west from Maitland Avenue toward Lake Sybelia. In the photograph below, dated 1915, Pinder stands in a boat on Lake Sybelia at the foot of West George Avenue. Also visible in this picture is the pump house of the American Fruit Growers, an organization of citrus growers located in Maitland.

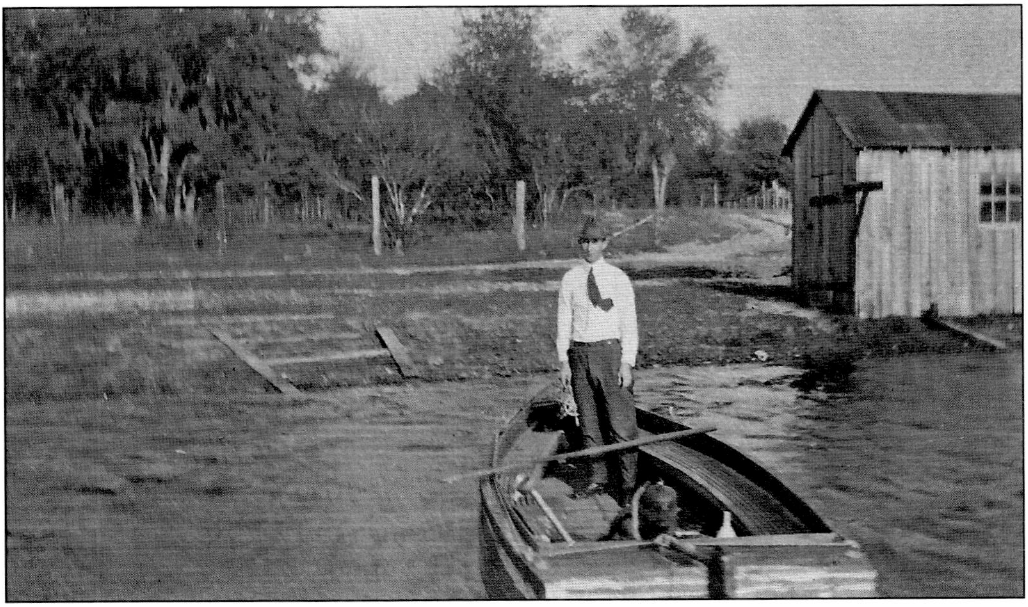

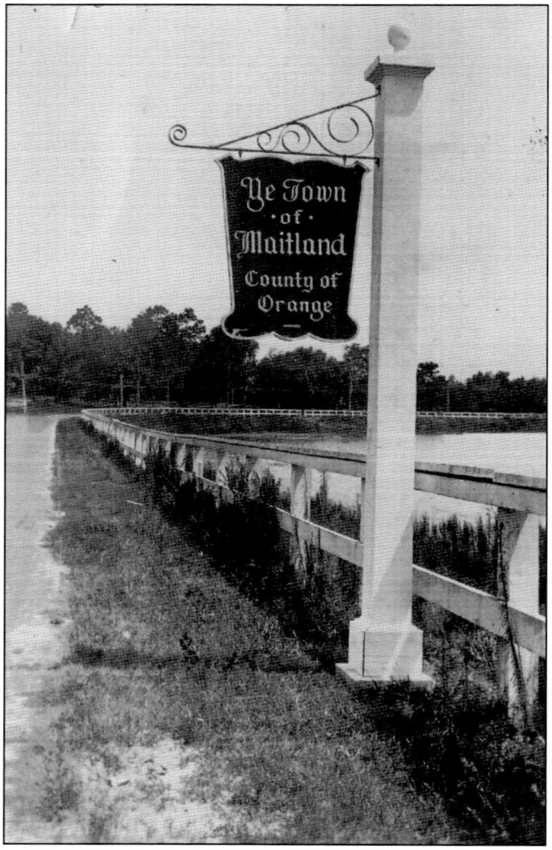

By the 1920s, Maitland was sharing the economic prosperity of the era and moving into the modern age. Although this road sign on Maitland Avenue near Lake Faith declares it to be "Ye Town of Maitland," the community truly was joining the gradual trek toward urbanization. Instead of horses and carriages, cars and trucks traveled on the streets, more and more of which were becoming paved and lined with poles carrying electrical and telephone lines. The photograph below of the intersection of Maitland and Horatio Avenues, once a shady spot, demonstrates the changes that came into the city, bringing with them a diversity of businesses and residents.

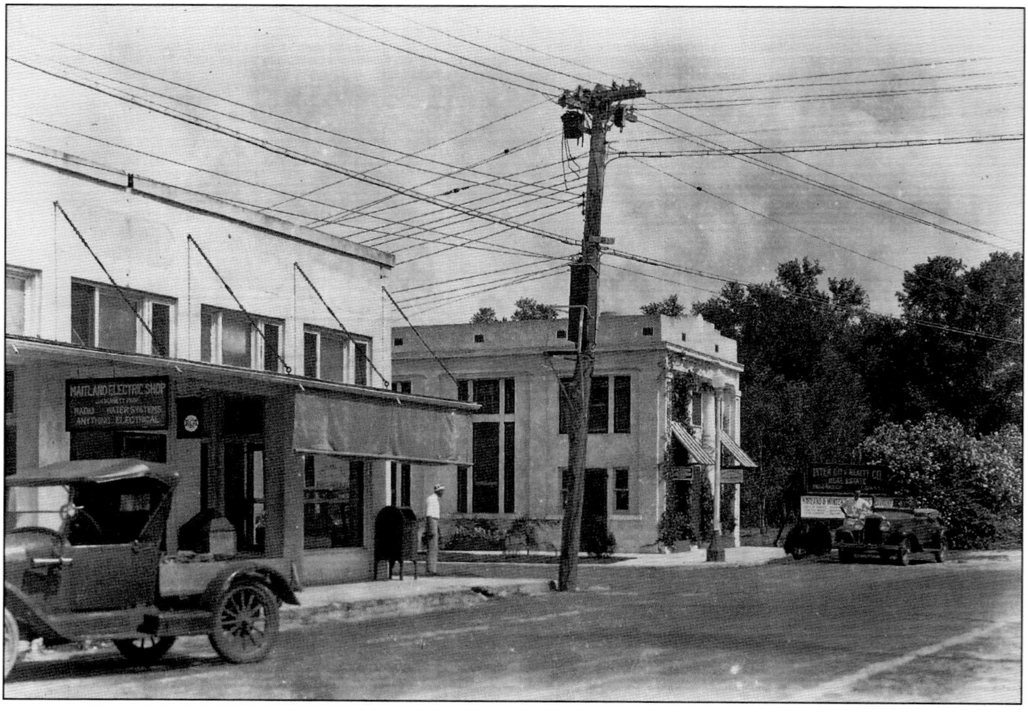

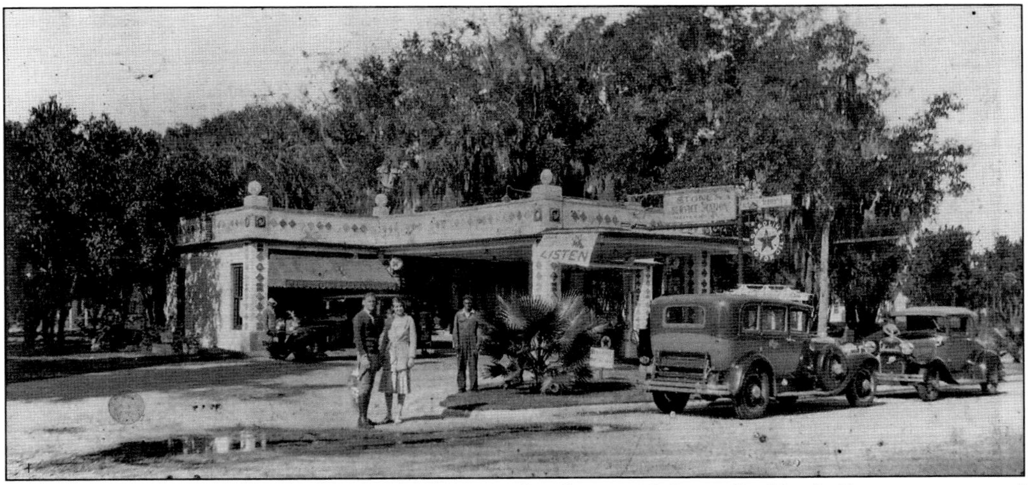

The Alvord Alonzo Stone family came to Maitland in 1883 from Guilford, Connecticut, and quickly became involved in the growing community. By the 20th century, their descendants were involved in several business interests, including citrus growing, a service station, and a store. Stone's Service Station was long a landmark in the city. This image from 1920 shows the station, which included a repair garage and a grocery store. It was located on U.S. 17-92 and was billed as "the one-stop station"—a modern crossroads store that also sold groceries, tires, and batteries. Residents could purchase a variety of items at the store, a precursor to today's big-box stores. Stone operated the business for 31 years before selling it in 1959 as a restaurant site.

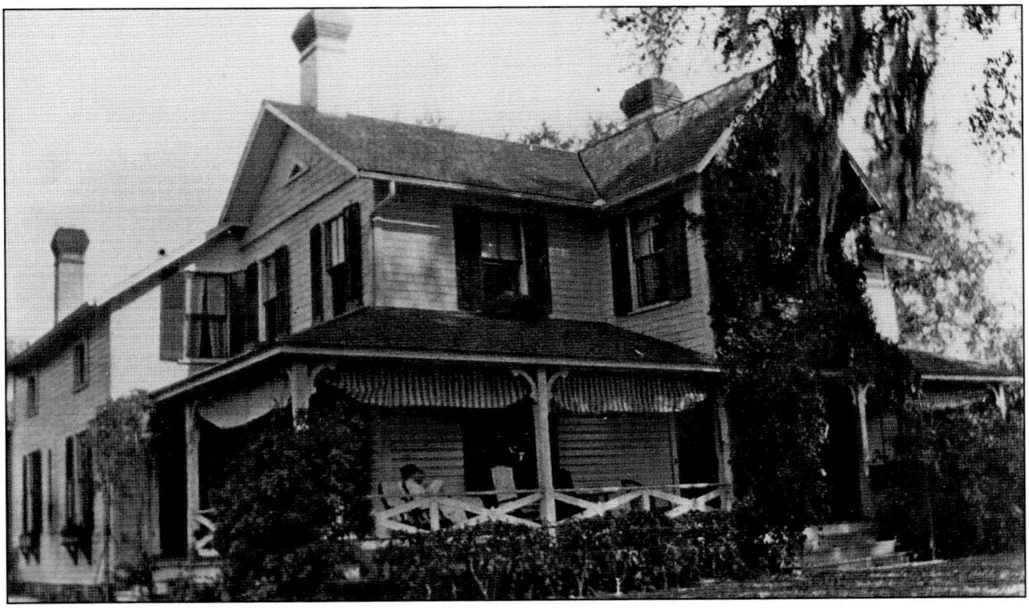

Chadbourne Hall, pictured here in 1923, became a winter home in the 1930s for various writers and notables, including American author Winston Churchill, who leased it from owner Dr. Kenneth Kilbourne. The house was part of property on the west shore of Lake Catherine bought in 1878 by Capt. Josiah Eaton, of Calais, Maine, who came to the Maitland area after the Civil War. Eaton was involved in the city's early days, serving as its first mayor. Initially Eaton, a former naval paymaster, built a one-room cabin with a swinging table and bed like those found on a ship. In 1880, his nephew, Eleazer Boynton of Massachusetts, built the existing wooden two-story house, sold in 1921 to Kilbourne. Today it is a private residence.

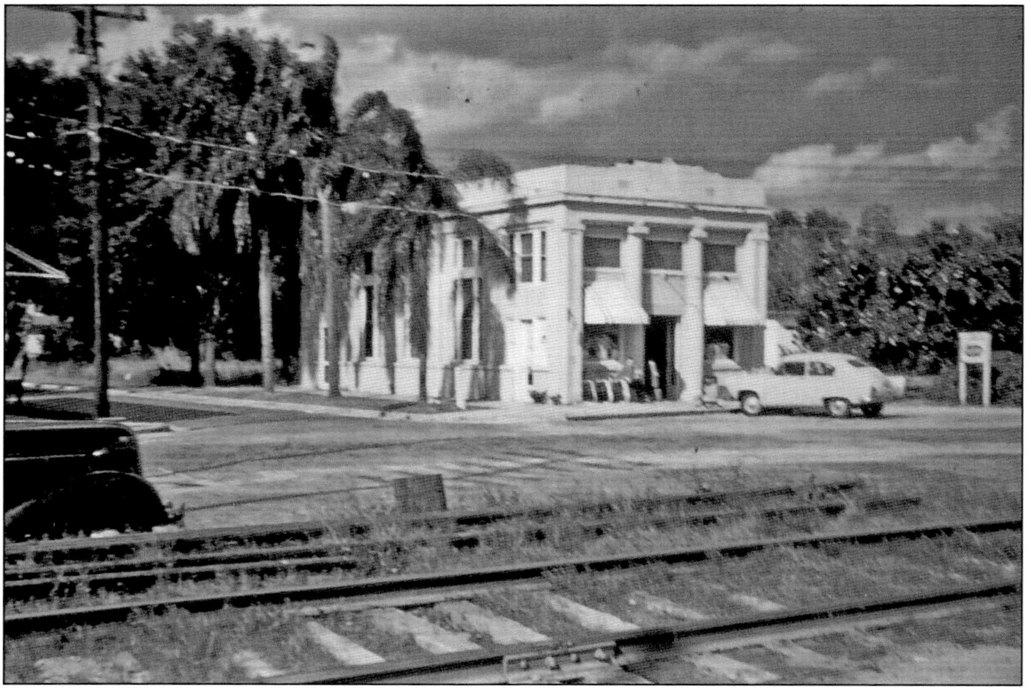

These photographs offer two early views of what is now known as the Bank of America Building, located at 105 North Maitland Avenue—a site that has been home to several businesses of central importance. In 1911, a post office was built on the property, but it was destroyed by fire in 1923. Two years later, the current building was constructed to house the Bank of Maitland, providing the first local banking for residents who previously had to travel to Winter Park or Orlando for such services. It closed during the Great Depression. In the 1930s, the building was home to Benson's Pharmacy (as pictured here, below), and in the 1960s, it was Jerry's Bicycle Shop. In 1978, the building once again became part of a bank—Barnett Bank—and its interior was restored to its 1920s design and decor. Remodeled once again in the 1990s, the building continues to operate as a bank and is a busy corner in the city's business life.

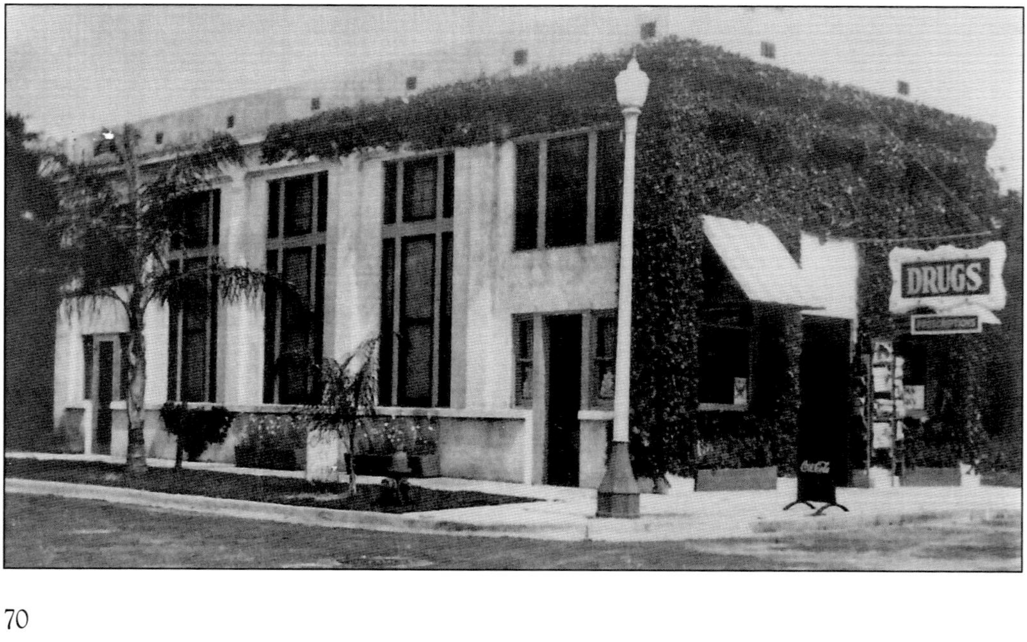

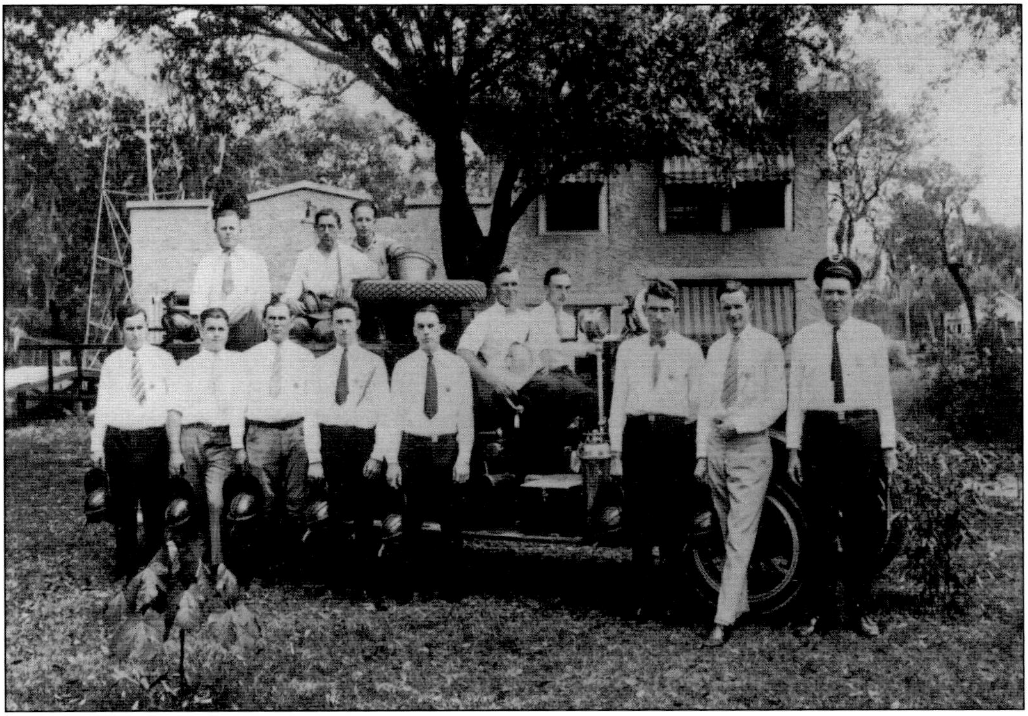

The Maitland Fire Department, founded in 1925 as a volunteer group, has long been a vital part of the city's services to its residents. Many members were local businessmen who offered their time to the city's protection. This April 5, 1929, scene is the oldest known photograph of city firefighters with their truck behind town hall. Today the all-professional department employs a total of 45 people and offers rescue and fire services along with a number of community services. From left to right are (first row, standing) Irb Snodgrass, Jack Horner, Joe Thomas, Laurence Parker, Clyde Clark, Roy Kyle, Ed Owens, and police chief Mose Bryant; (second row, seated) fire chief John I. Strong and driver Arthur Wellons; (third row, standing) Hope Small, Joe Bennett, and Phil Witlis.

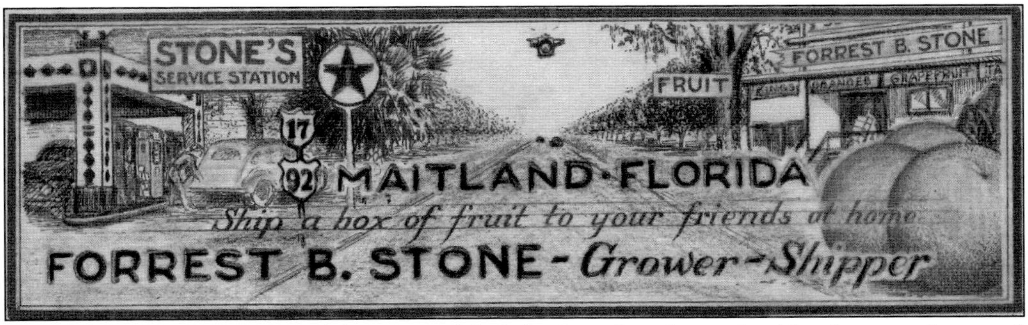

Florida's citrus growers created distinctive labels for fruit they shipped to Northern markets, and the Stone family was no exception. This label clearly illustrates their many interests—from Stone's Service Station on the left to the family's fruit stand across the street on U.S. 17-92, depicted on the right. "Ship a box of fruit to your friends at home" was the motto for this label. No doubt many Maitland residents and visitors did just that.

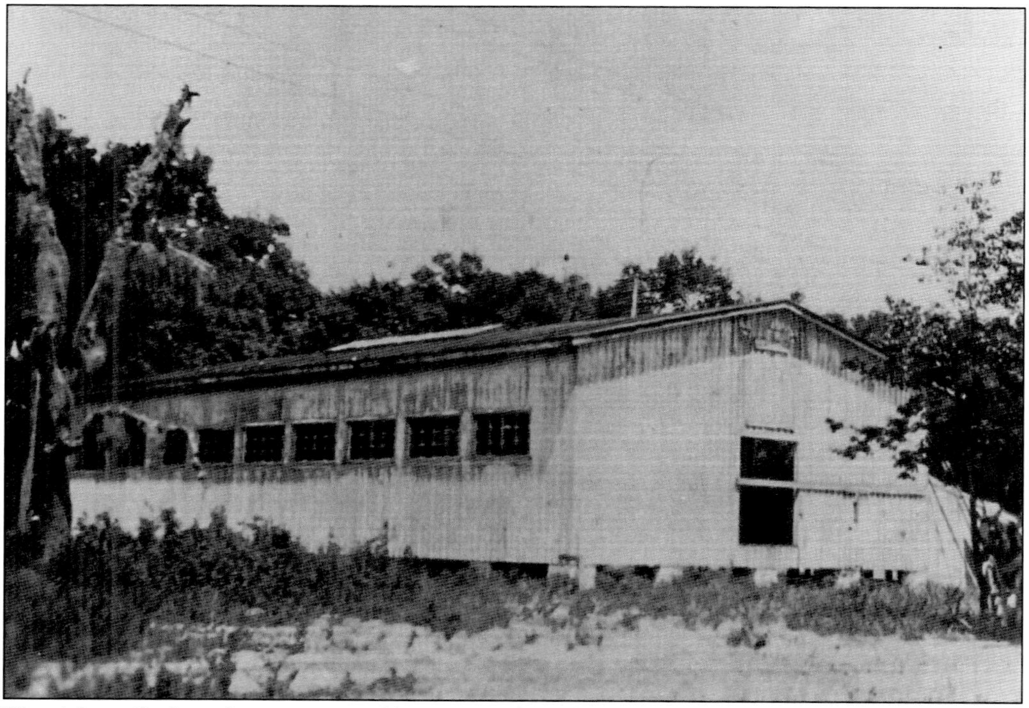

The Adams Packing house, pictured here around 1925, was one of several citrus processing firms in the Maitland area. It was located on Maitland Avenue, south of the current municipal complex. Its founder, Frank Adams, arrived in Lake Maitland in 1881 from New York City and grew citrus on property on east Horatio Avenue known as Adams Groves. In an early sales brochure from Adams Groves, the region was touted as being healthful and "famous for the quantity and quality of its fruit." The packinghouse was torn down in 1926 to make way for Central Park.

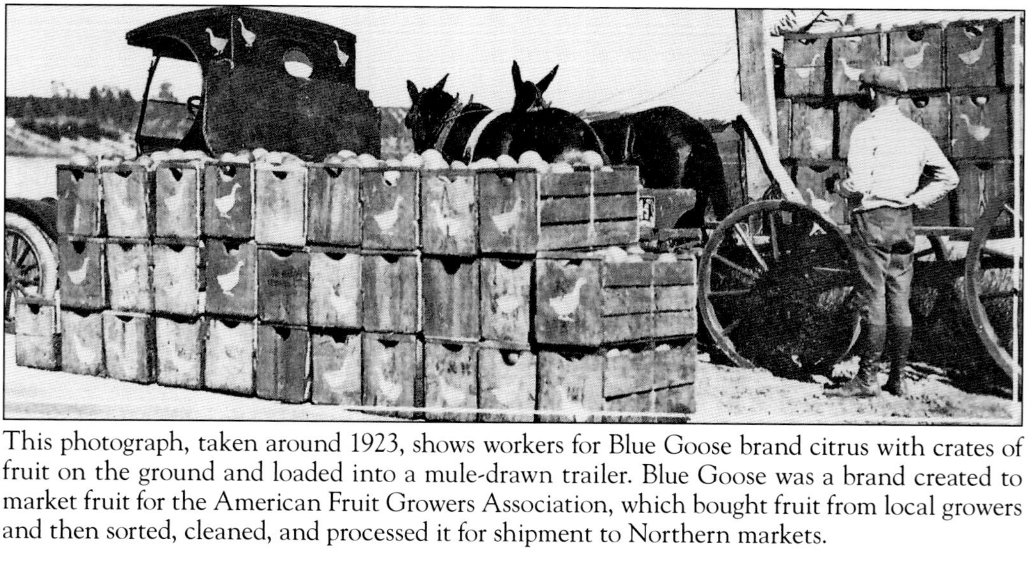

This photograph, taken around 1923, shows workers for Blue Goose brand citrus with crates of fruit on the ground and loaded into a mule-drawn trailer. Blue Goose was a brand created to market fruit for the American Fruit Growers Association, which bought fruit from local growers and then sorted, cleaned, and processed it for shipment to Northern markets.

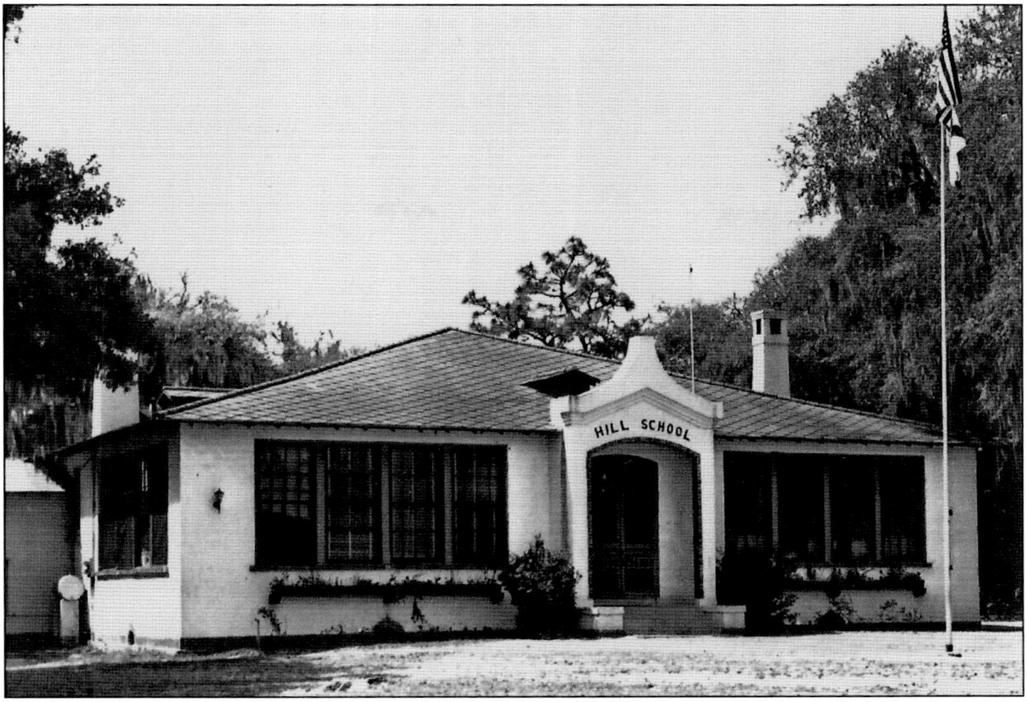

In 1923, the Maitland Hill School was built for $8,000 to educate Maitland's growing population of children. It was named after Sumter Brock Hill, a citrus grower, who donated the land. Many of his grandchildren and great-grandchildren would attend the school in future years. The above image, taken around 1935, shows the exterior of the school, located on West Sybelia Avenue. It served children through fourth grade and was recognized with high honors for its achievements—credited in 1927 for being one of the best schools in Florida. It was torn down in 1975. The photograph below, taken soon after the Hill School's opening, shows Rita Mae Bennett on one of the school's swings.

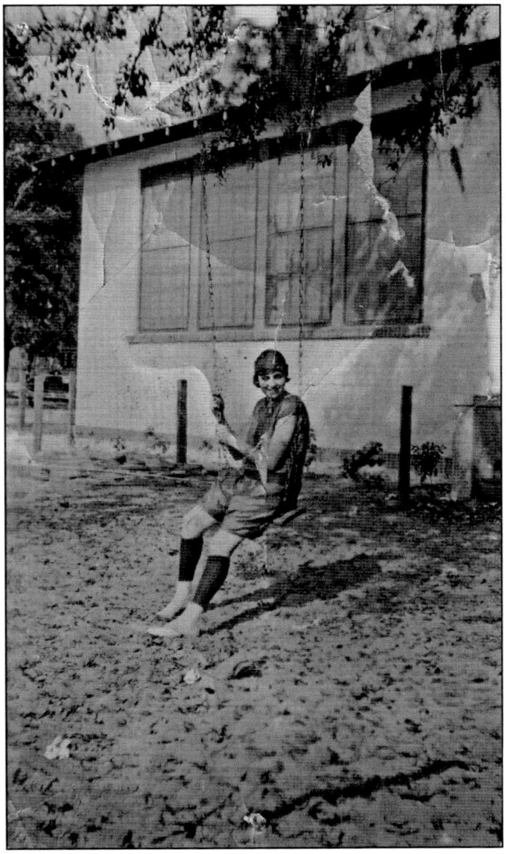

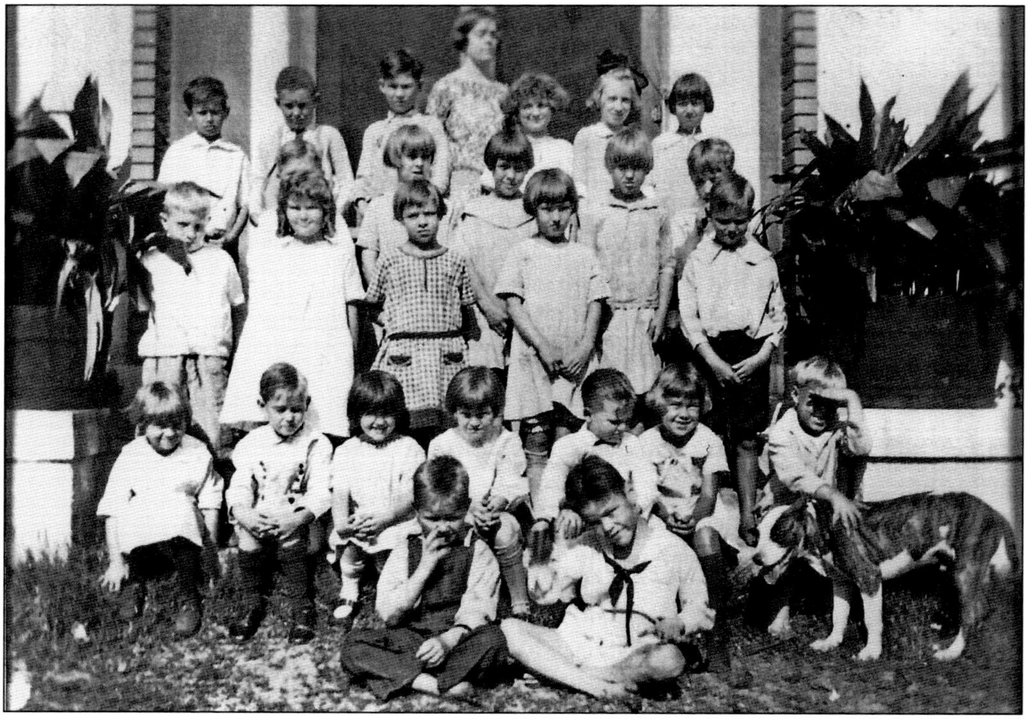

Sitting and standing on the front steps of the Hill School are Una Fugate and the school's first- through third-grade class in 1925. This group of 25 is not identified, but they were among the first to take classes in the new school; and it looks like they found a canine companion as well.

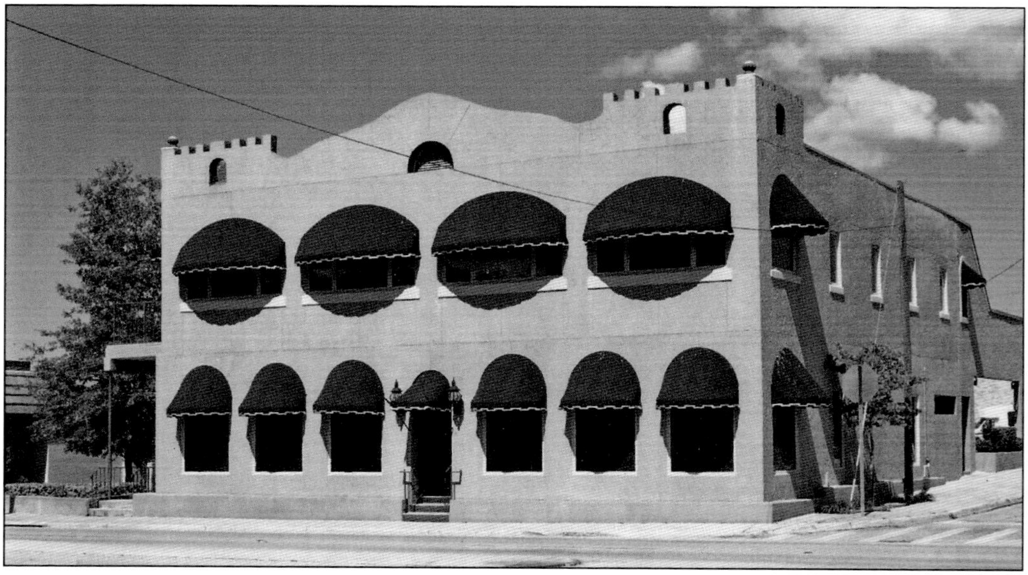

The White Way Building was constructed in 1925 on the site of Maitland's second schoolhouse. It was initially used by the White Way Motor Company and Filling Station with John Nelson as the proprietor. The White Way Restaurant, run by F. H. Manning, operated out of the southwest corner of the building. In 1994, the interior of the building was remodeled and its exterior restored to its original appearance in the Mediterranean Revival style. A law firm now occupies the building, located at 300 North Maitland Avenue.

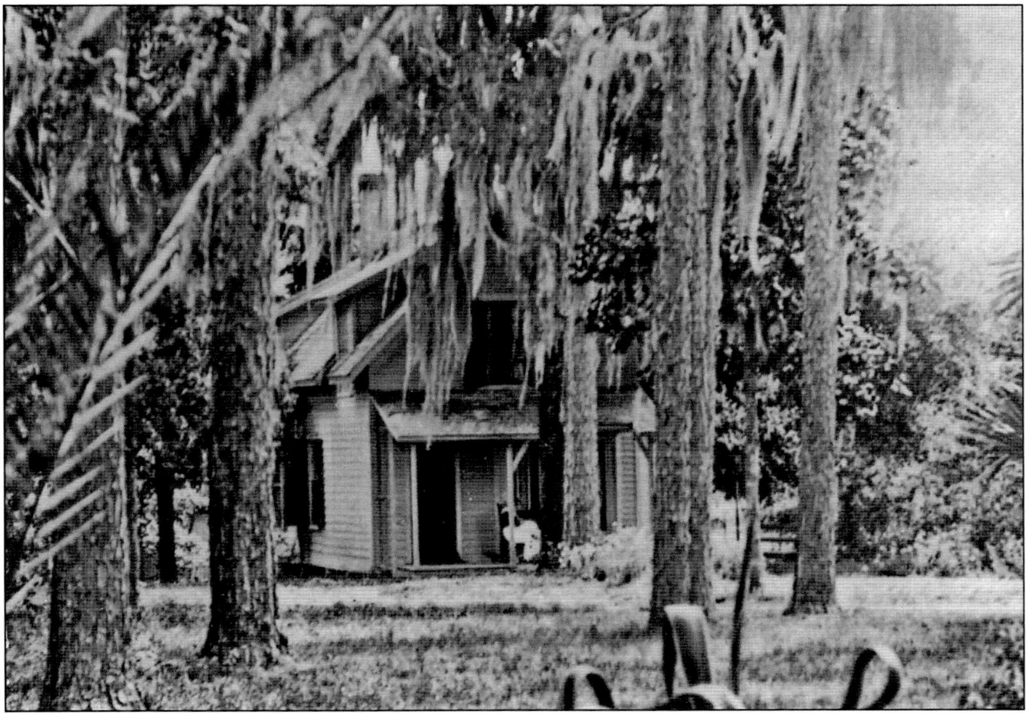

Judge Bolling Baker lived in this home on Lawrence Avenue (now Lake Street), built in 1879 and located between the rail line and the winter home of Bishop Henry Whipple. The Bakers were noted members of the community, especially Baker's daughter Elizabeth, who taught at the Maitland School on Maitland Avenue and continued to live in the house after her father's 1880 death until the 1930s. Baker was an attorney who practiced in Alabama and Florida before the Civil War, during which he was a member of the Confederate Cabinet. The Whipple and Baker houses have since been replaced by the Maitland Shores Apartments.

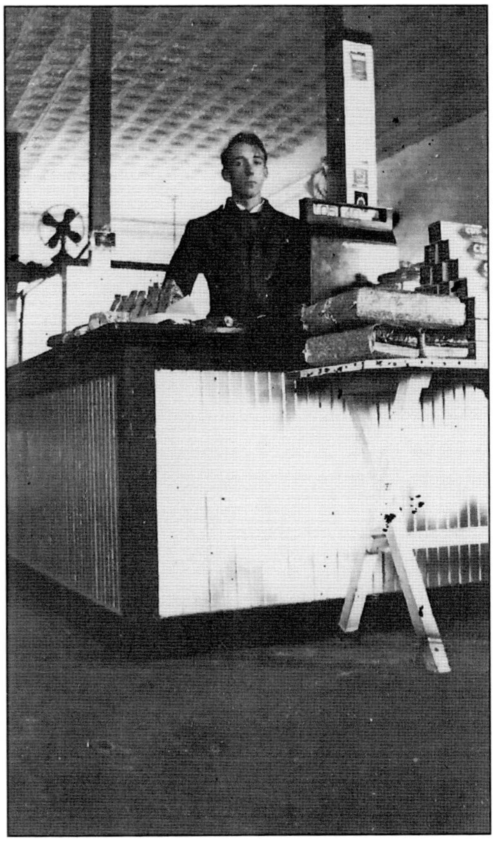

Richard Pinder, the son of John Pinder, is shown here around 1934 working at the counter of Johnny Stover's Store. Located next to the post office at the southwest corner of Maitland and Horatio Avenues, the store provided a number of goods and merchandise to the local population.

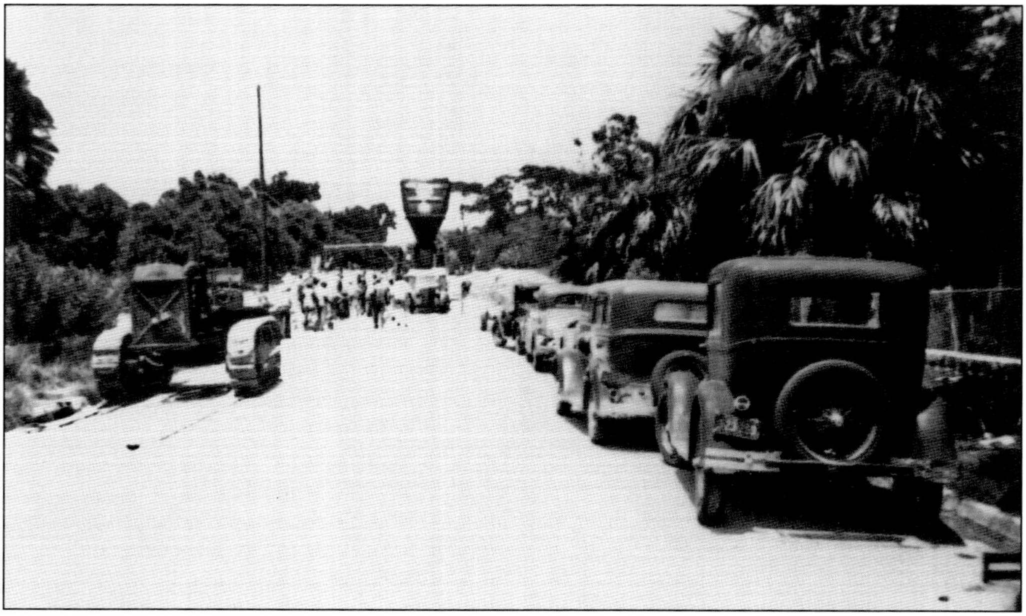

By the 1930s, the city had three major streets—Horatio and Maitland Avenues and U.S. Highway 17-92—that were lifelines for business, travelers, and residents. In 1924, the city could boast of 5 miles of brick-paved streets. Within a decade, however, the city already needed to widen some streets to accommodate its booming growth. These photographs from 1938 show the "before and after" of a road-widening project on U.S. Highway 17-92. The view looks north along the highway between Park Lake and Lake Maitland. Although the trains would continue to travel through the area, the automobile would reign from here on, and it still dominates the city's transportation landscape.

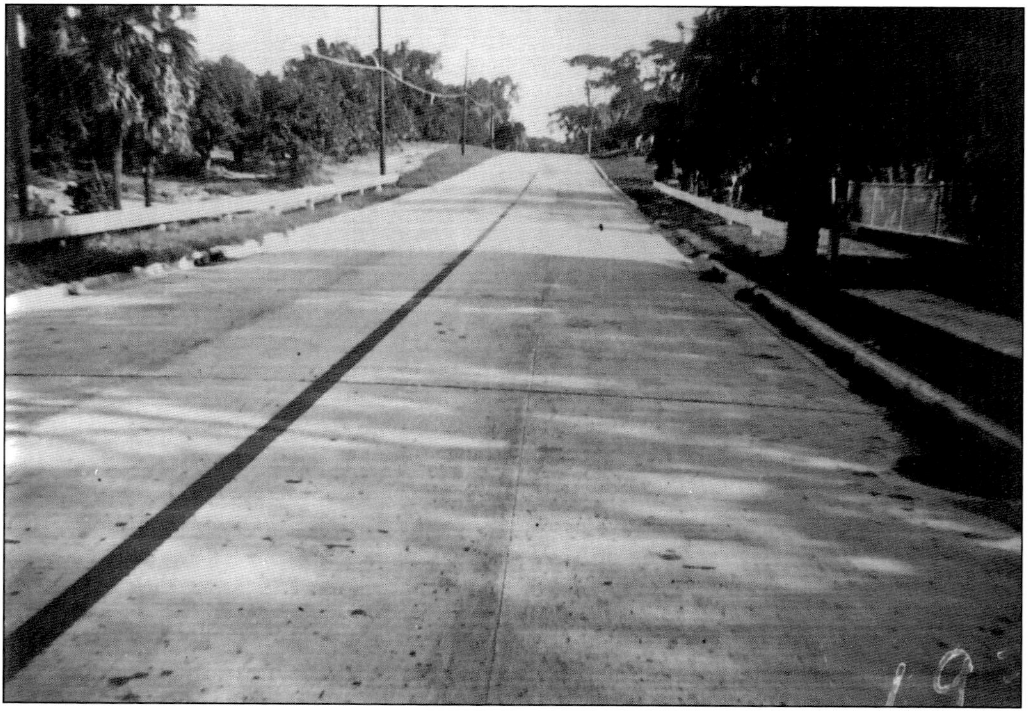

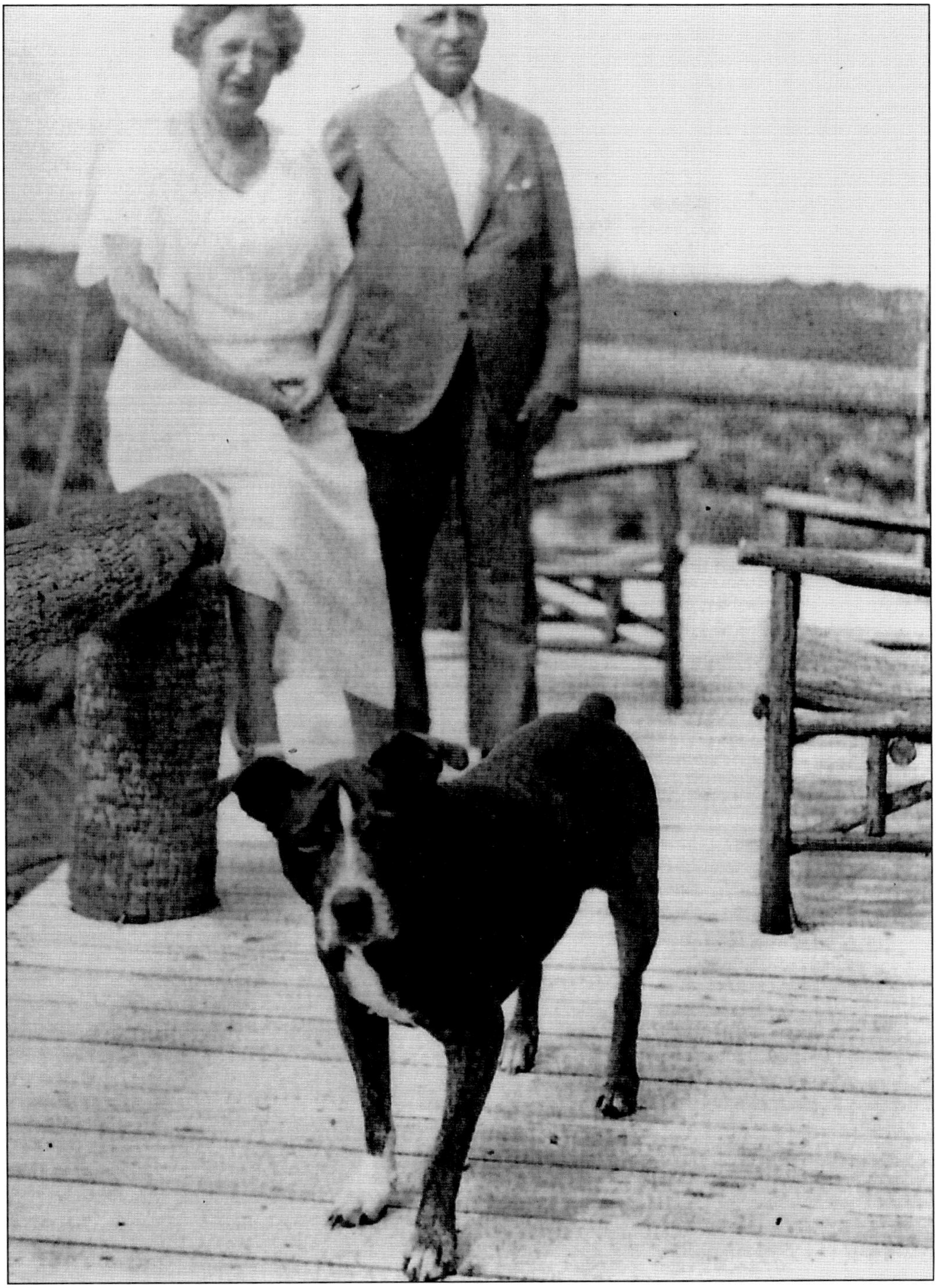

Elizabeth McConnell and Edward Hall, joined by Caesar the dog, enjoy a sunny day in 1935 at New Smyrna Beach. Another important feature of the Maitland area was its proximity to East Coast beaches, particularly once roads and automobiles became the prime mode of transportation, making the beach an easy day trip for city residents. Hall, once a Chicago banker, moved in 1915 to Maitland, where his family grew citrus.

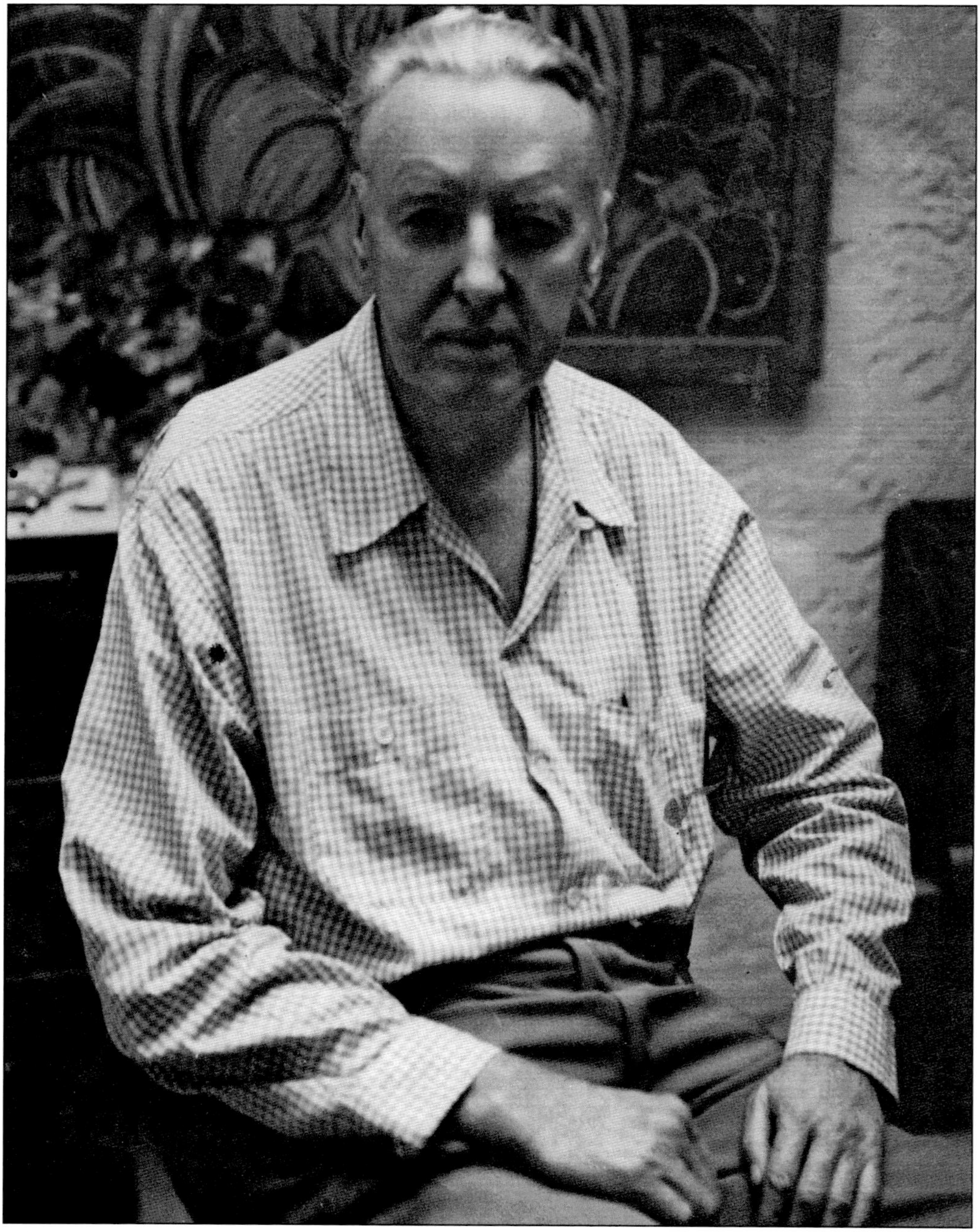

Jules Andre Smith, known as Andre (1880–1959), a noted artist, architect, and author, first visited the Maitland area in the 1930s. He was so charmed by the area that he returned to establish an artists' studio and residence that opened in 1938, originally calling it the Research Studio. After Smith died in 1959, the studio complex stood empty until the City of Maitland purchased it. In 1971, a group of concerned citizens formed the Maitland Art Association and leased the property from the city, reopening it as the Maitland Art Center at 231 West Packwood Avenue. During its many years, the Art Center has hosted a number of noted painters, sculptors, and printmakers, and it continues to attract resident artists and offer art instruction. (Courtesy Maitland Art Center.)

Andre Smith was involved with the nearby community of Eatonville, the oldest incorporated African American city in the United States. He was friends with many of the residents there, including noted author Zora Neale Hurston, and used scenes from the city in his work, as these paintings demonstrate. The first, titled *Church Scene, Eatonville*, was created around 1940. Smith used bold colors to show churchgoers gathered outside the tall wooden church, which is surrounded by pine trees. The second painting, untitled and undated, is of a residence in the nearby city. Smith, who attended Cornell University to study architecture, later became more interested in art, particularly etching, for which he won a gold medal at the San Francisco Exhibition of 1915. He also worked in oil—the medium for these paintings—as well as watercolor, sculpture, and printmaking. (Both courtesy Maitland Art Center.)

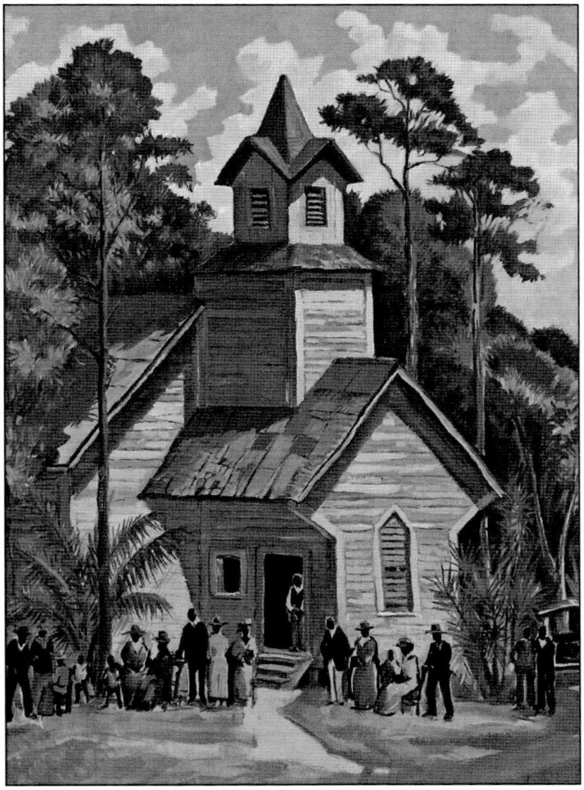

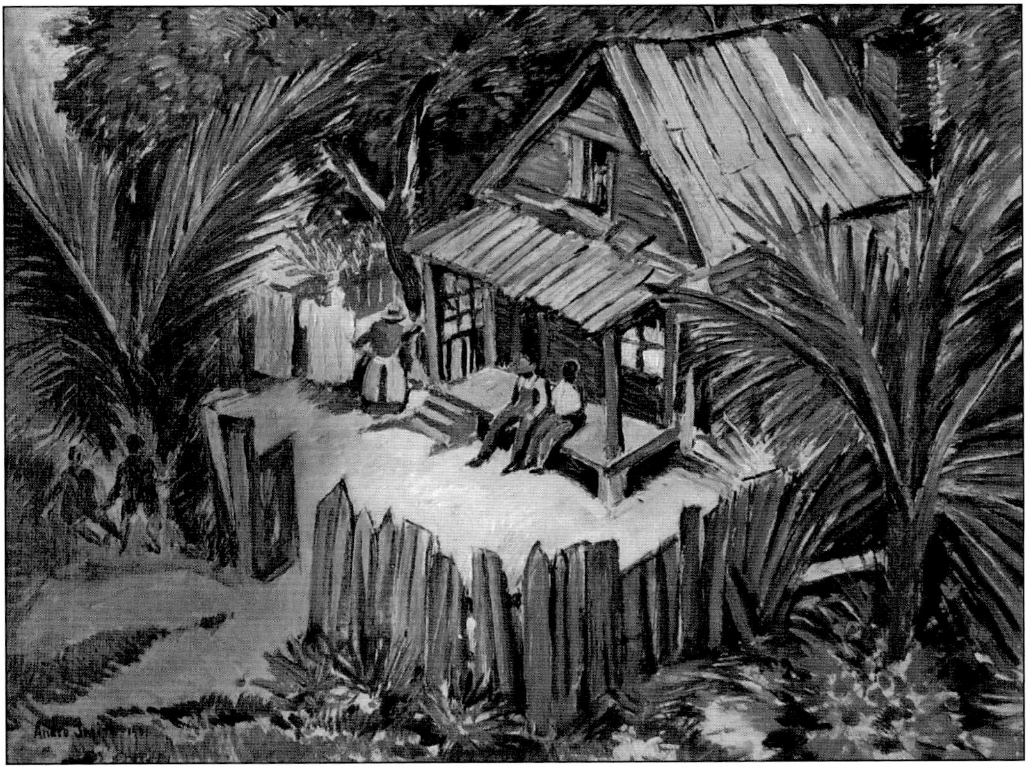

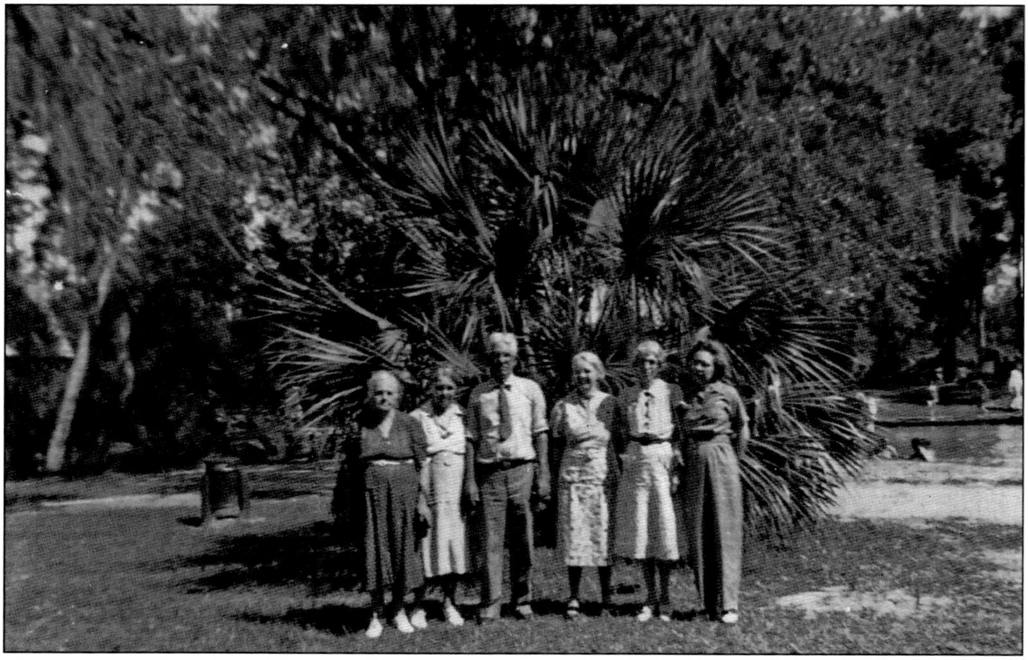

The Claude J. Woodward family is shown above in a July 1940 photograph in front of their family home in Maitland. Woodward served as stationmaster of the Maitland depot office of the Atlantic Coast Line Railroad from 1920 to 1965 and was very involved in city activities. He served 10 years on the town council and was Maitland's mayor for four years. As the photograph below shows, the Woodward family had a great sense of humor—these are their dogs in a moment of happy relaxation.

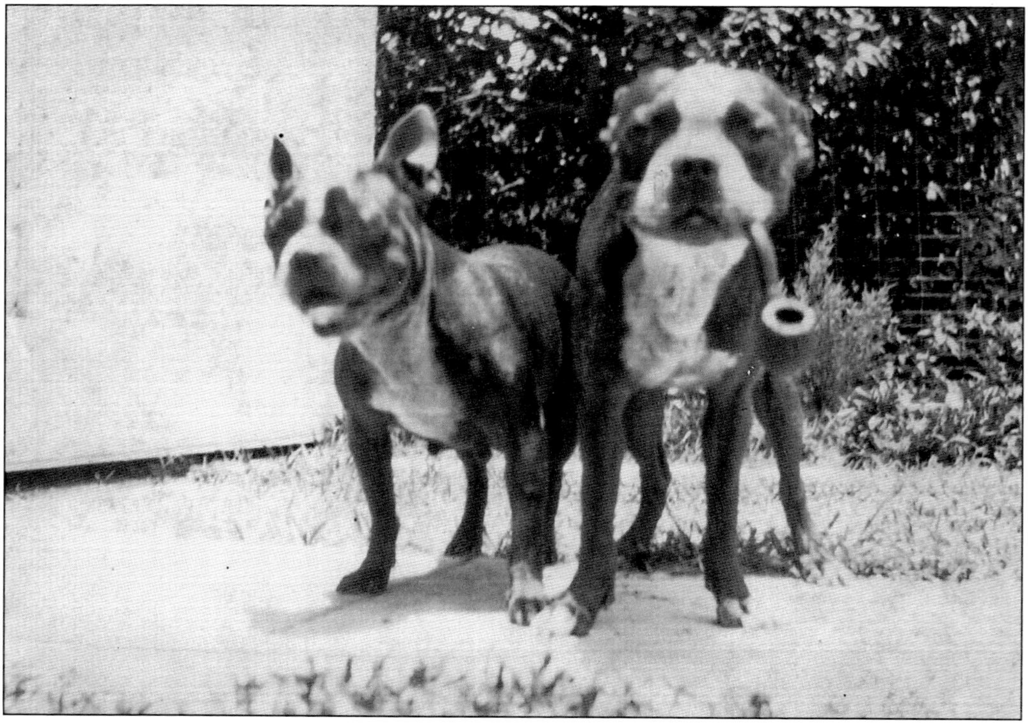

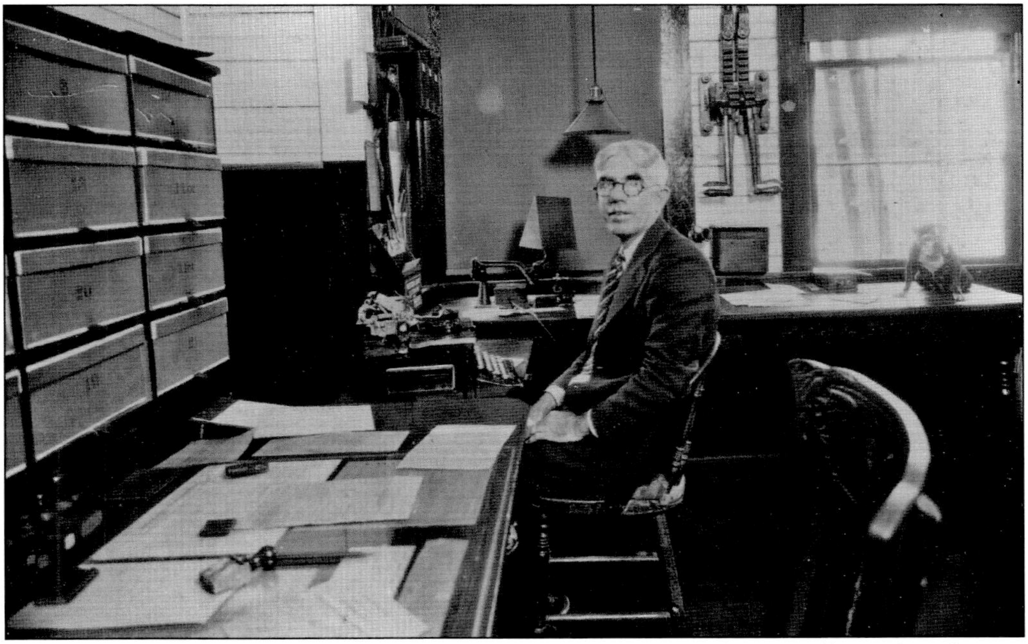

Pictured here is Claude J. Woodward at this desk in the Maitland depot office, where he was stationmaster for 45 years. In this role, Woodward used a tall semaphore (a signal device) located near the tracks to tell oncoming trains to stop or heed conditions. A bay window was built in his office, so he could see trains arriving in the station. Woodward's other duties included managing depot operations, passenger ticketing, arranging outbound citrus and freight and inbound shipments, and handling all telegraph messages.

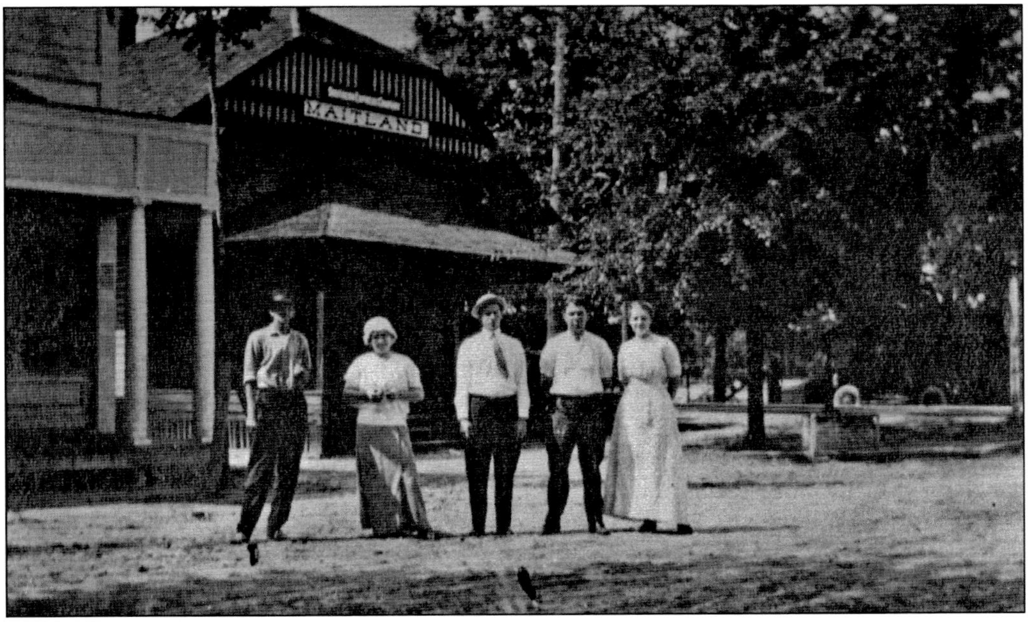

This photograph, with Woodward in the center and others unidentified, offers a view of Maitland in the early 20th century. The group is standing on East Horatio Avenue with the old railroad station behind them. The white building on the left is the general store constructed by George T. Stith.

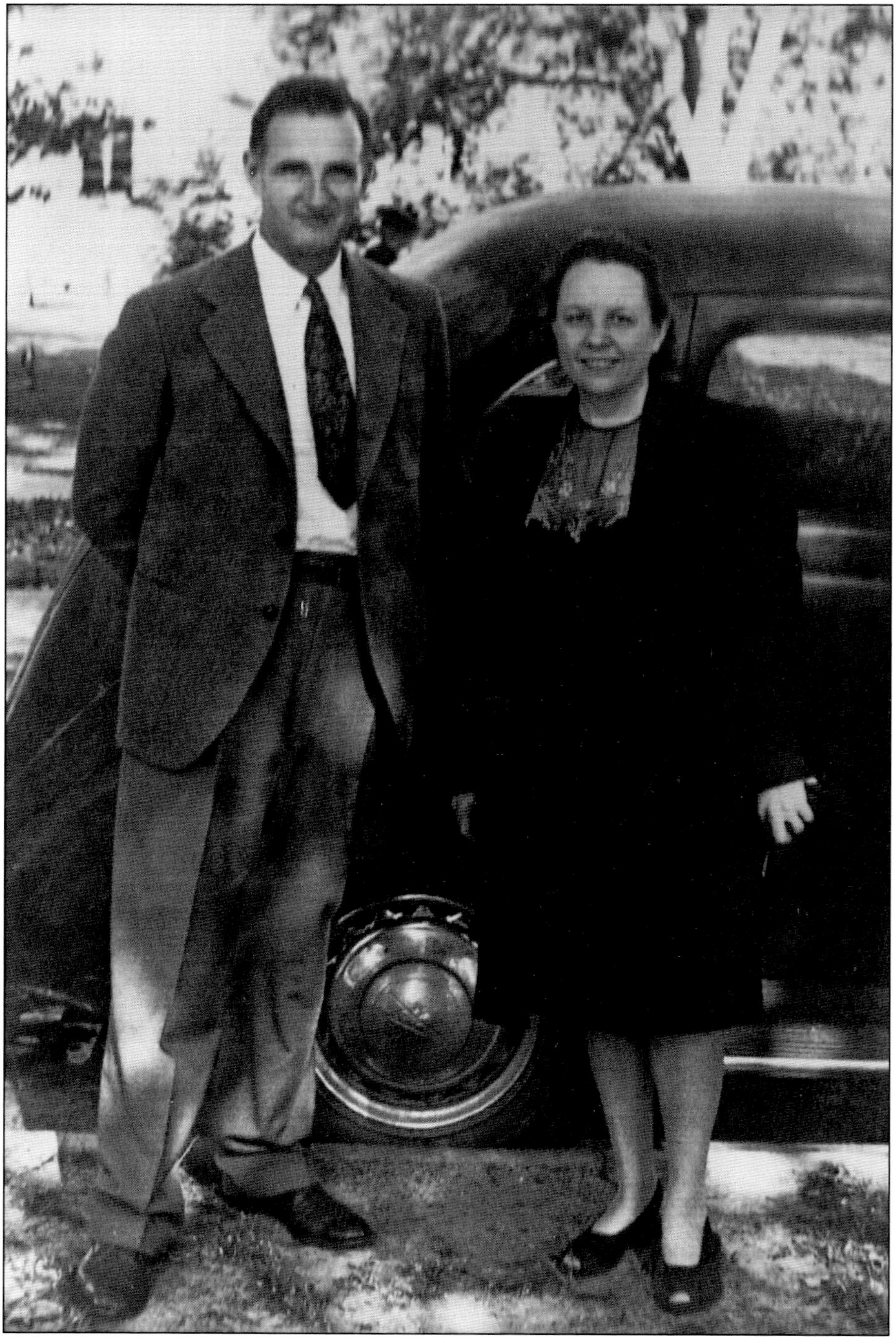

The Stone and Hill families made an important impact on the growth of Maitland through their local businesses and commitment to the community. Shown in this photograph from around 1948 are Forrest Brewer Stone and his wife, Georgianna "Dixie" Hill Stone. The granddaughter of pioneer James Erwin Hill, Georgianna Stone was a talented artist whose drawings of early Fort Maitland were used in a book about the same. She also created many of the graphics used in her family's business.

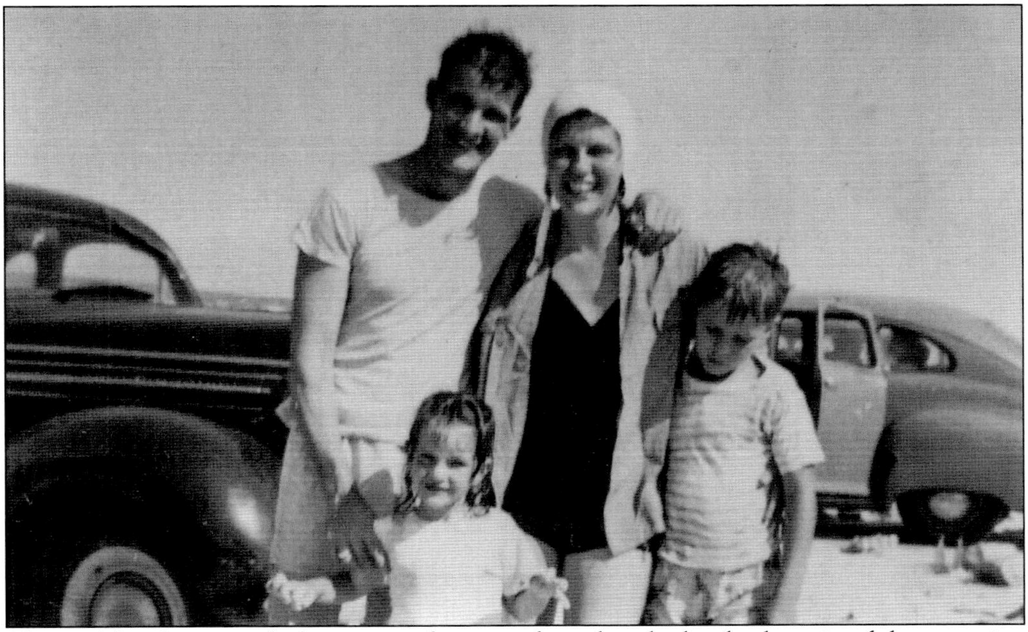

The area's beaches not only drew visitors from out of state but also locals who enjoyed the recreation they afforded. In this photograph from 1949, the Hulbert family—Russ and Isabelle and their two children, Jim and Grace—enjoy an outing at Daytona Beach, their favorite spot, having traveled from their Maitland home in their family car to park on the beach.

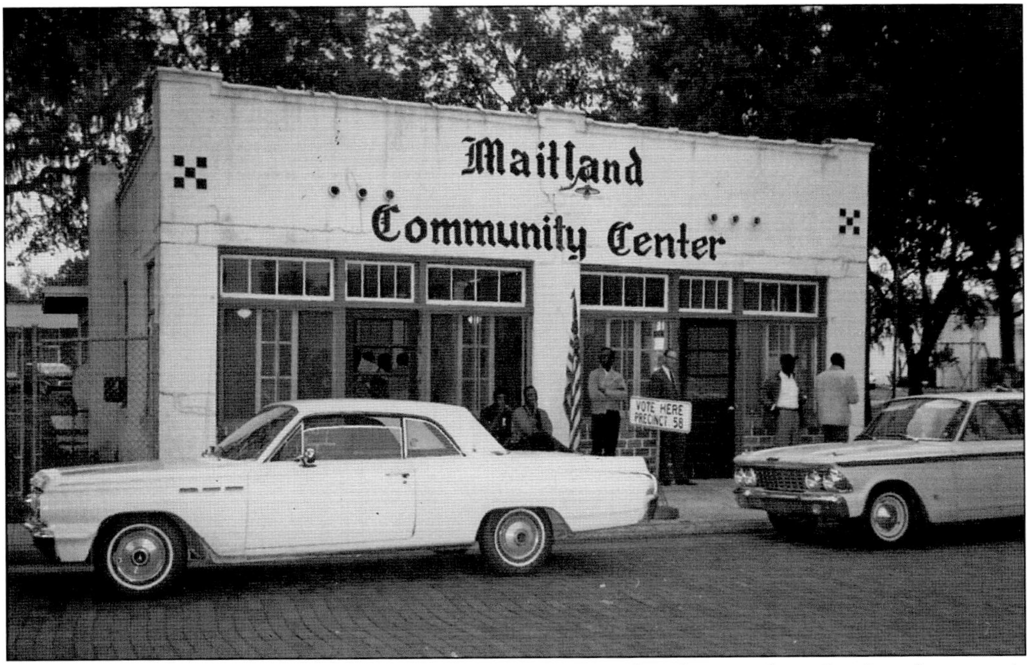

The Maitland Community Center offered citizens a central gathering place. In this photograph from the 1950s, residents prepare to vote on election day at the building, located on Inter Street, which was a few feet west of what is now Independence Lane. Many meetings, dances, and gatherings were held at the center. It was replaced by a large, spacious civic center near the shore of Lake Lily that was built in 1964 and remains in use today.

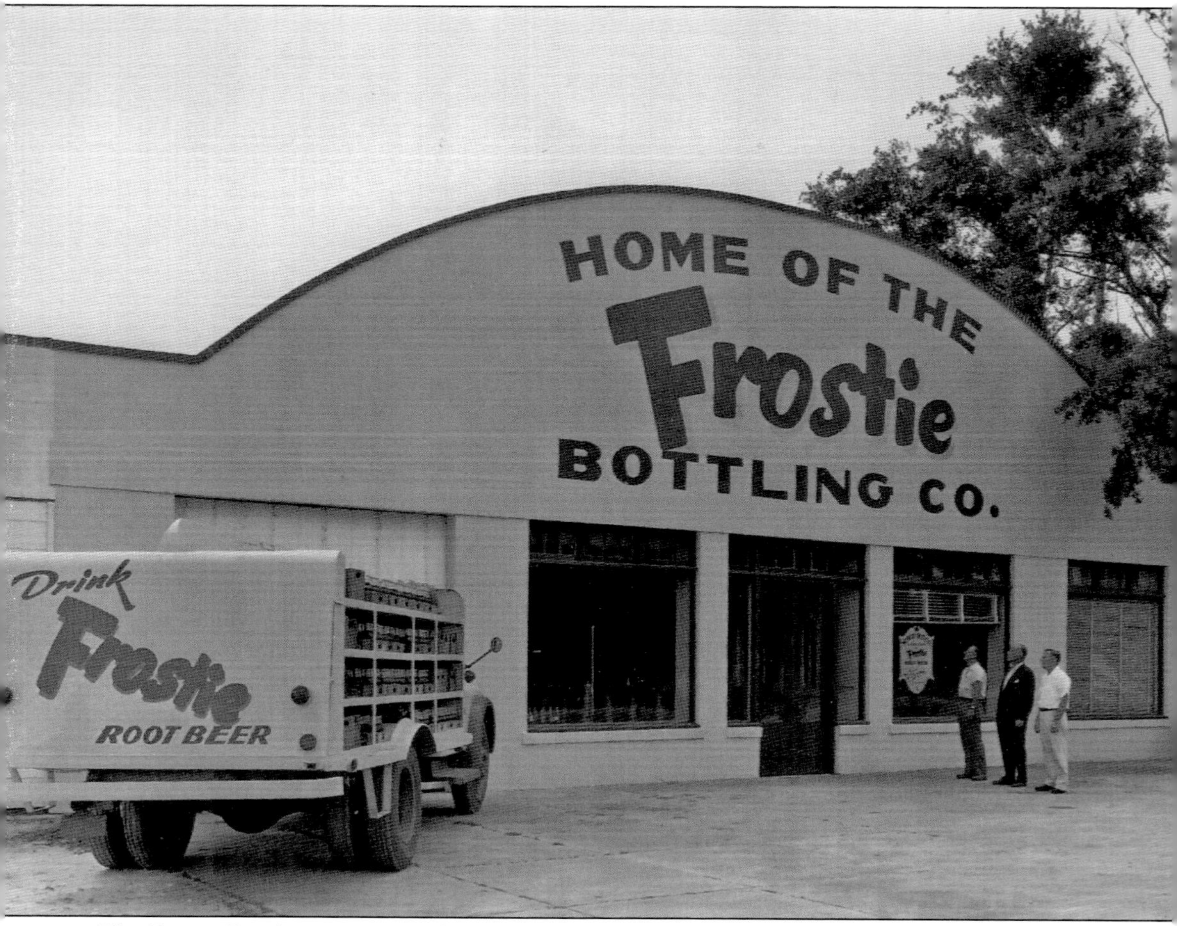

The Frostie Bottling Company, located near the intersection of U.S. Highway 17-92 and George Street, was a landmark in the Maitland community. Its root beer—and later its ginger ale—were a source of welcome refreshment and favorites of local residents. This photograph from the 1950s shows the exterior of the building. Nearby a delivery truck offers the promotion, "Drink Frostie Root Beer." At the far right in the group of three men is owner Andrew E. Grimm.

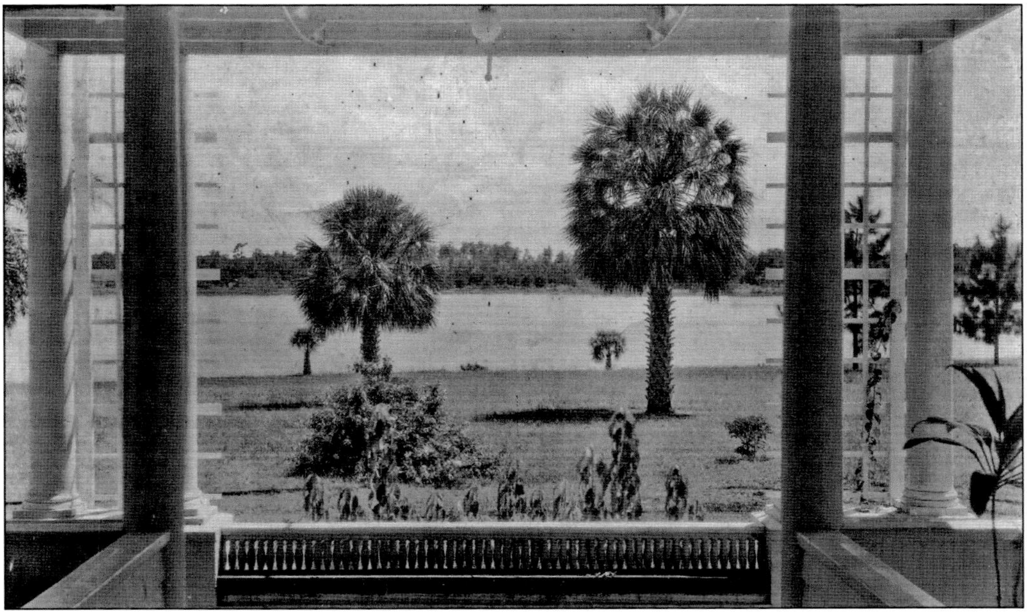

Dr. Russell H. Nevins, a New York doctor and surgeon, first purchased this property in 1877. In 1878, he built a large beautiful home overlooking Lake Faith and Lake Seminary in the area north of the city called Woodbridge. By 1882, he owned an ice factory there with John Prentiss, but three years later, an explosion destroyed the factory. Dr. Nevins returned to New York City shortly after that and resumed his medical career. These photographs from March 1958 show the view of the home from Lake Faith and a view to the lake from the house's porch, then occupied by different owners. (Both courtesy Rollins College.)

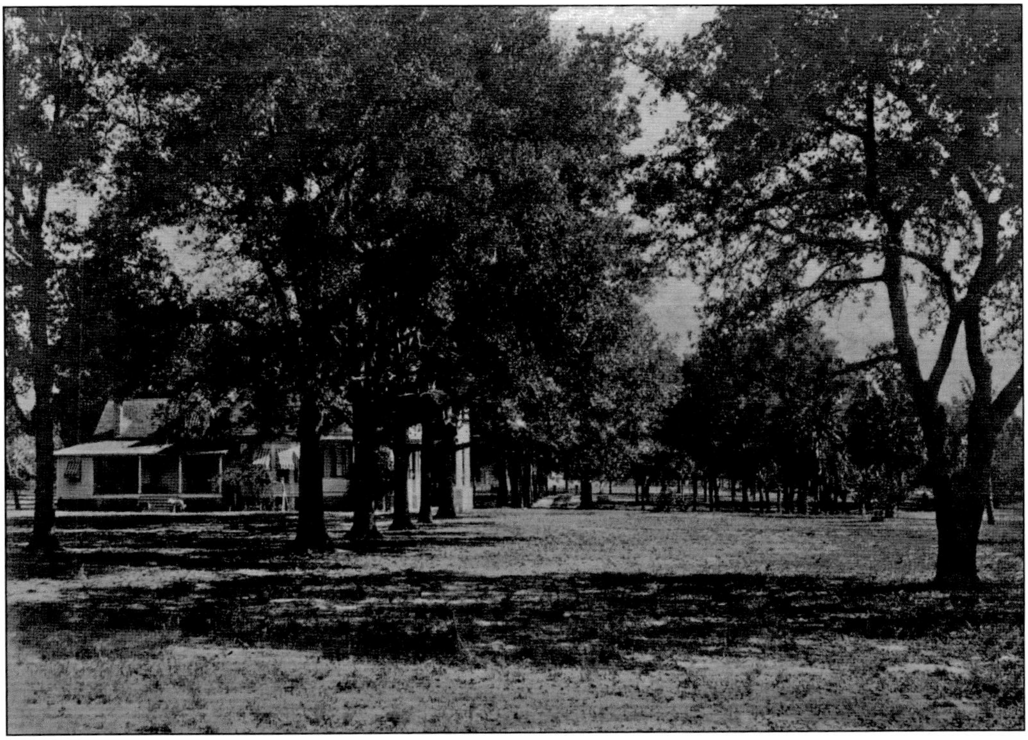

In this undated photograph, young Virginia Clare Pinder, daughter of John and sister of Richard, poses for the camera. Visible in the background is Maitland School, the school that once provided an education for the city's children through grade four.

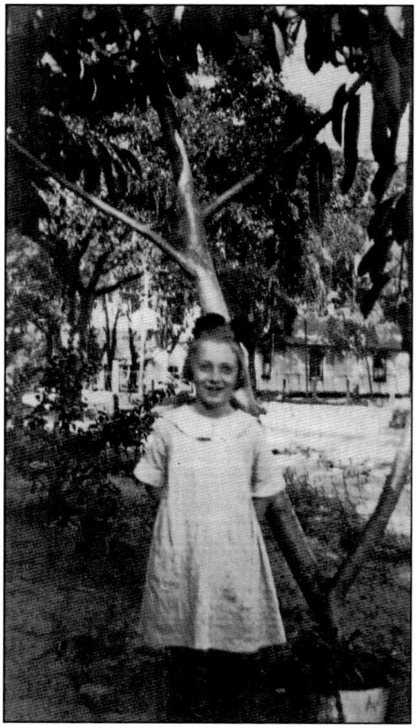

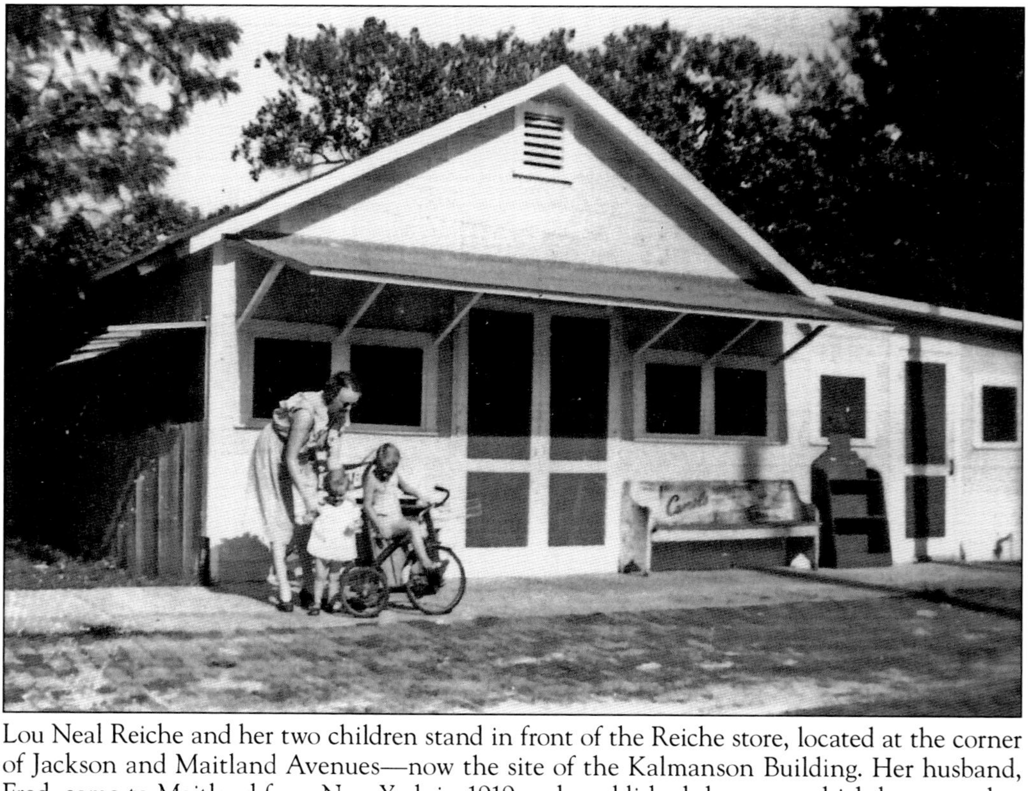

Lou Neal Reiche and her two children stand in front of the Reiche store, located at the corner of Jackson and Maitland Avenues—now the site of the Kalmanson Building. Her husband, Fred, came to Maitland from New York in 1919 and established the store, which became a bar in the 1950s.

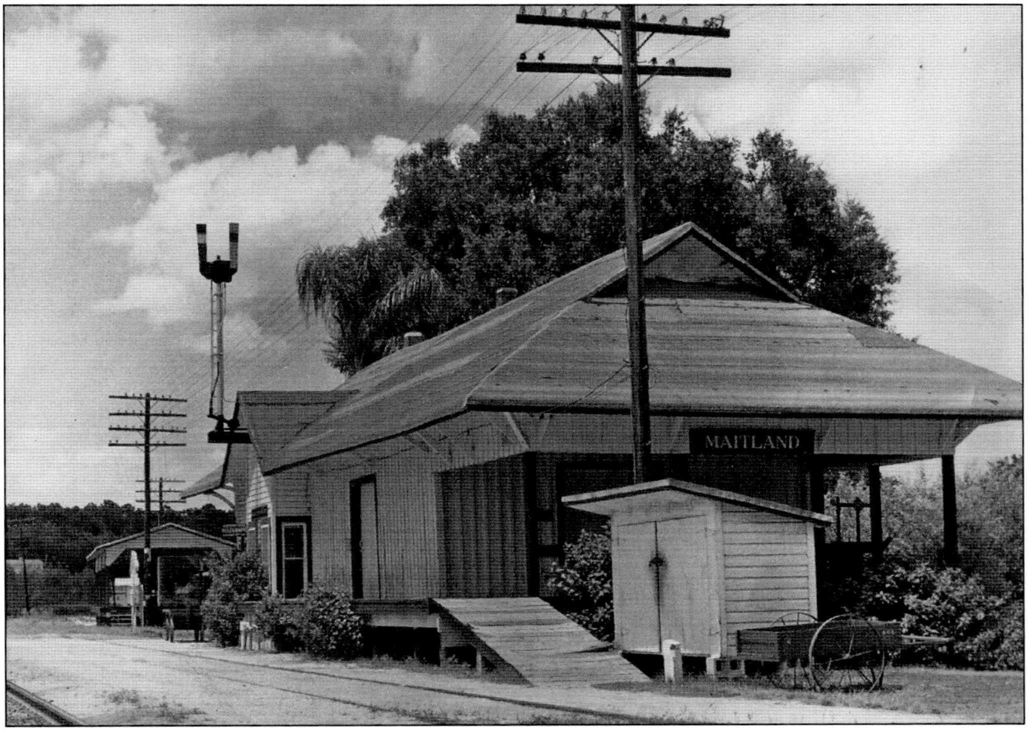

The city's depot remained an important aspect of Maitland life well into the mid-20th century. This photograph of the building shows the depot, connected to the rest of the world by rail line and by telegraph lines strung on nearby towering pine poles. Maitland residents found it interesting to stop at the depot and listen to signals that came in by Morse code and watch the telegraph operator interpret them into messages for local residents.

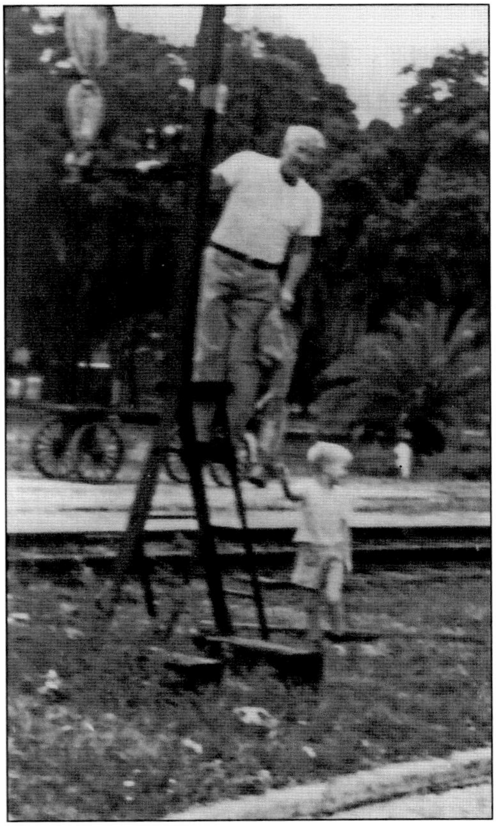

The depot also was the central delivery point for mail dropped off by train. As shown in this 1952 photograph of Carl Reiche, workers placed bags of outgoing mail on a catch pouch crane located near the tracks. It was retrieved by catcher arms on passing trains. Any bags with incoming mail were thrown onto the loading dock of the depot, where they were picked up and taken to the post office. There the mail was sorted and held for pickup by residents and visitors. Prior to the train's arrival in Maitland, mail was delivered once a week by post rider or horseback from Mellonville, near current-day Sanford.

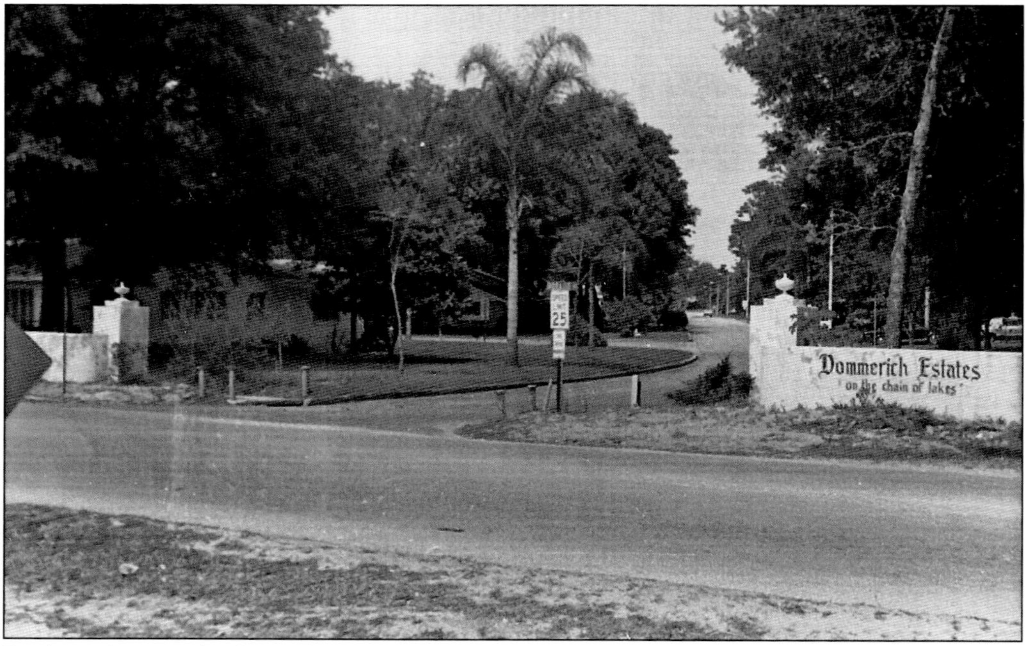

By the 1950s, Maitland was changing dramatically. Subdivisions, such as this view of the entrance to Dommerich Estates at the corner of Horatio and Seneca Avenues, replaced agricultural fields and, in this case, the actual expansive estate of the Dommerich family known as Hiawatha Grove. This subdivision along with many others sprouted up where citrus once grew to serve a growing population, spurred in part by the opening of the Martin Marietta Corporation's new division in the Orlando area. Employees there were advised to live within 7 miles of the company's plant—and Maitland provided the perfect site for relocating families, who came in groups of 200 to 300 people at a time. Others also found the city to be a perfect place to raise their families, leading to the construction of associated businesses and schools.

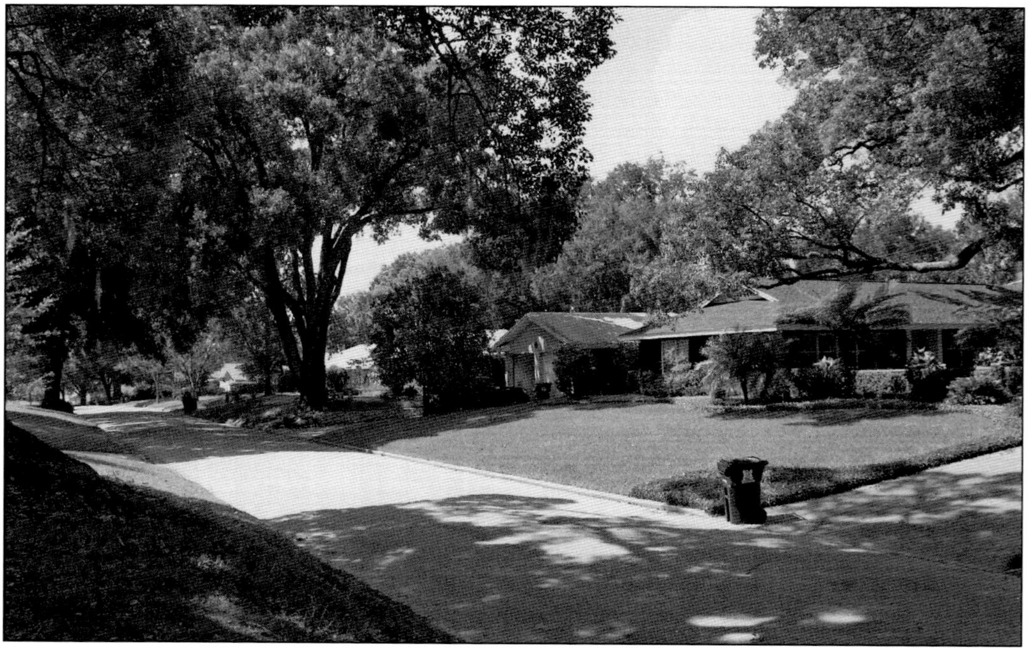

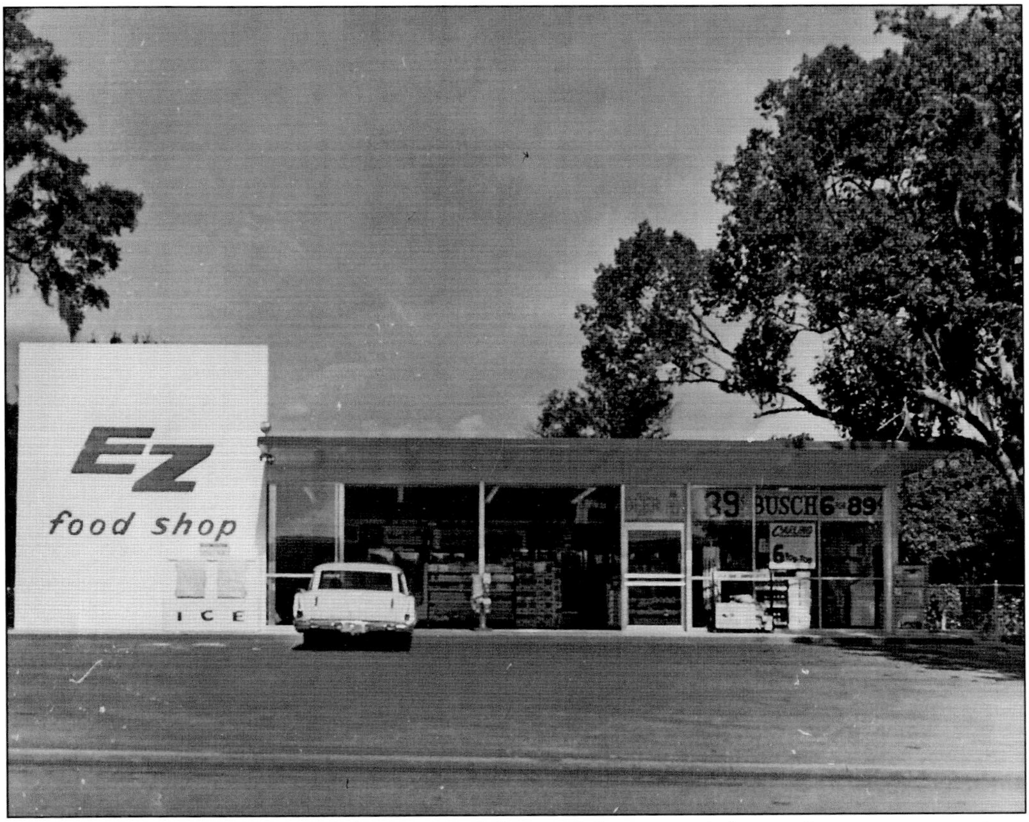

With an influx of residents and the more mobile era of the automobile, new businesses came into the Maitland area to accommodate their needs. Featured above is the E-Z Food Shop, located at the corner of Horatio and Swoope Avenues. For most of the city's history, general stores flocked to this area, the heart of the city. The arrival of convenience stores was a sign of modern times.

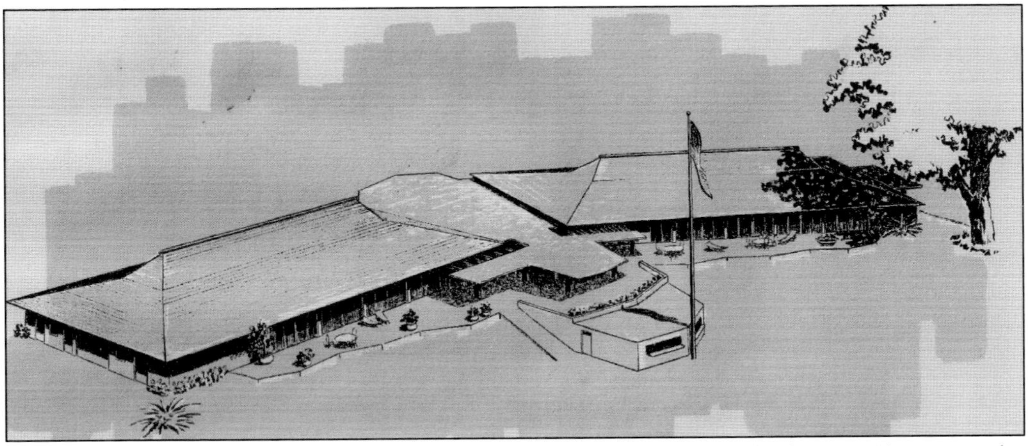

This is an artist's rendering of the Maitland Civic Center, which was built in 1965 to serve the needs of the growing community. A group of concerned citizens held a series of fund-raising events to raise the money for the independent, non-profit gathering place, located at 641 South Maitland Avenue, on the shores of Lake Lily. Through the years, the Maitland Civic Center, including its ballroom, stage, kitchens, and banquet facilities, has been the site of numerous events, including antique, train, stamp, doll, and craft shows.

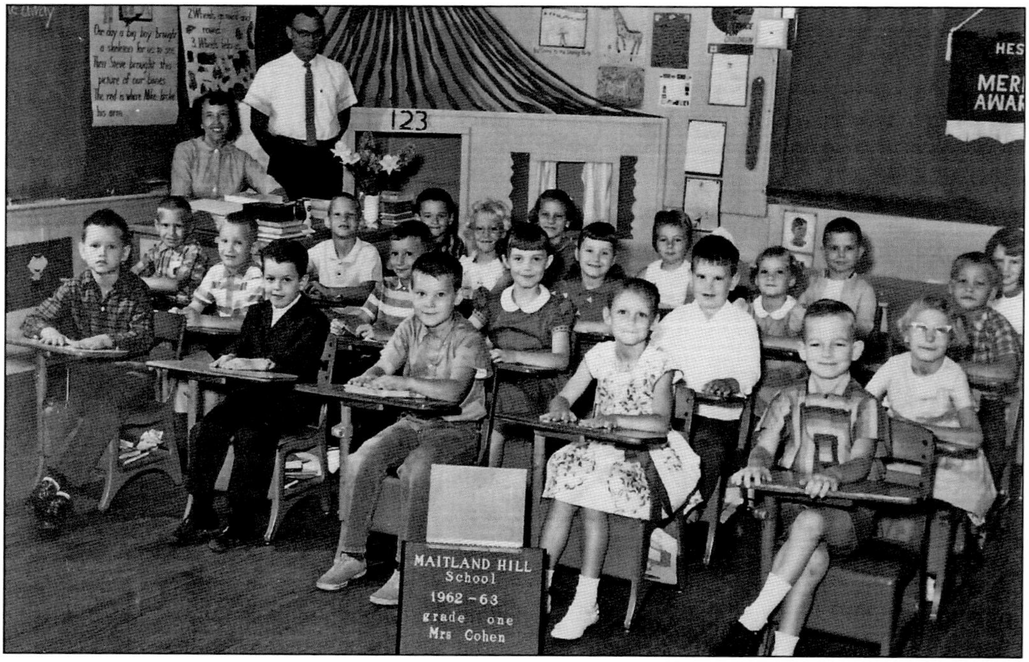

Nell Cohen's first-grade class at the Maitland Hill School, from 1962–1963, poses for a photographer. The 21 students are not identified, but their classroom demonstrates many of the features such as metal desks, textbooks, and wall displays offered in the 1960s. With the city's growth, a number of schools now serve its students, including two elementary schools and a middle school. In 1968, Cohen founded Park Maitland School, a private school in Maitland that serves children from preschool to sixth grade.

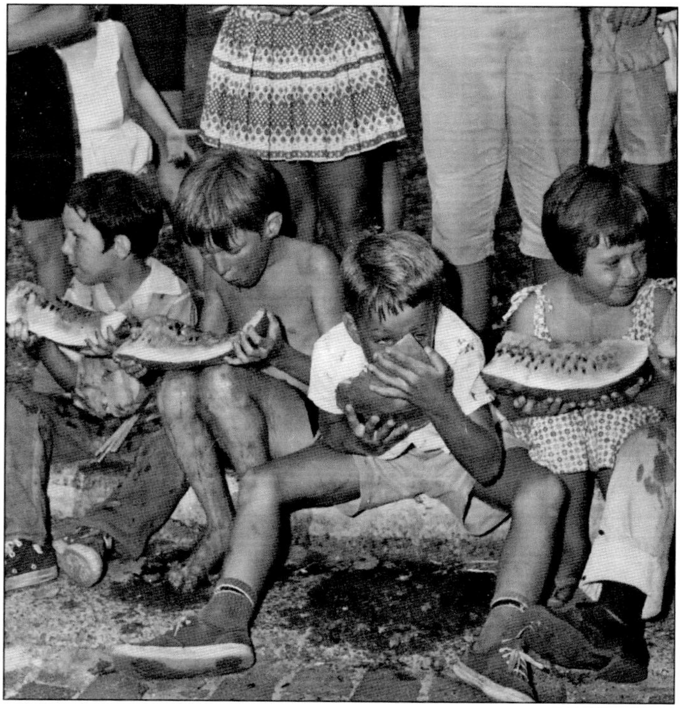

There is nothing more American than the Fourth of July, and in the city, it was celebrated as Maitland Day. Every year from 1958 for the next 25 years, the Maitland Chamber of Commerce sponsored a host of activities that began with a parade featuring as grand marshal Orange County sheriff Dave Starr riding his horse. The parade's finale featured convertible cars in which rode contestants for the Miss Maitland title. Tents and booths were set up at Lake Lily for residents to enjoy as part of the celebration. This photograph from 1962 shows youths gleefully participating in a watermelon-eating contest.

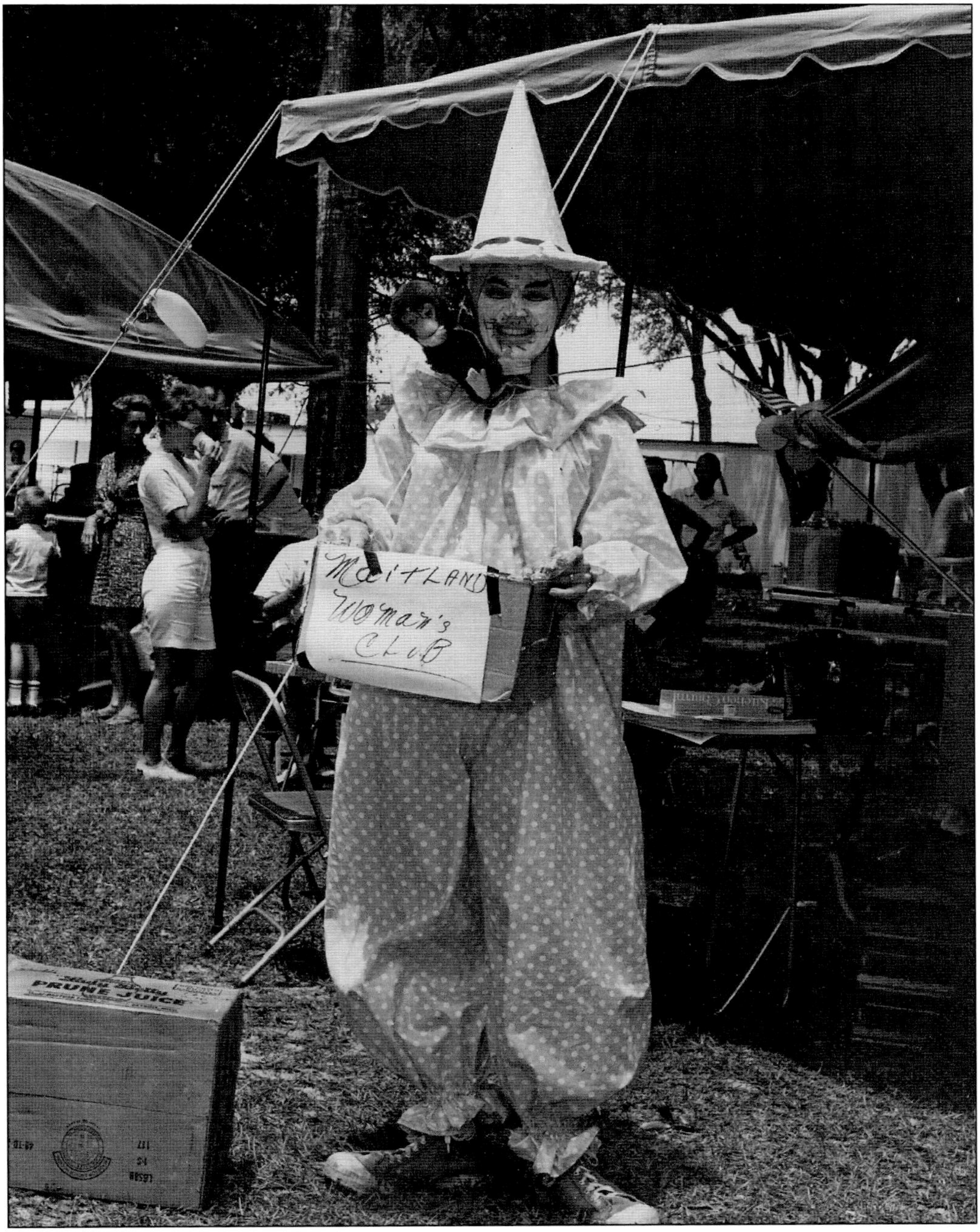

What would the Fourth of July be without a happy, festive clown? Here Maxine Parker, a member of the Maitland Woman's Club, takes a moment from entertaining residents in 1962 to smile for the camera. The Woman's Club, established in 1948, has long been committed to supporting the community and actively supports a number of cultural, civic, and philanthropic groups in the area. Every year, the club provided a patriotic-themed booth at Lake Lily, and members handed out items such as flags and flag pins to passersby.

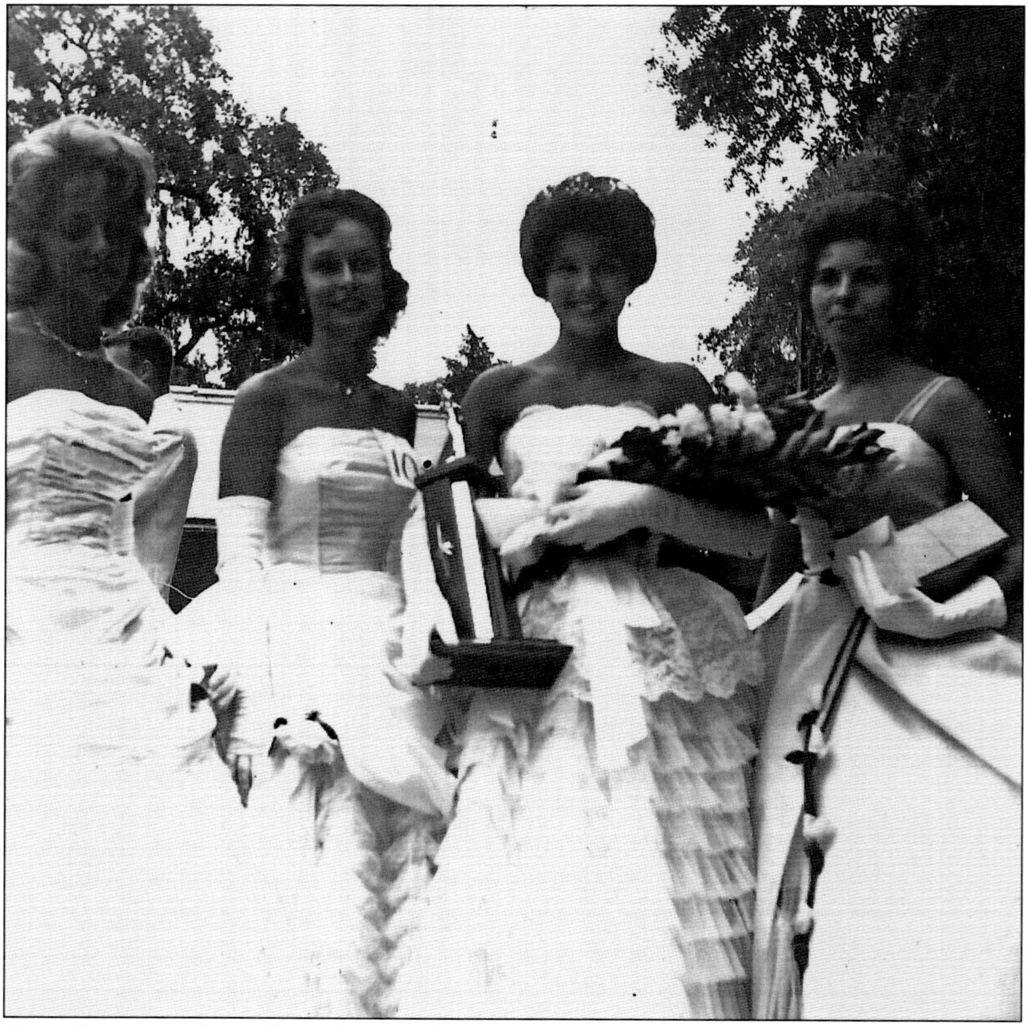

One of the annual rituals in the city's life was the crowning of Miss Maitland as part of the Maitland Day festivities. Every year, a young woman would win the crown in a pageant contest, claiming the title from the previous year's winner. In 1962, the honors went to, from left to right, Diane Beiger, Miss Maitland 1961; Dolores Myers, second runner-up; Paula Hicks, Miss Maitland 1962; and Ruthie Troiano, first runner-up.

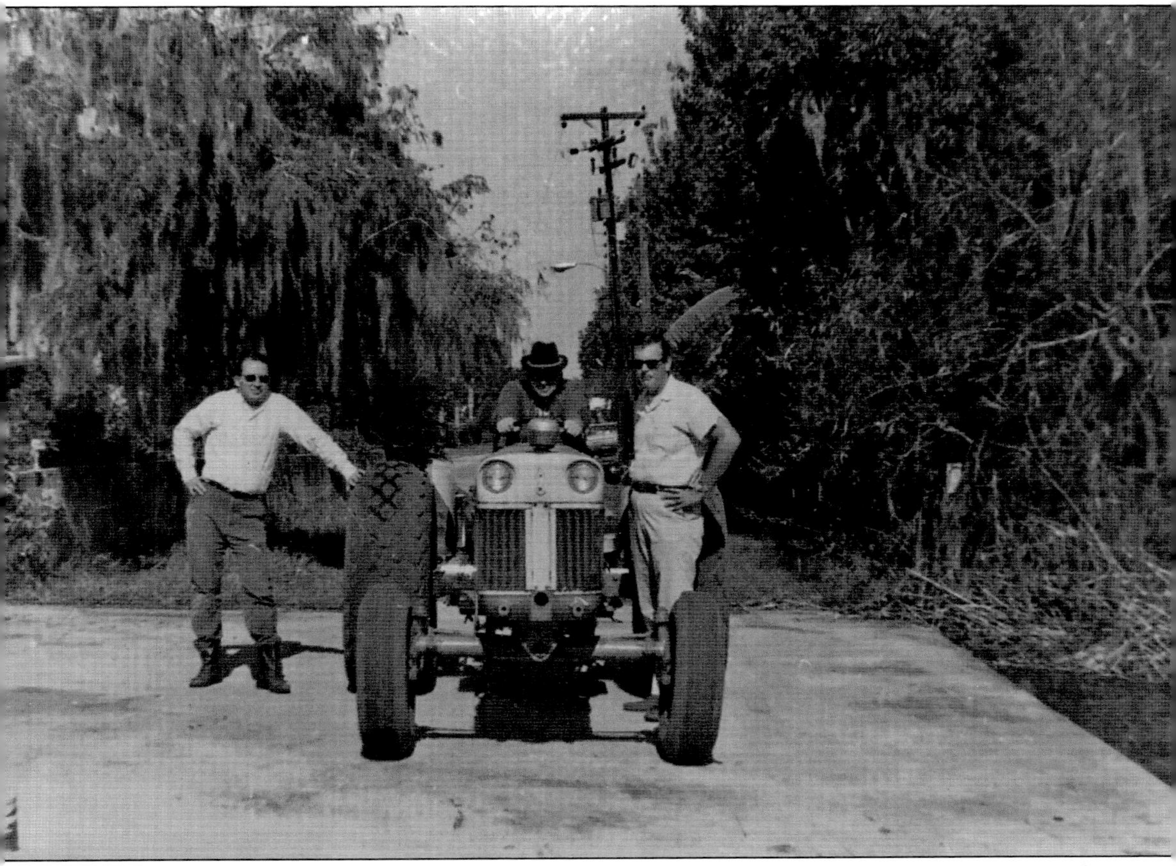

Maitland has long been blessed with active civic groups and clubs, such as these members of the Jaycees. In July 1969, the group became concerned about trash, rats, and high growing grass and weeds on Dog Island, a 1-acre island in Lake Maitland that has long been a regular stopping point for boaters, picnickers, water skiers, and campers. They loaded up equipment, including this tractor, shown with, from left to right, Ed Stuart, Dr. Bill Lee, and Bill Vinton. Later that year, the Jaycees held their annual Labor Day Picnic on the island, offering food, games, and fun to all who ventured to the cleaned-up isle.

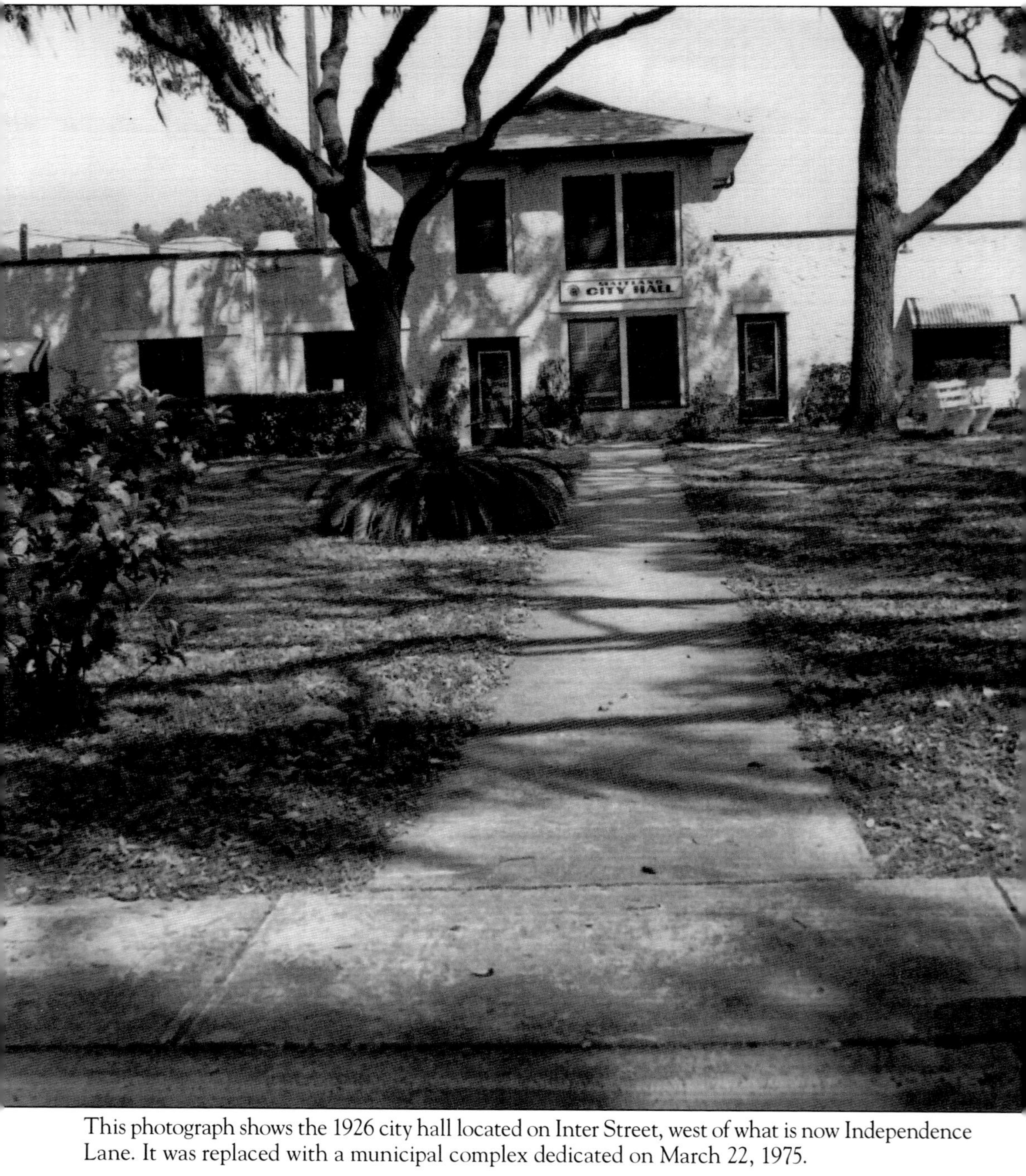

This photograph shows the 1926 city hall located on Inter Street, west of what is now Independence Lane. It was replaced with a municipal complex dedicated on March 22, 1975.

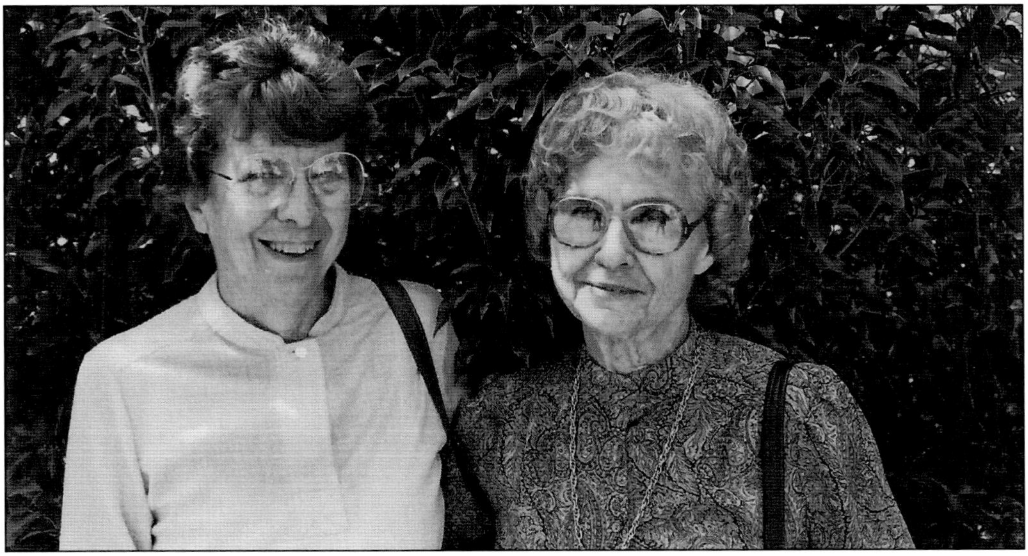

From the early residents who beautified the city with oaks lining the streets to the many city volunteers today, Maitland has a tradition of active citizenry. Civic involvement was a way of life for longtime residents Marjorie Tope (left) and Rita Parker, photographed in 1976 during a planning session for the Maitland Historical Museum. Both were active in the historical society, served on the board, and helped with publications. Tope and Parker were vital in obtaining the Lake Lily home of pioneer William Waterhouse and restoring it into a museum. Through the years, they were involved in the cultural and community affairs of the city, serving on various boards and committees.

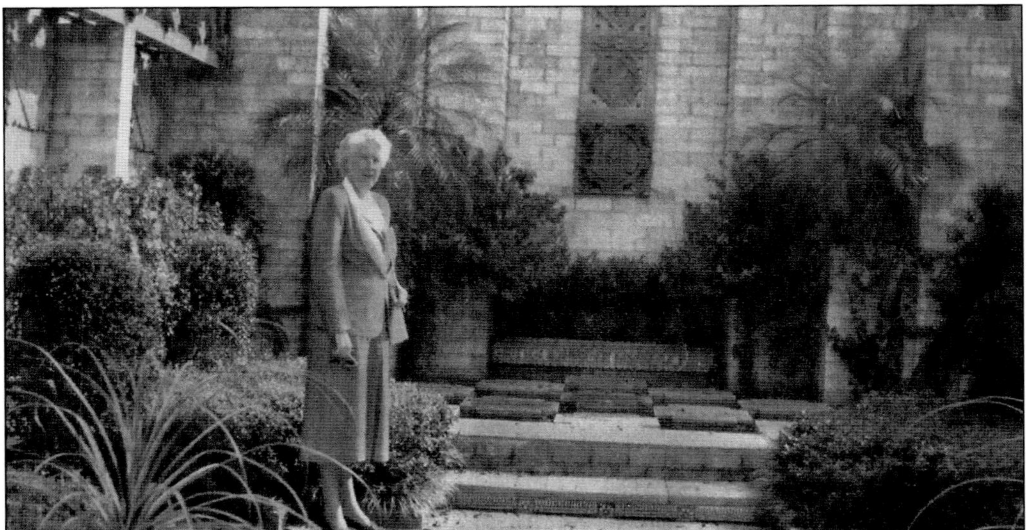

Helen Waterhouse, granddaughter of William Waterhouse, an early Maitland pioneer, is pictured in this *c.* 1971 photograph in the Maitland Art Center Chapel. The brainchild of noted artist Andre Smith, the artists' studio complex opened in 1938. It was financially backed in part by Mary Curtis Bok, the widow of philanthropist Edward Bok. At the complex, "Bok Fellows"—specially chosen artists—were given room and board during winter months and encouraged to experiment in many different art forms. Today the complex offers classes and exhibitions of various artists as it celebrates Smith's vision.

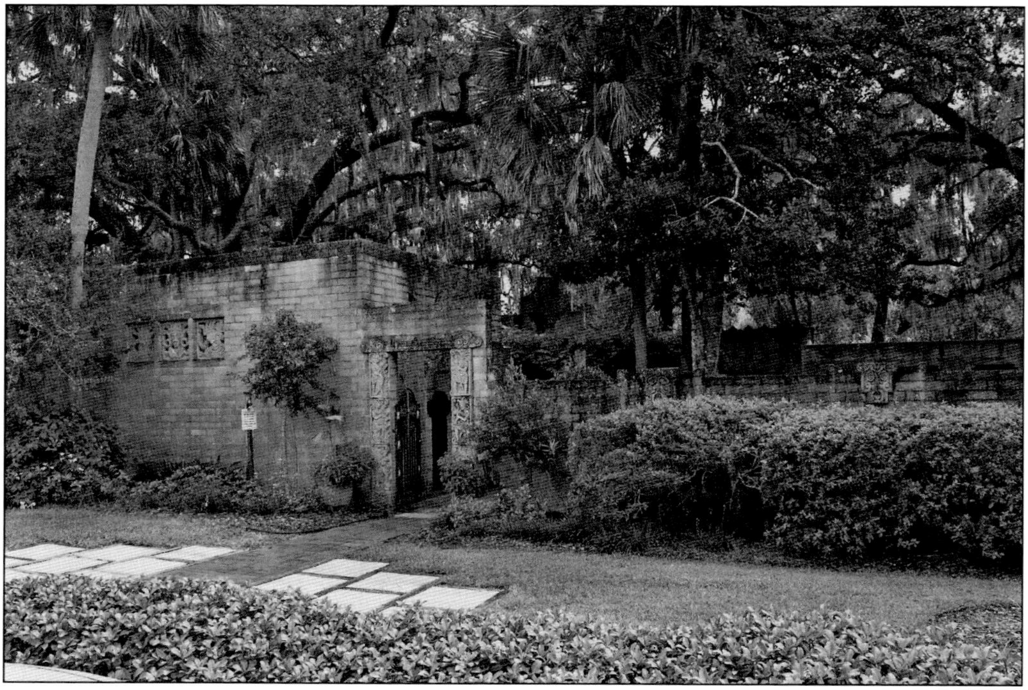

These photographs show the chapel building and pool at the Maitland Art Center. The buildings in the Art Center complex, personally designed by founder Andre Smith, make it one of the few surviving examples of "fantasy" architecture in the Southeast, featuring Mayan/Aztec motifs, much of it carved by Smith. Its 23 separate structures are linked by lush gardens and beautiful courtyards. Stylized faces, animals, birds, and plants also are represented in the garden and chapel areas. In recognition of its unique style and historic contribution to the community, the Maitland Art Center is listed on the National Register of Historic Places.

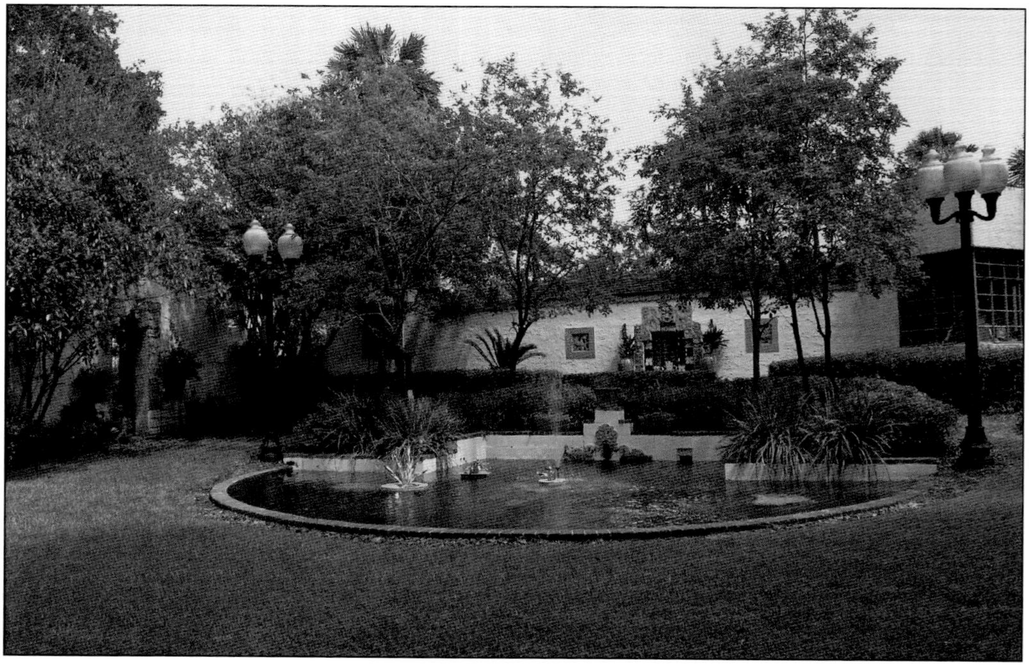

Five

The Modern City

By the late 20th century, Maitland was undergoing a great change, adding municipal buildings and businesses that brought a new character to the city. As the area's population rose from dramatic changes in the region such as the opening of Walt Disney World, growth stretched the city's boundaries to meet those of its neighbors. The development of Interstate 4 to the west of the city also heralded a new transportation system for visitors and attracted commercial development to its corridor. By the 1970s, the city was home to several banks and 12 new subdivisions. Most of the city's orange groves, whose blossoms once perfumed the spring air, were gone, as were many of the city's landmarks. The community remains a cultural center that offers residents many opportunities to engage in history and the arts. From its humble beginnings around a sweet-smelling lake, to a wooden fort, to a citrus center, to a suburban center, Maitland has kept the same basic close-knit community character and natural beauty. Continuing to change with the times, Maitland looks to the future with its residents in mind as it plans for a new town center and further development in the dawning century.

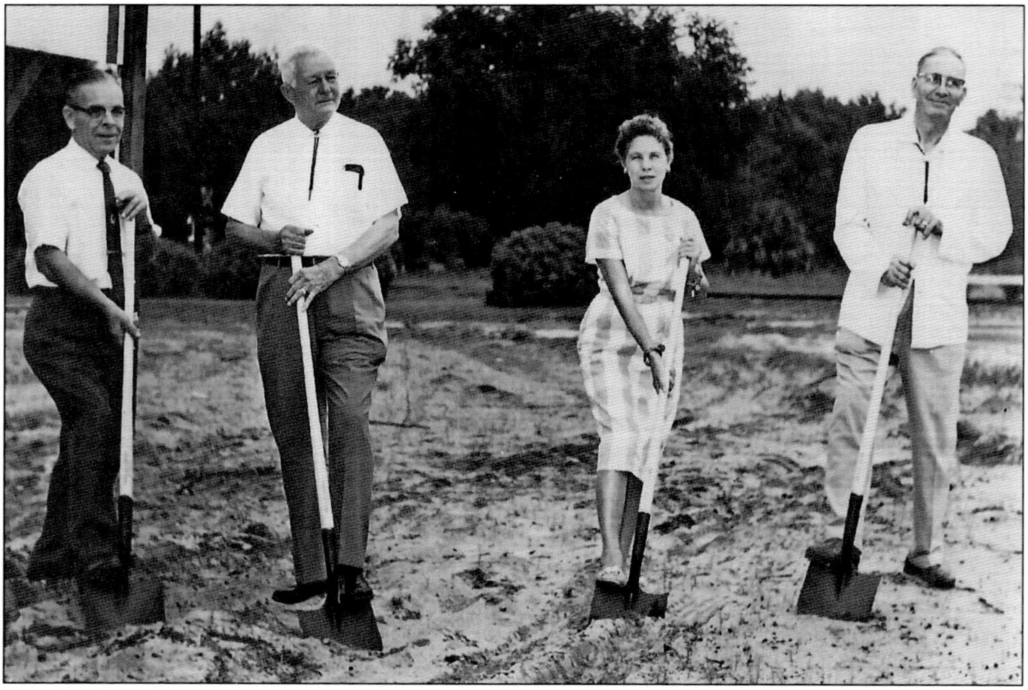

Maitland residents have long relied on postal delivery to stay in touch with friends and relatives and to conduct their business. By September 1961, just three years after formally shortening the city's name to "Maitland," ground was broken for a new post office to be constructed at Packwood Avenue next to the railroad tracks along Maitland Avenue. On hand to help with the celebration were four of the city's former postmasters: from left to right, John T. Stover, appointed postmaster in 1949; Edward T. Owen, appointed 1935; Agnes Moreman Kohloss, appointed 1922; and Wilson A. "Gus" Moreman, appointed 1913. Also pictured are employees of the post office in front of the 1961 building. The current post office is located on Maitland Avenue at George Street.

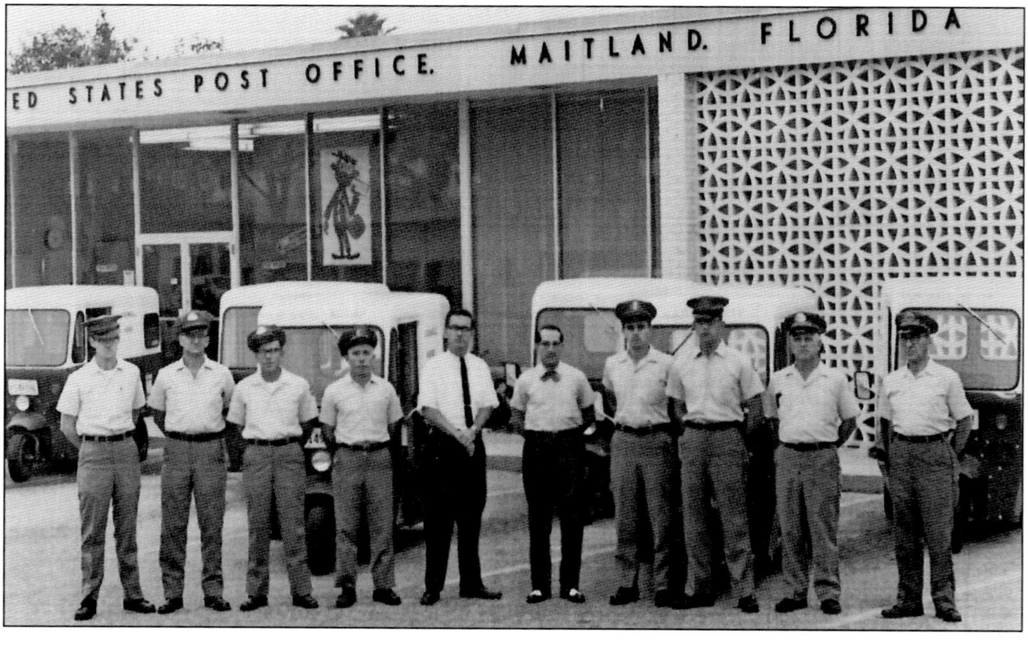

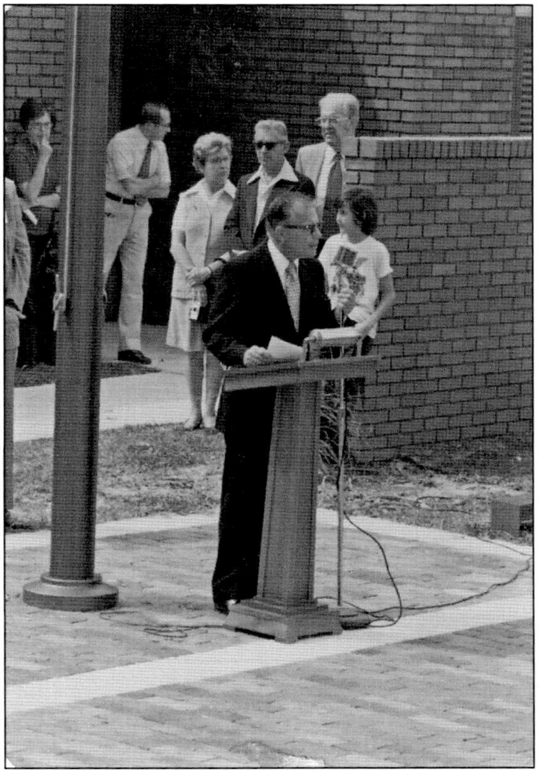

A sign of modern times in Maitland was the construction of a new city municipal center, located at 1776 Independence Drive between Packwood and Horatio Avenues. Its dedication, on Saturday, March 22, 1975, became an afternoon celebration for residents that featured a speech by Mayor Homer Hough (shown above) and a performance by a choral group from a local school. The new complex included buildings to house the police and fire departments and a new city hall. To celebrate its entry into city life, a flag was raised (below) in front of the building.

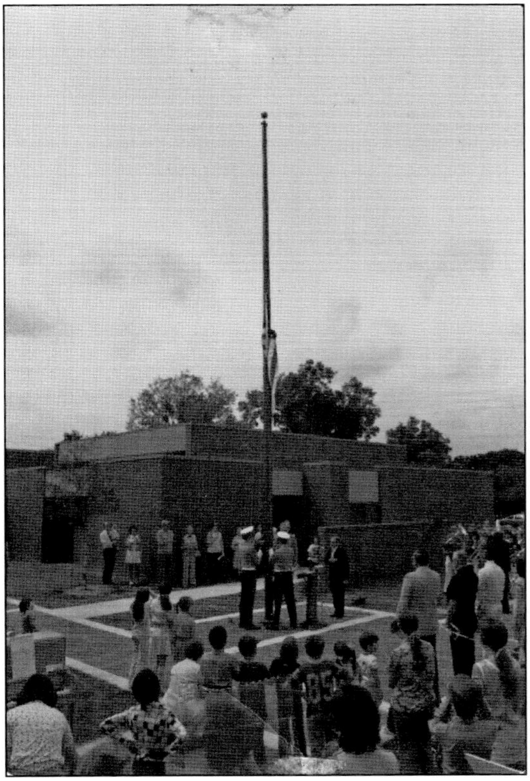

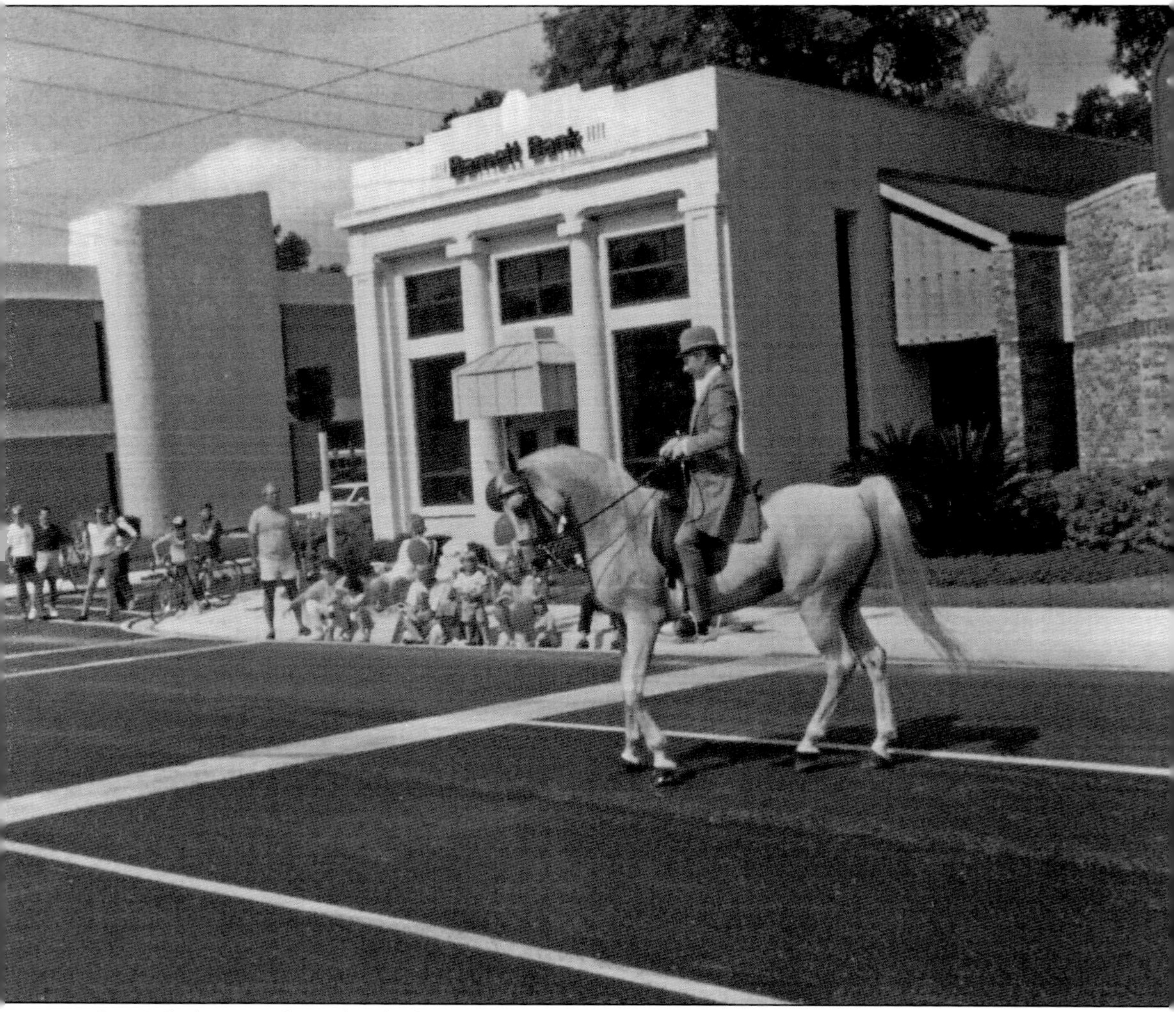

In 1985, the city of Maitland celebrated what few Florida cities can claim: its centennial anniversary. For four days, residents enjoyed memories of the city during the past century, with a picnic and symphony concert and the dedication of the fountain in Lake Lily. As this photograph shows, the highlight of the festivities was a July 20, 1985, parade through the old downtown—here at the corner of Maitland and Horatio Avenues. The Saturday morning parade proceeded all the way to Lake Lily, once a central recreation site for area residents. There a number of exhibits and activities, including game booths, hot air balloon rides, an ice cream social, an automobile show, Confederate and Union military demonstrations, and fireworks, were presented to entertain everyone enjoying the celebration.

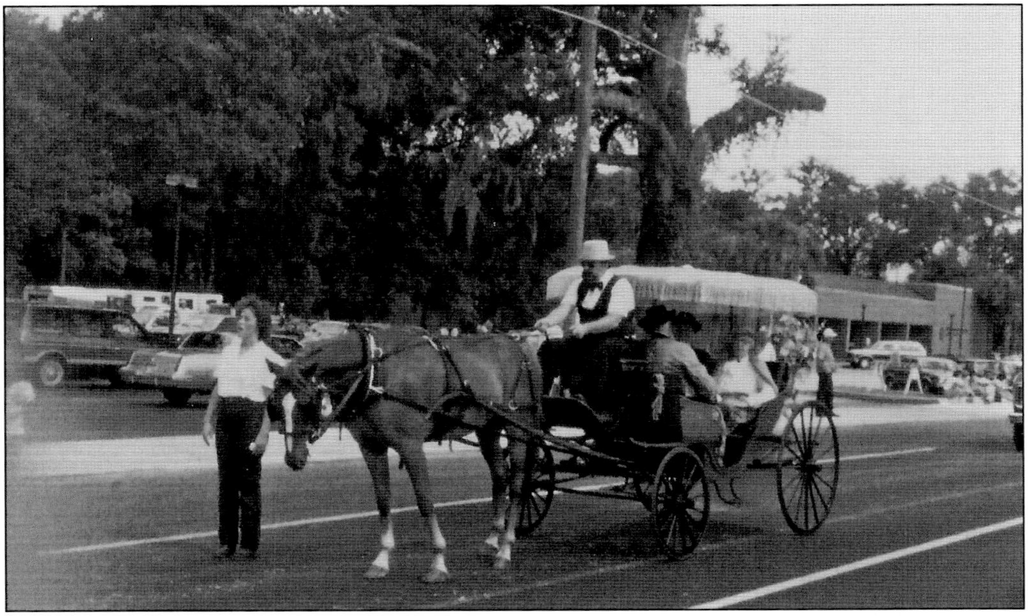

One entrant in the Centennial Parade was a horse and buggy sponsored by the Maitland Historical Society, which commemorated the days when this was the area's main means of transportation. As the photograph below shows, two descendants of pioneering Maitland families, Isabelle McNair Hulbert (left) and Helen Waterhouse dressed in style, Waterhouse wearing her grandmother's old clothing, to celebrate the day and remind residents of the city's long and rich history. As part of the four-day celebration of the city's 100th birthday, residents were invited to remember the city's past with a tour of historic sites and the Maitland cemetery, where many of the area's pioneers were buried.

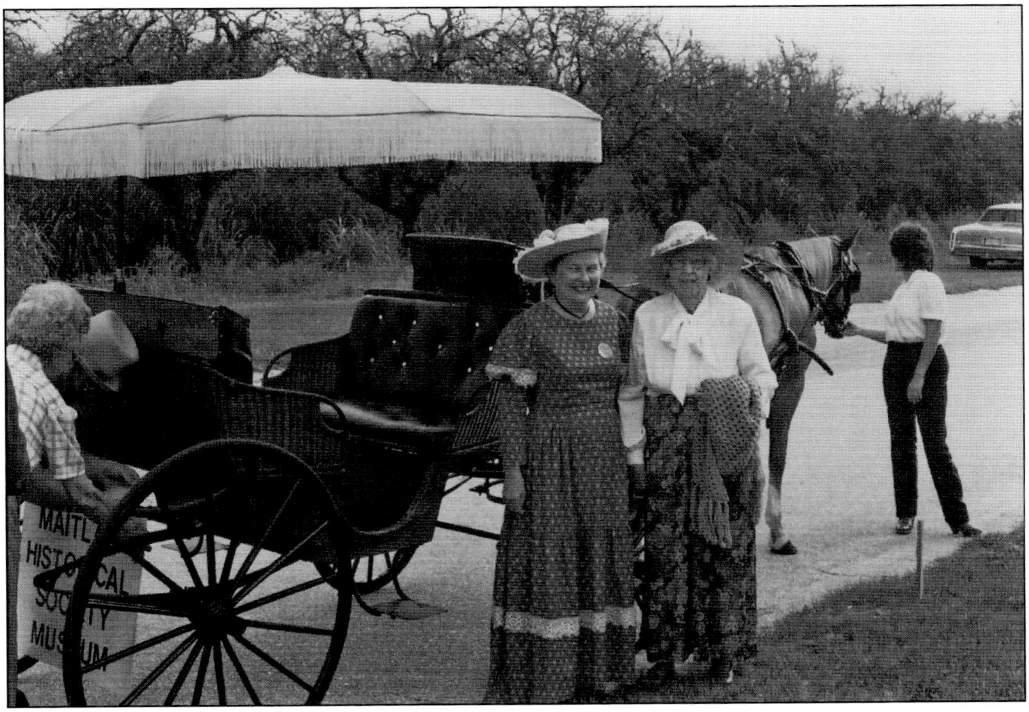

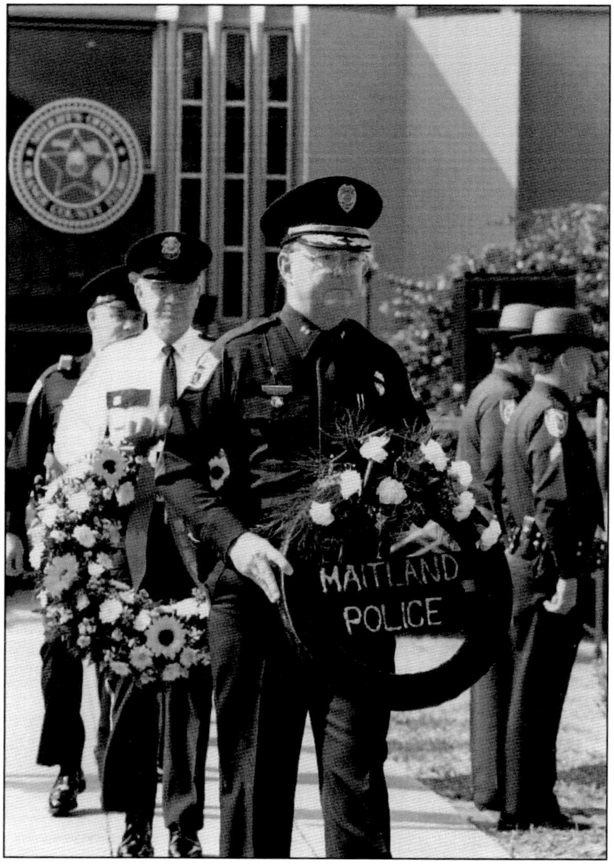

The Maitland Police Department is not only a vital city department but is well loved in this tight-knit community. Police chief Ed "Butch" Doyle is shown in the 1990s carrying a wreath with his department's name during an Orange County ceremony that memorializes Central Florida's law enforcement officers. The photograph below, from 1988, shows two of Maitland's motorcycle officers as they ready to leave on patrol on the Maitland Center Parkway. Officers Bob Poalillo (left) and John Schardine were two of four officers who patrolled the city's streets on motorcycles.

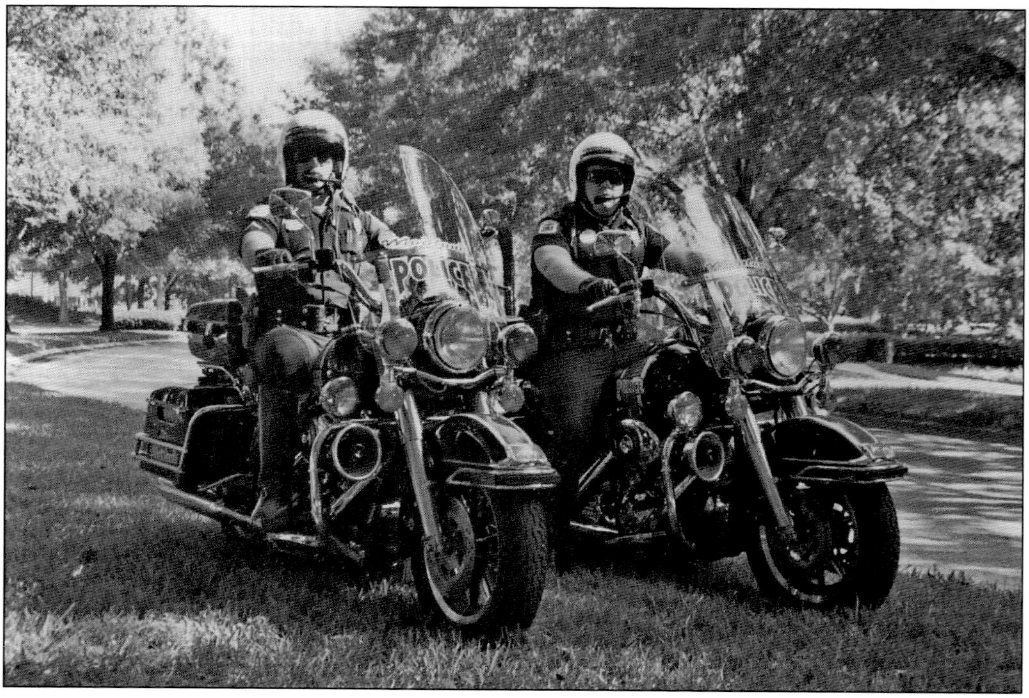

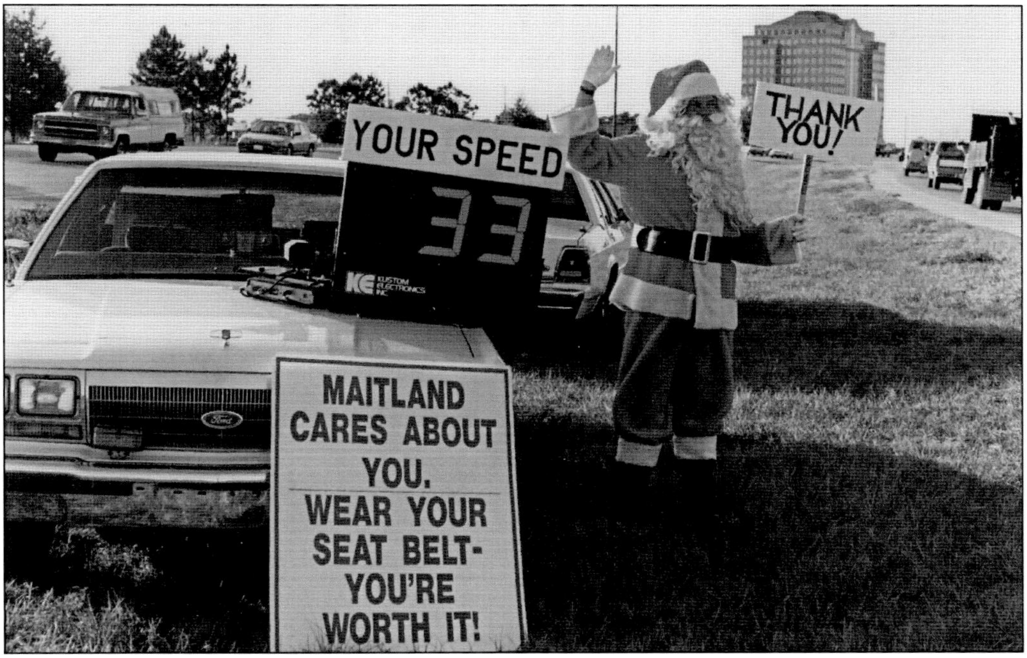

Maitland's police are an integral part of the community, whether they are patrolling streets or lakes or taking part in community events. In the above photograph from December 1988, Community Relations Officer David Robb—also known as Santa Claus—waves to motorists at the intersection of Maitland Boulevard and Lake Destiny Drive.

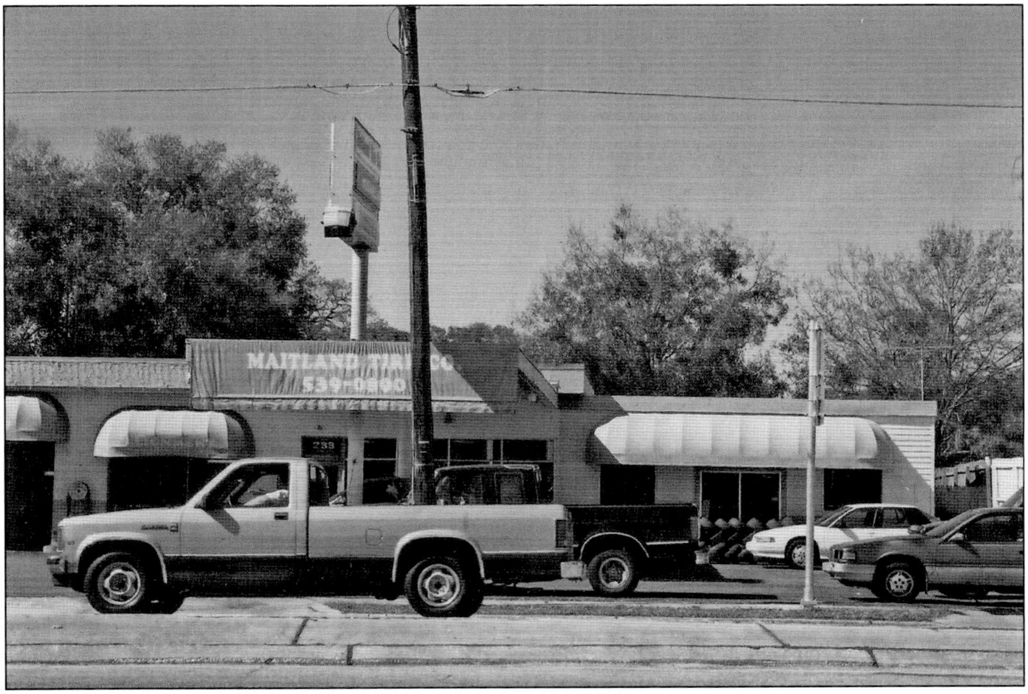

Through the years, Maitland has been home to many locally owned and operated businesses. Maitland Tire Company, shown in this 1995 photograph, has long served residents from its location at 233 North Orlando Avenue (U.S. Highway 17-92).

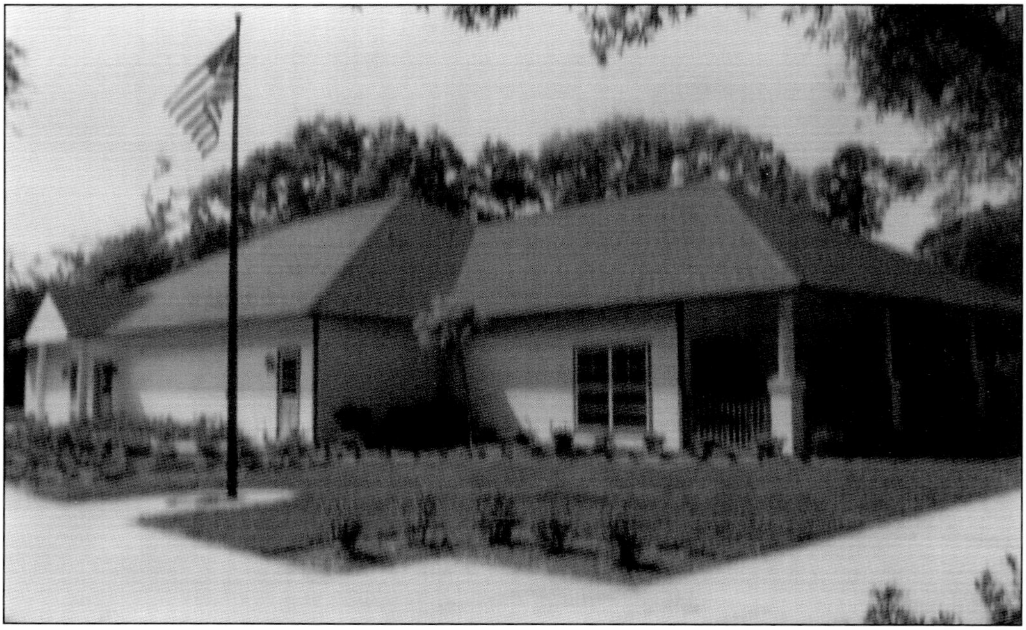

The modern Maitland Senior Center, which opened in 2002 and is operated by the city, is an important gathering place for the city's residents. Each week approximately 250 people come to the building, located at 345 South Maitland Avenue, to enjoy a variety of activities, including lessons in cooking, writing, fitness, yoga, knitting, and music.

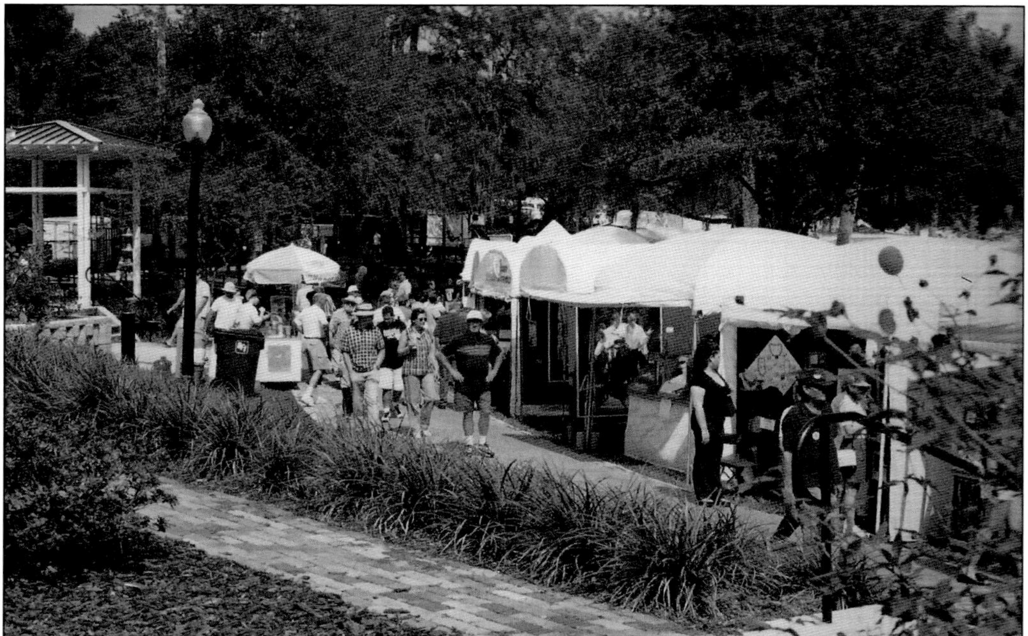

Community festivals of all kinds around Lake Lily are a Maitland tradition. Since 1976, the Maitland Rotary Club has sponsored a popular autumn art festival on the shores of Lake Lily. The festival has become an important part of the art community, offering awards for artists who work in a variety of media from oil to watercolor to sculpture and more.

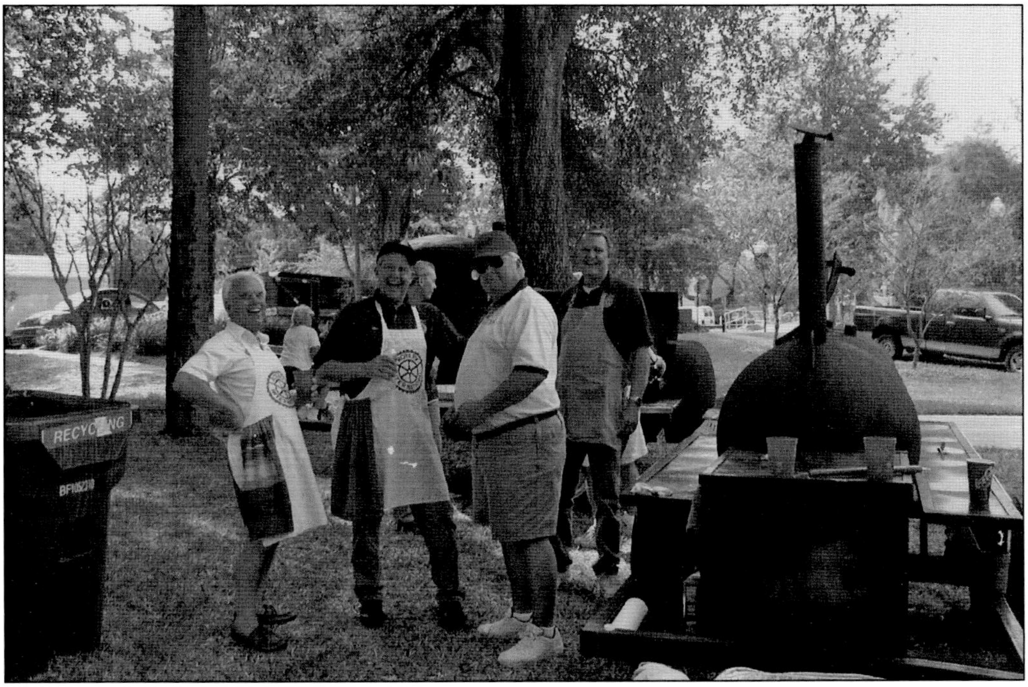

Members of the Maitland Rotary Club don their finest gourmet attire in order to man the barbeque and food stations at the annual autumn art festival. In the spirit of giving and civic participation so important to the city, all of the proceeds from the festival's parking, food, and poster sales are donated to local charities. In the above photograph, from left to right, Rip Voorhees, Bob Mellen, Tom Burruss, and Jim Dowden have a laugh while working at a barbeque cooker during the festival in the late 1990s. The below image from around 2000 shows another group of Rotary workers: from left to right, Graham Hamilton, Rob Lesperance, Brian Bone, and Roger Zalneraitis.

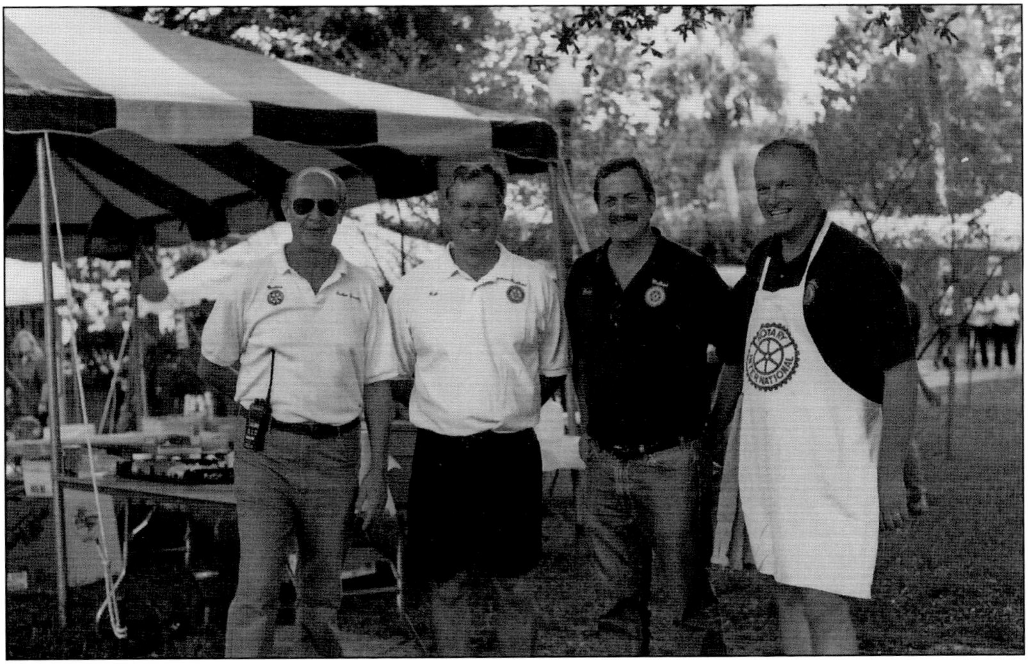

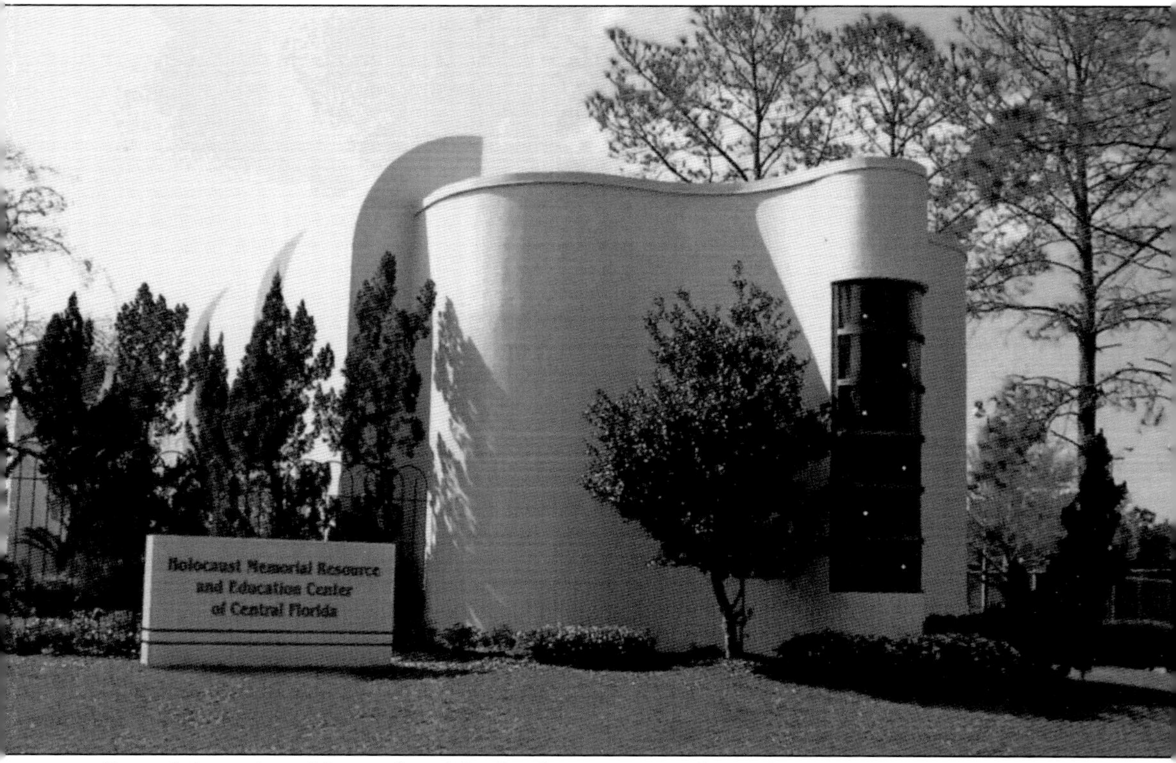

One of the cultural "musts" in Maitland is a visit to the Holocaust Memorial Resource and Education Center, located at 851 North Maitland Avenue on the campus of the Jewish Community Center of Greater Orlando. The Holocaust center uses a variety of resources, education programs, community outreach, and public events to provide an overview of the Holocaust and is a memorial to its millions of victims. The center includes a library with more than 5,000 volumes and 500 videotapes that are available for the public and researchers interested in the Holocaust. The Jewish Community Center opened in 1973 in a wooden house in an orange grove but has blossomed into a 68,000-square-foot facility with a variety of programs to serve more than 20,000 Jewish and non-Jewish members in the community.

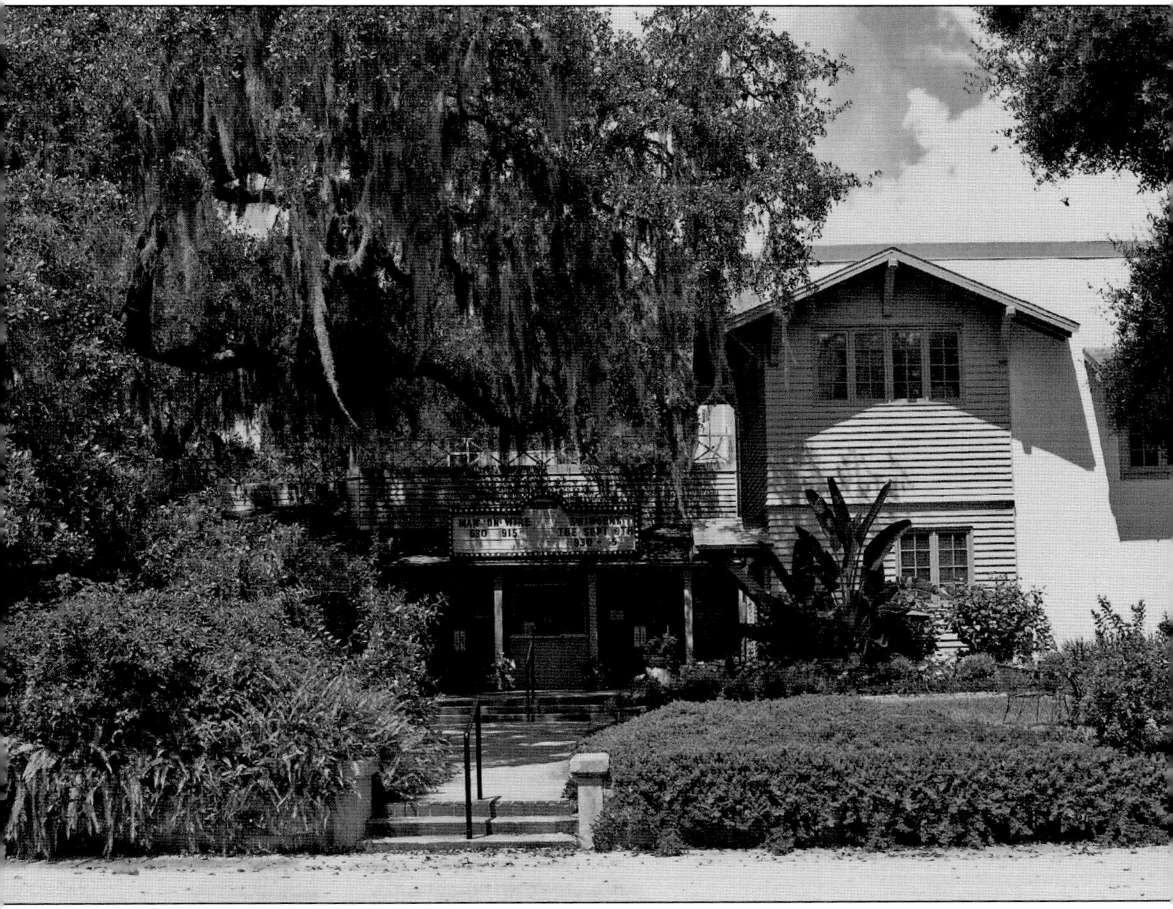

Located on Highway 17-92, the Enzian Theater was founded in 1985 by Tina Tiedtke and the Tiedtke family. Initially it was a repertory house that offered classic films and some live music. Four years later, it began showing first-run independent films with the motto "Film Is Art." Through the years, the Enzian Theater has been the site of many special events and now is home to the nationally renowned Florida Film Festival, founded in 1991, which brings noted directors, producers, and film stars—along with an estimated 25,000 film fans—to the campus for 10 days each spring.

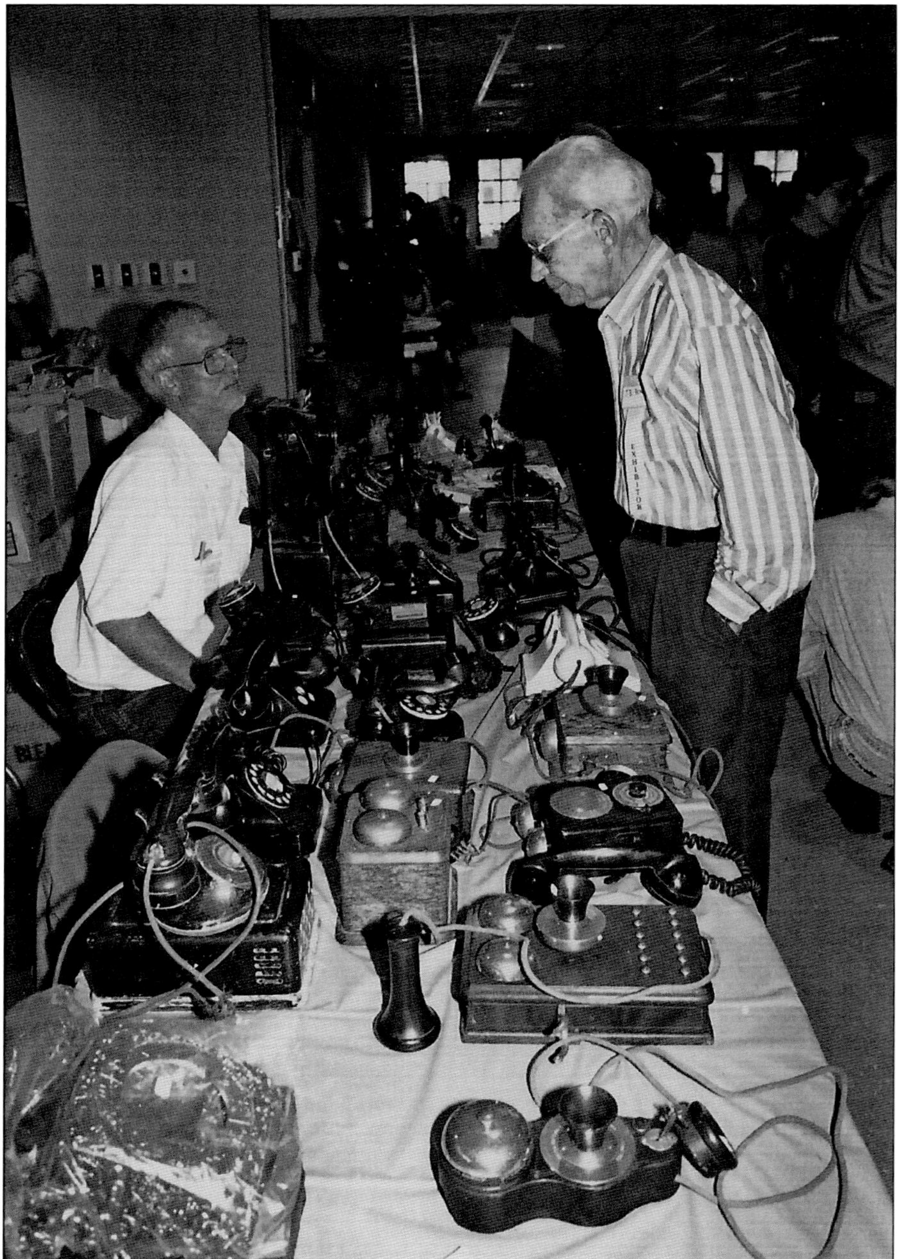

An annual cultural tradition every January is the antique telephone show at the Maitland Civic Center. In this undated photograph, two unidentified men discuss the many old styles of telephones that date back to the late 1800s with the advent of the communications system. In celebration of this event, the Maitland Historical Society opens the doors to its Telephone Museum, located behind the historical museum at 221 West Packwood Avenue, so that visitors can look at memorabilia dating from 1910. That year, Maitland resident Carl Galloway installed the area's first telephones in his father's grocery store and in the homes of several store customers so they could quickly place orders. The enterprise eventually became the Winter Park Telephone Company, then Sprint, then United Telephone.

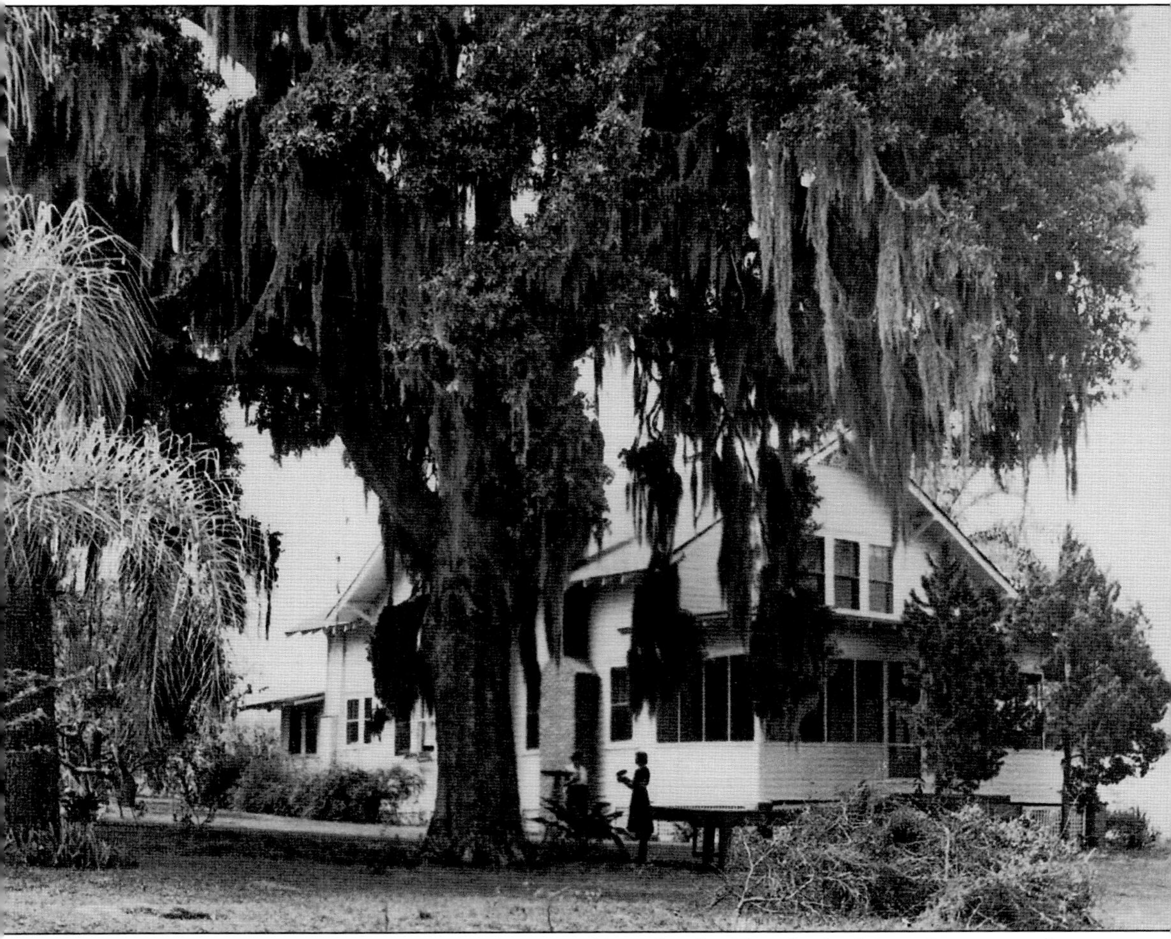

Once a family home, this building now houses offices for the Florida Audubon Society and its Center for Birds of Prey. The two-story home, located on 2.5 acres on the southeast shore of Lake Sybelia, was built in 1924 for the Patterson family. In 1958, the Florida Audubon Society bought the property and used it for offices and as a meeting place. Four years later, the campus became a refuge and rehabilitation center for raptor birds, including bald eagles, owls, falcon, and hawks—many of them locally rescued after becoming injured or sick. Children and visitors can see a number of different birds and learn more about them through educational programs.

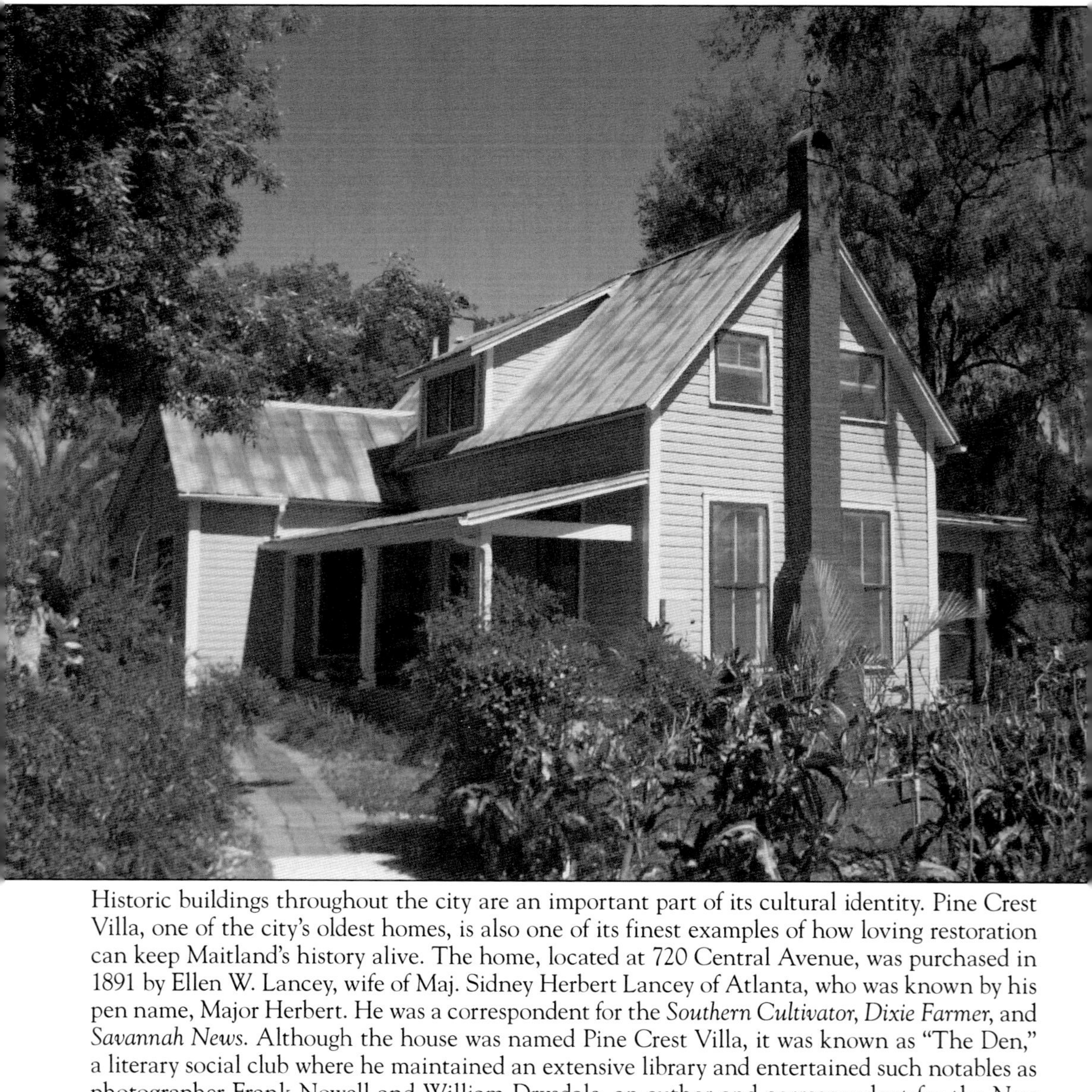

Historic buildings throughout the city are an important part of its cultural identity. Pine Crest Villa, one of the city's oldest homes, is also one of its finest examples of how loving restoration can keep Maitland's history alive. The home, located at 720 Central Avenue, was purchased in 1891 by Ellen W. Lancey, wife of Maj. Sidney Herbert Lancey of Atlanta, who was known by his pen name, Major Herbert. He was a correspondent for the *Southern Cultivator, Dixie Farmer*, and *Savannah News*. Although the house was named Pine Crest Villa, it was known as "The Den," a literary social club where he maintained an extensive library and entertained such notables as photographer Frank Nowell and William Drysdale, an author and correspondent for the *New York Times*.

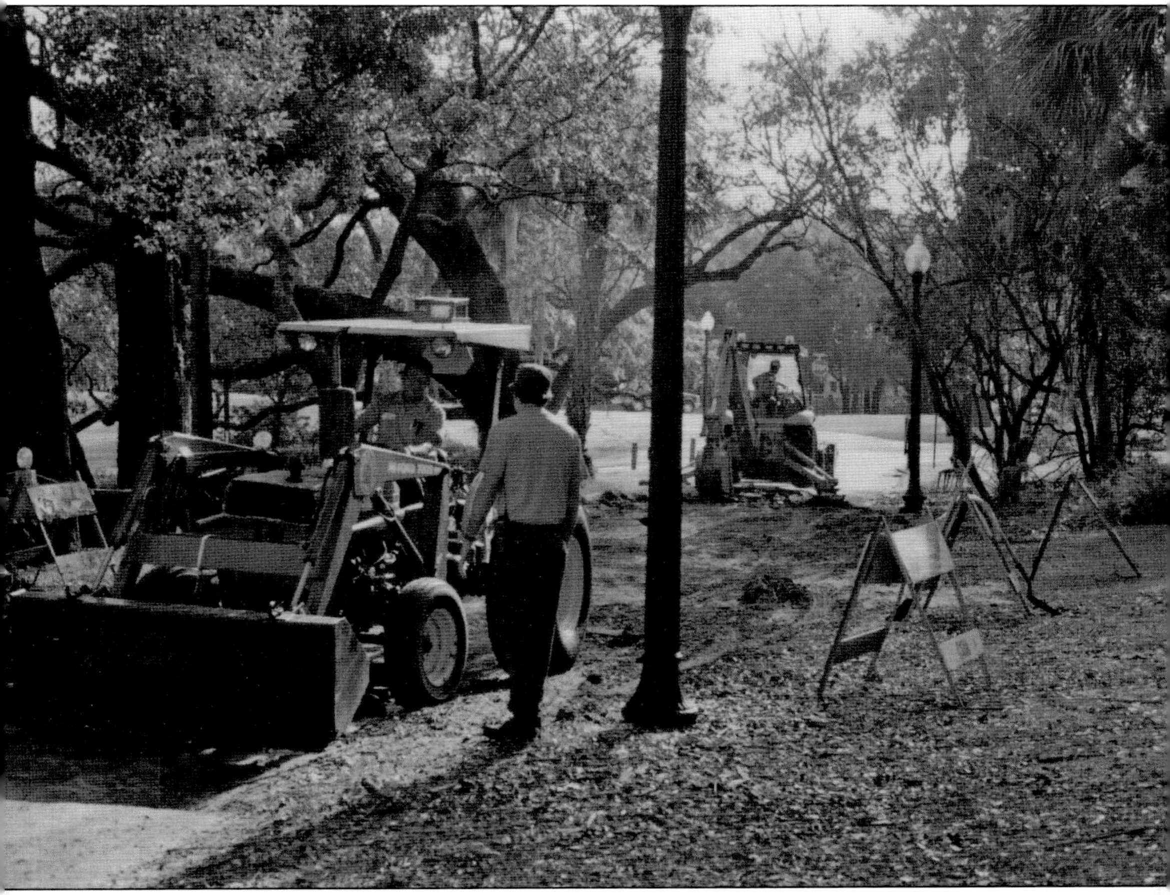

One of Maitland's hidden cultural treasures was uncovered in 1998 with the removal of asphalt to reveal the original Dixie Highway, the first brick-paved road in the State of Florida. The original road was 9 feet wide and extended along the west side of Lake Lily, linking Winter Park and Maitland north to the border of Orange and Seminole Counties. The entire road, designed to be a tourist route, stretched from Canada to Miami when it was completed in 1925. The road was paved in the 1960s, losing much of its original charm, but with its restoration, it has regained its original glory and continues to be an important part of the community as bikers, joggers, and families use it while enjoying Lake Lily.

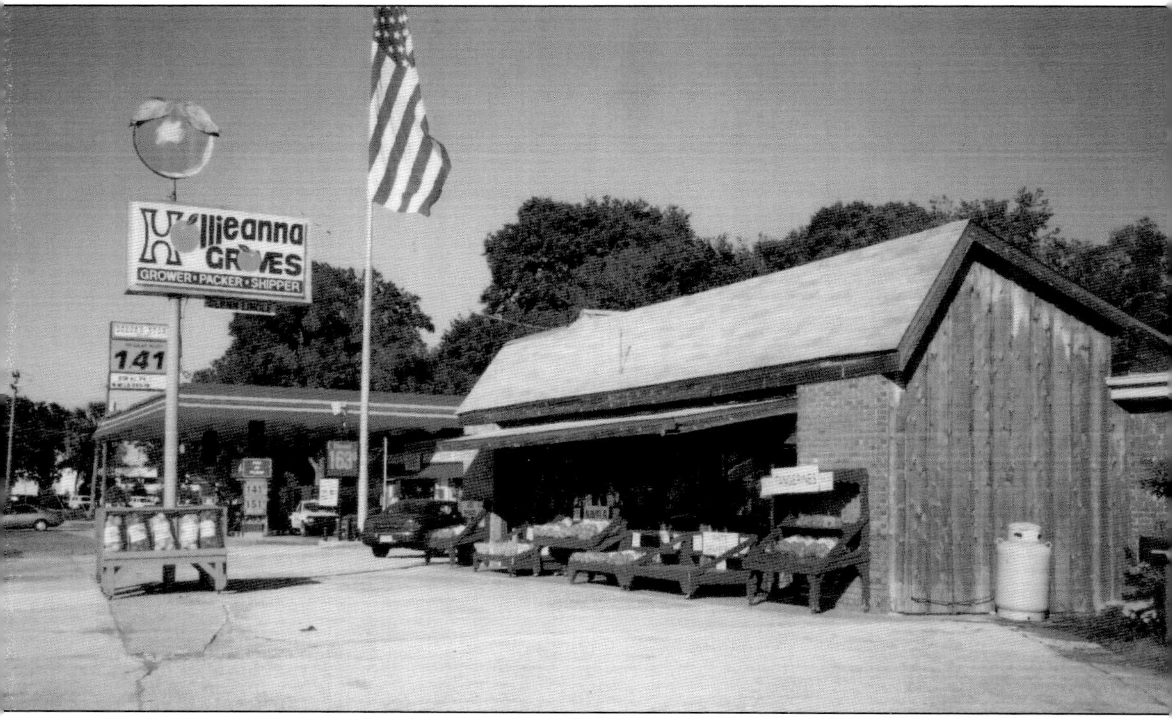

Maitland was once a major part of Central Florida's citrus industry, but that business has waned with damaging freezes and the replacement of old groves with subdivisions. Hollieanna Groves, located on U.S. Highway 17-92, is the last citrus packinghouse in the city, a reminder of agriculture's glory days in the area. Since 1954, the Lingle family has owned and operated the outlet, which features fruit picked from their groves, packed at the shop, and then shipped to customers in a variety of destinations. The location was once on the prime tourist route—before the advent of Interstate 4 in the 1970s—but it continues to thrive with local and out-of-state orders.

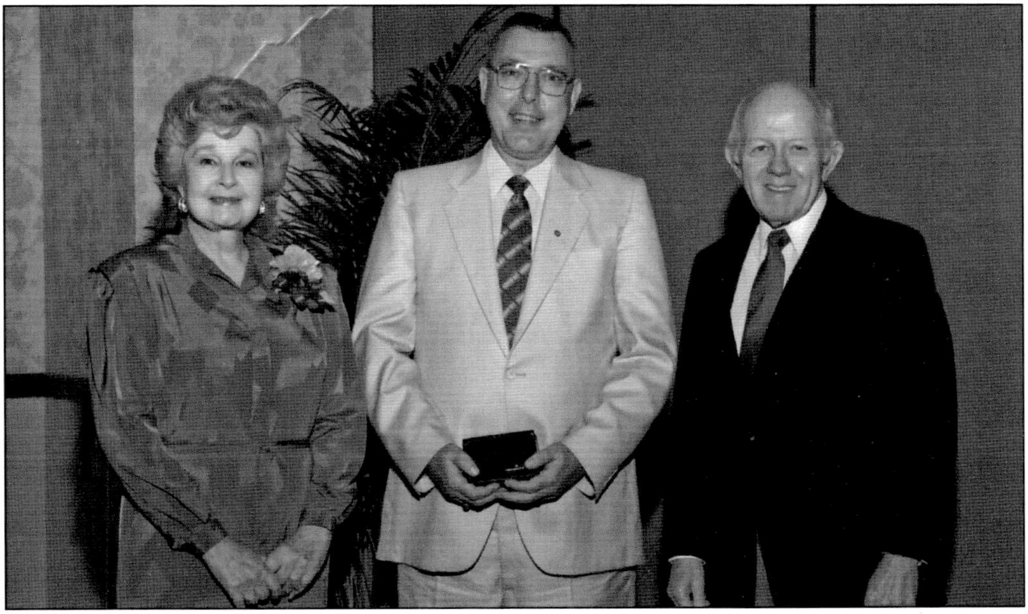

For many years, Gooding's was a household name among Maitland residents, who enjoyed shopping at what was then the area's first gourmet supermarket. Located on U.S. Highway 17-92 at Packwood Avenue, the store opened in 1964 and offered something local residents had never experienced before—a scratch bakery in which donuts and breads were baked on the premises. Shown in the above photograph from the early 1970s are three familiar faces from the store: from left to right, Mary Louise Gooding, store manager H. Darcy Bone (who served as a city commissioner and mayor), and founder James E. Gooding. The Goodings were generous donors to many Maitland causes and donated the Lake Lily Fountain to the city. Below, around 1980, Bone (right) greets Florida governor Bob Graham, who manned the delicatessen counter in one of the many "work days" he held during his administration. Many prominent area politicians dropped in to greet Graham as he sliced lunch meat for customers. Store officials announced the closing of the Maitland store in 2005—the end of a long legacy.

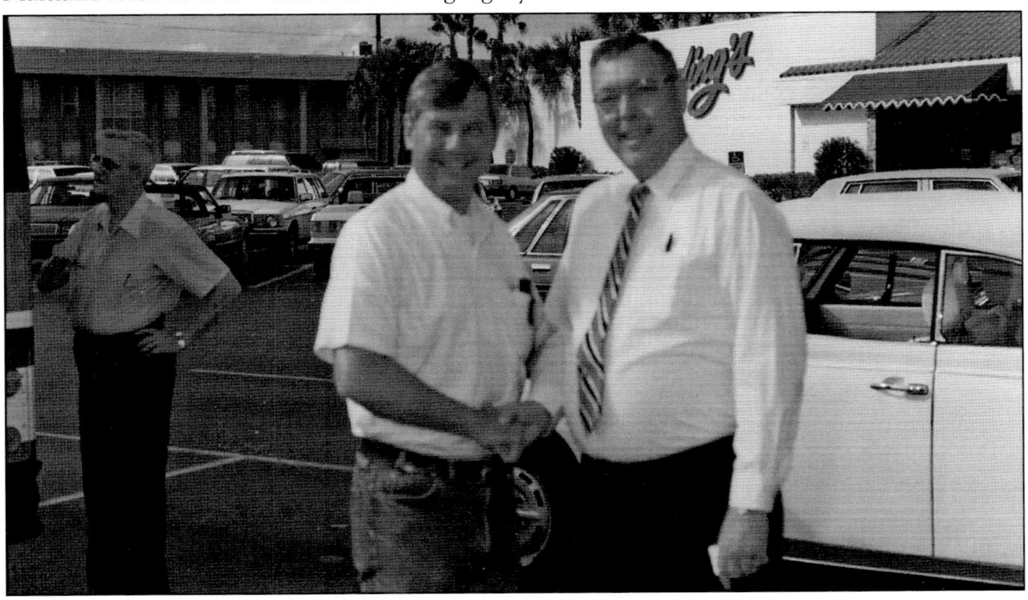

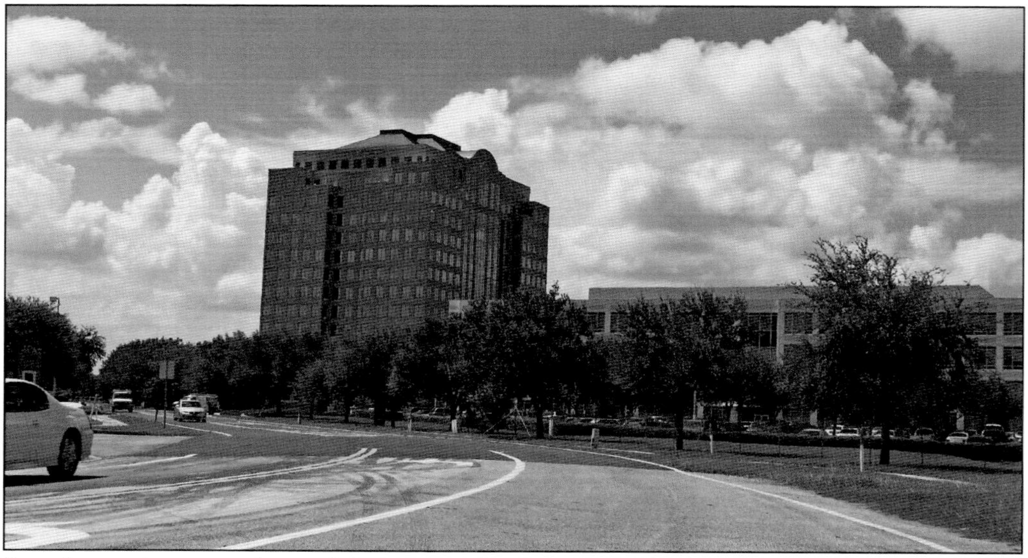

Significant change in the city's business industry came in the latter part of the 20th century. Maitland's borders expanded to the west, past Interstate 4, to include the Maitland Exchange area of towering office buildings and retail outlets. Initially plans called for I-4 to come directly through the center of the city, paralleling the railroad track and U.S. Highway 17-92. Much rejoicing was heard when the final path was chosen to the west of Lake Sybelia. With the road construction came a push for new growth. In the late 1970s, a Georgia firm developed Maitland Center, which continues to grow and is one of the leading office parks in the southeastern United States.

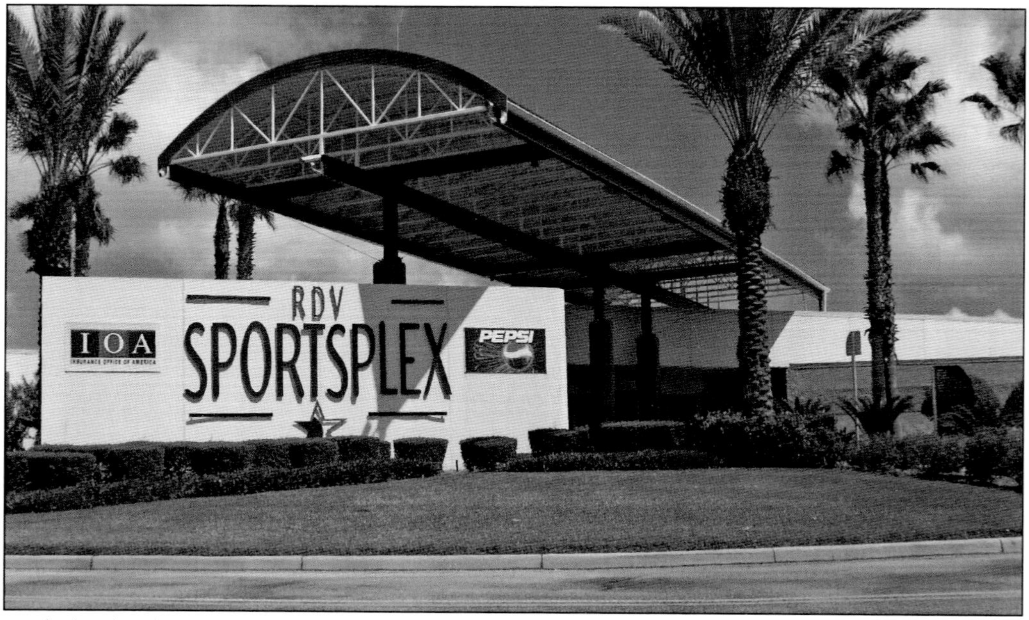

With the development to the west of Interstate 4 came a variety of other facilities, most notably the RDV Sportsplex, opened in February 1998. The $60-million, 365,000-square-foot building at the corner of Maitland Boulevard and Keller Road provides a range of training and fitness programs and facilities, including ice skating, tennis, shops, medical offices, a spa, and restaurants. The building also is the corporate and training home of the Orlando Magic professional basketball team of the National Basketball Association.

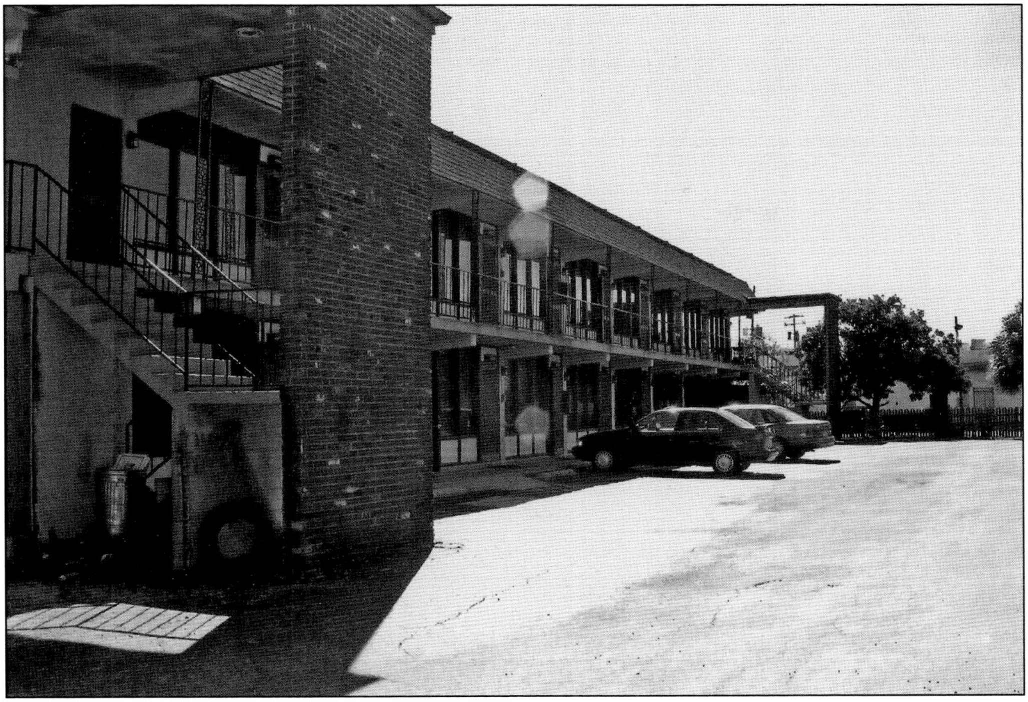

Maitland's plans to redevelop the city center on the east side of I-4 in the early 21st century meant the demolition of several older buildings. The El Rancho Motel, which once urged visitors to stay there at night and "see beautiful Orlando in the daytime," was removed as part of the project. Also taken down was the China Jade, for many years offering cocktails and a buffet of Mongolian barbeque. A Publix Super Market, whose sign is pictured below, was built on the site of these former businesses.

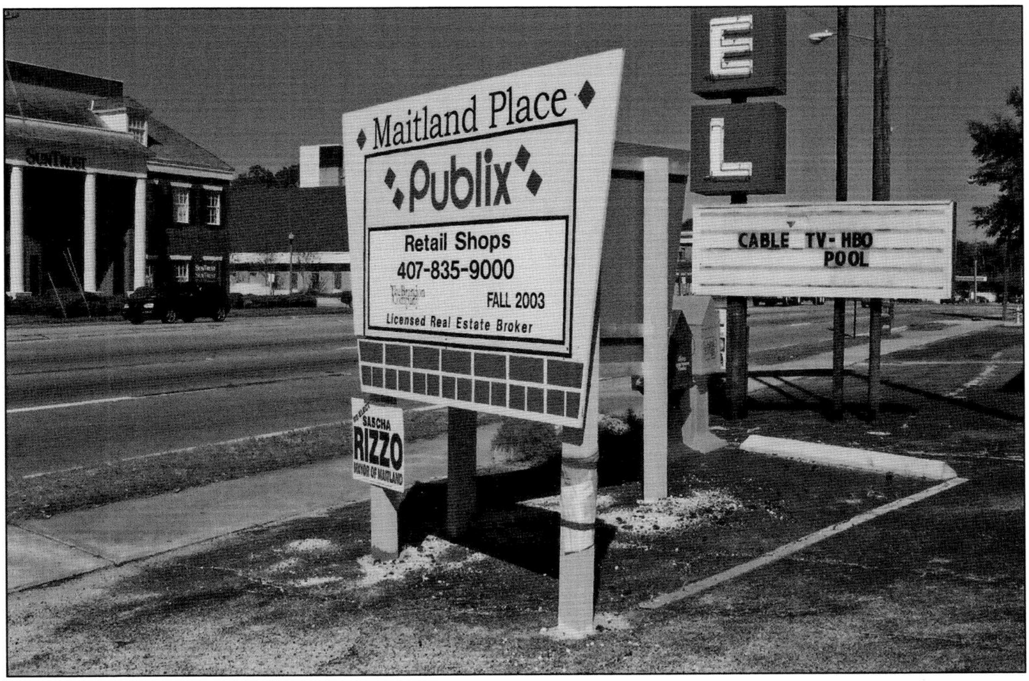

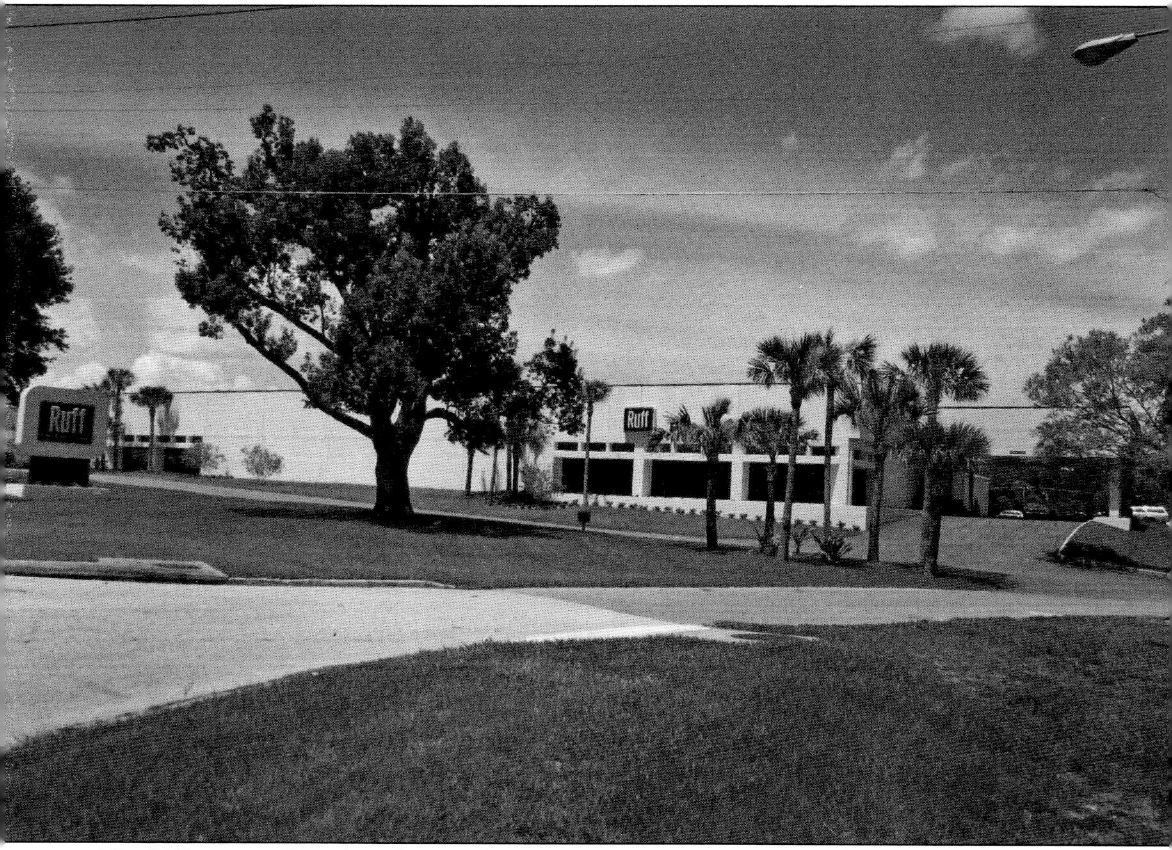

The Village at Lake Lily, a $100-million project that includes apartments, condominiums, and retail space, has replaced a number of older businesses and buildings, including that which once housed Thomas W. Ruff and Company, shown in this photograph. The Ruff Company once offered office furniture from its location on U.S. Highway 17-92 on the southern shore of Lake Lily. The new construction that replaced it is part of the city's downtown redevelopment project that includes reconfiguring some streets in order to create a central business district to serve residents into the 21st century. The face of Maitland is once again changing, which makes preservation of its history even more important.

Six

Then and Now

In its long and colorful history, the city of Lake Maitland, now known by its shortened modern name of Maitland, has undergone vast changes. Much like other Florida communities, the city has gone from a largely rural, agricultural settlement to a thriving metropolitan area. As these next few pages illustrate, oak-lined dirt streets have been paved, then widened, then paved again to accommodate new growth that brought with it a current population of more than 16,000 residents. Stately old wooden lakefront homes have given way to modern mansions and, in some cases, high-rise condominiums. And yet Maitland has retained the natural charm that first lured people to the area. The train is no longer the center of the city's commerce, but the horns of passing freight and passenger trains still resound daily through the city. Many descendants of Maitland's founding families continue to live in the area, worship in local churches, and celebrate special occasions with large parties under its graceful trees. Maitland has established a Cultural Corridor that includes the Waterhouse Residence and Carpentry Shop Museums, the Maitland Public Library, the Maitland Senior Center, the Maitland Historical and Telephone Museums, and the Maitland Art Center. Maitland's A-rated public schools and several excellent private schools continue to attract young families to the city. The Maitland of the 21st century may be greatly changed from that of a century ago—so much so that early settlers might not recognize it—but its people still hold the same dream of finding a happy, rich life within its borders.

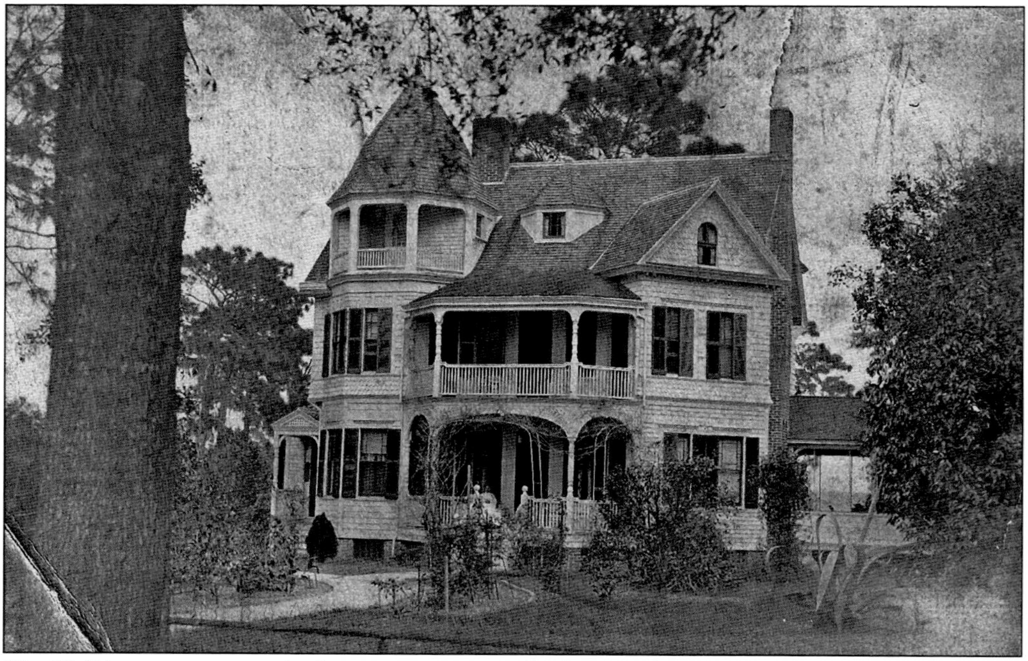

The Hall house was a stately three-story mansion built around 1877 on the western shore of Lake Maitland near the site of the old Fort Maitland. It was built by Charles H. Hall, a banker and retired mining engineer from Ishpeming, Michigan, who wintered many years in the area and grew oranges on the property. Hall donated the land for the Episcopal Church of the Good Shepherd and funded a scholarship at Rollins College in nearby Winter Park. In 1960, the Hall house was damaged by fire and subsequently was demolished. Today it is the site of the nine-story West Cove condominiums. The building was constructed in 1973 along what is now U.S. Highway 17-92, a busy six-lane road that bisects the city.

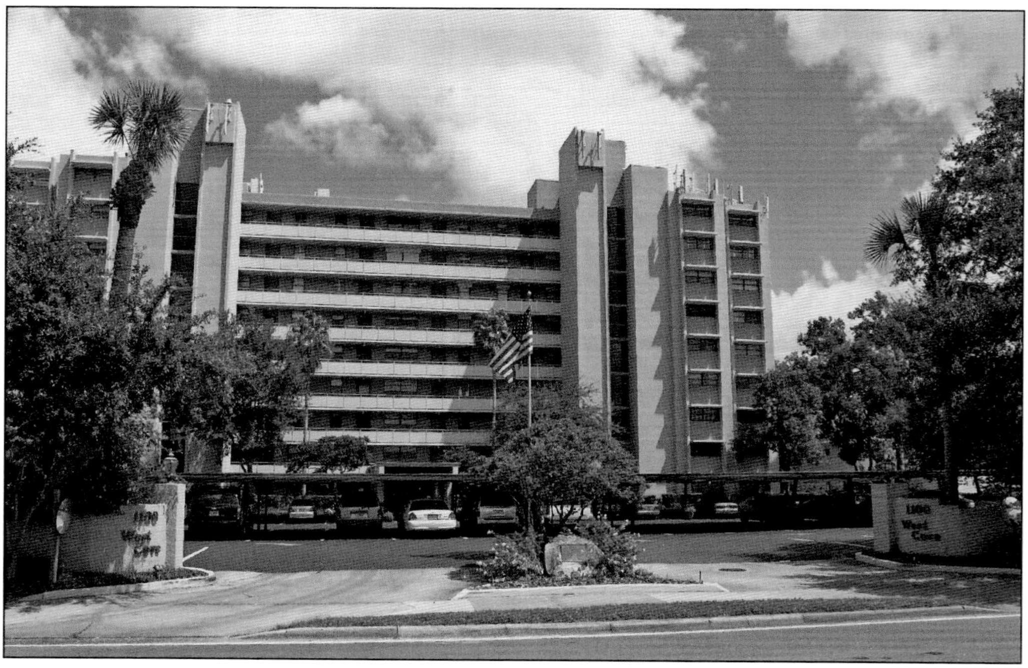

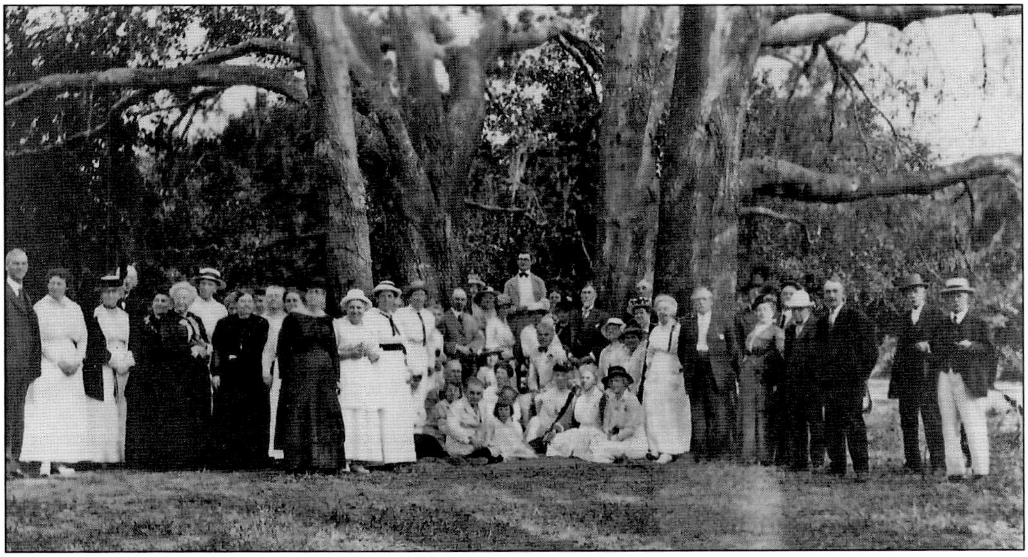

The lovely estate Under Oaks is located on the north shore of Lake Maitland. It originally was constructed in 1882 as a winter home for Dr. Albigence Kingsley of Elizabeth, New Jersey. As this photograph shows, every spring, the Kingsley family held a picnic for about 100 friends on their front lawn. The Hames family, the current owners, revived the Kingsley tradition with the outdoor wedding of Leigh Hames to David Dreisbach on April 12, 2008. About 400 guests watched as vows were exchanged under the estate's ancient oaks and then dined and celebrated late into the spring night under the stars. The wedding party was, from left to right, (seated) Lindsay Hames, Melissa Clemens, Bryan Dreisbach, Haley Rizor, Ginna Dreisbach, and Lee Bryan; (standing) Tyler McRae, Jesse MacDougall, Dr. Randall Martin, Amanda Ayers, Ryan Albert, Leigh and David Dreisbach, Lauren Hames, George Garcia, and Lisa Dreisbach. (Bottom image courtesy Leigh Hames Dreisbach.)

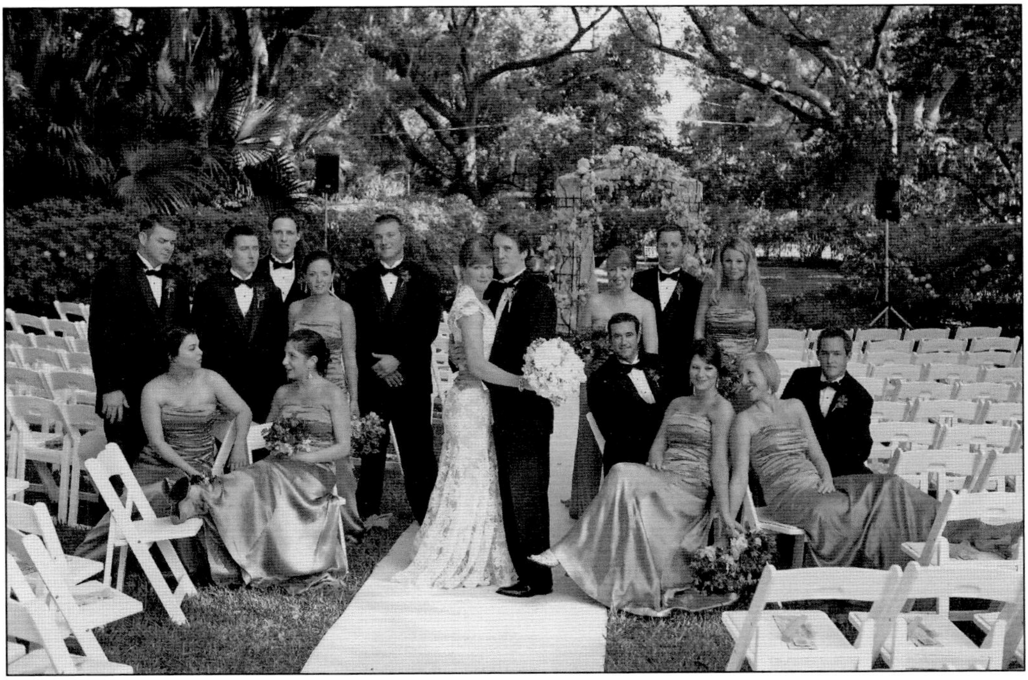

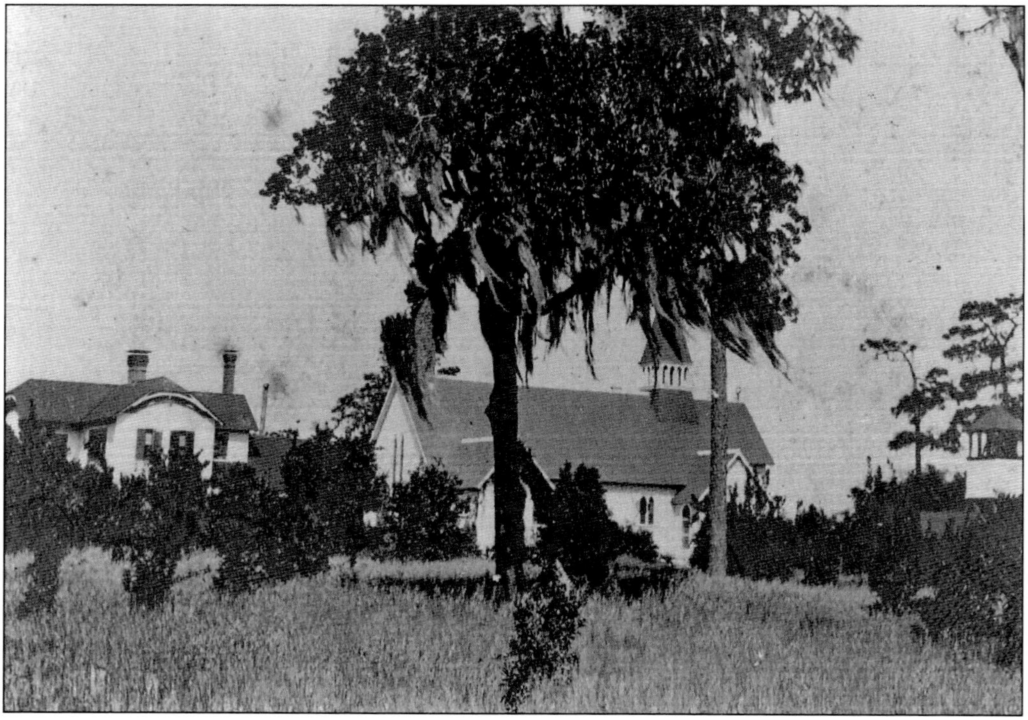

The Church of the Good Shepherd is the oldest standing church in Maitland and remains one of its loveliest landmarks. The white wooden church, built in the late Gothic Revival style, was consecrated in 1883 by the Right Reverend Henry B. Whipple, the Episcopal bishop of Minnesota, who wintered in the town. The old church is now used as a chapel and stands next to a newer church building, constructed in 1963 and designed by parishioner Nils M. Schweitzer, a noted local architect who trained with Frank Lloyd Wright. On March 16, 2008, the congregants along with the Right Reverend John W. Howe, bishop of the Diocese of Central Florida, gathered to celebrate Palm Sunday and the 125th anniversary of Good Shepherd—a milestone for the church and the Greater Maitland community. (Bottom image courtesy Church of the Good Shepherd.)

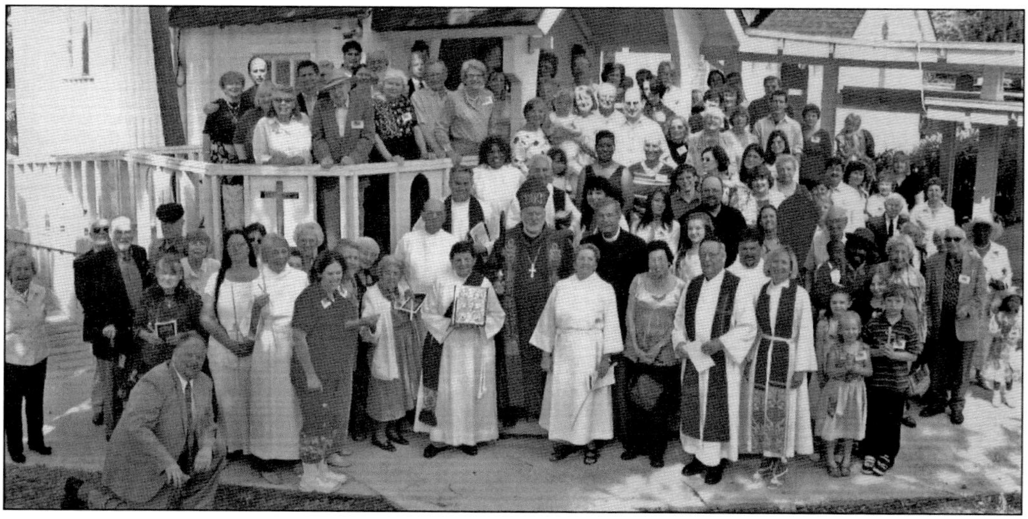

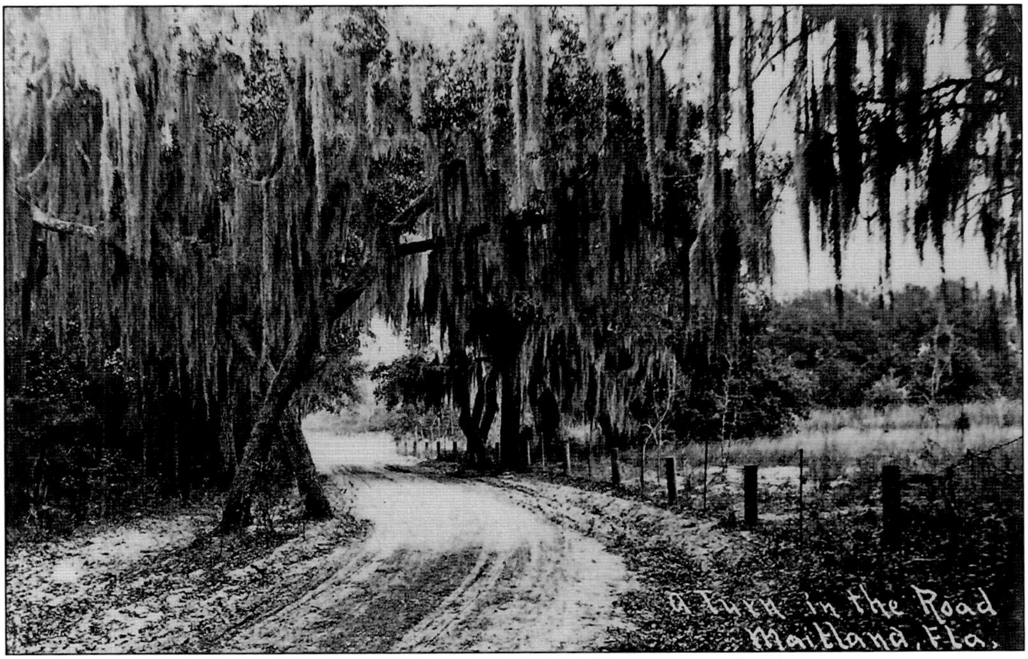

Horatio Avenue has long been one of the central thoroughfares in Maitland, connecting important roads, commercial areas, and the railroad. Once upon a time, it was a shady, dirt country road that passed through areas filled with citrus groves and agricultural fields. Named for early resident George Horatio Packwood, it has slowly been transformed into a modern, paved four-lane road featuring many traffic lights to contain and control its busy traffic. Its path now connects major commercial centers with municipal buildings and numerous subdivisions that house Maitland's growing population. These photographs demonstrate the transformation the street has undergone from its earliest days to the present.

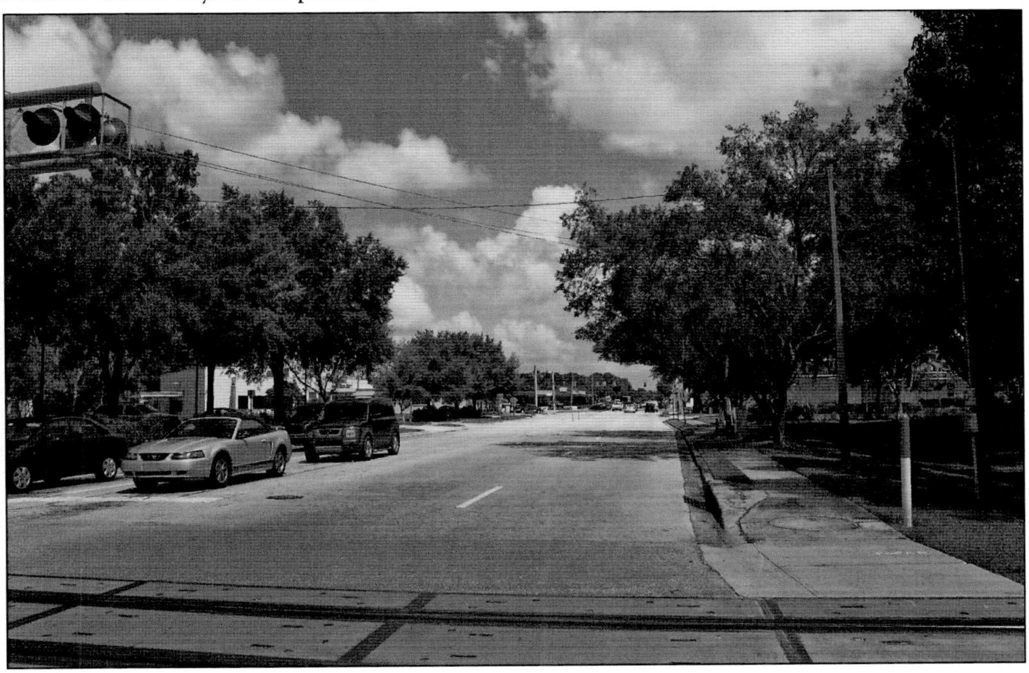

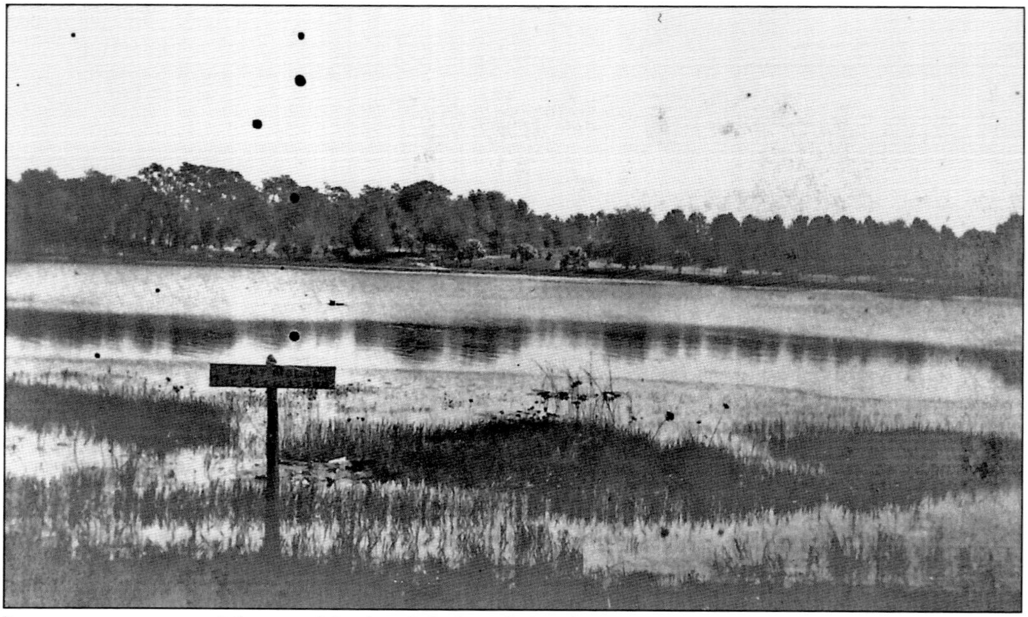

Long a centerpiece of the city, Maitland's Lake Lily has been an important recreation and gathering place for the city's residents. Almost perfectly round and a half-mile across, the lake once was known as St. John's Hole. Early African American settlers built shacks along its shoreline and used the lake for fishing and washing clothes. In 1886, area pioneer Edward C. Hungerford donated to the town of Lake Maitland the land that would become a park along the lake's edge. In later years, Dixie Highway, the first brick-paved road in Orange County, ran along the lake's west side. This early picture of the lake shows just how "wild" the area once was, with a sign warning, "Don't molest the alligators." Today the reptiles are gone and the lakefront has become a popular park and site for community festivals, including this 1991 Maitland Chamber of Commerce spring arts and crafts festival.

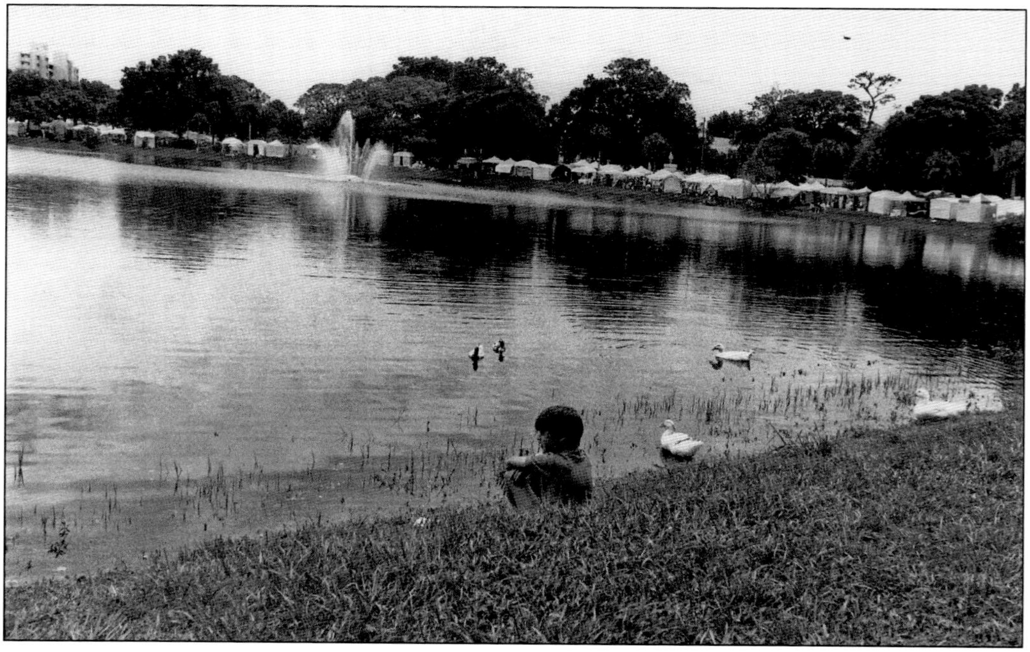

Seven

Preserving Maitland's History

The preservation of historic buildings, documents, and records is a mission of caring about a community, its people, and its heritage. Since 1970, the Maitland Historical Society has worked to bring the city's rich history to life for its many residents. Through its four museums, the society offers historical programs to the public as well as educational classes, exhibits, and speakers. Its growing archives contain a wealth of information about local families, places of worship, businesses, and community groups—and it always welcomes new contributions of material, talent, and resources from the public. These next pages highlight the Maitland Historical Society's facilities and its passionate corps of staff and volunteers who make all of its programs and operations possible.

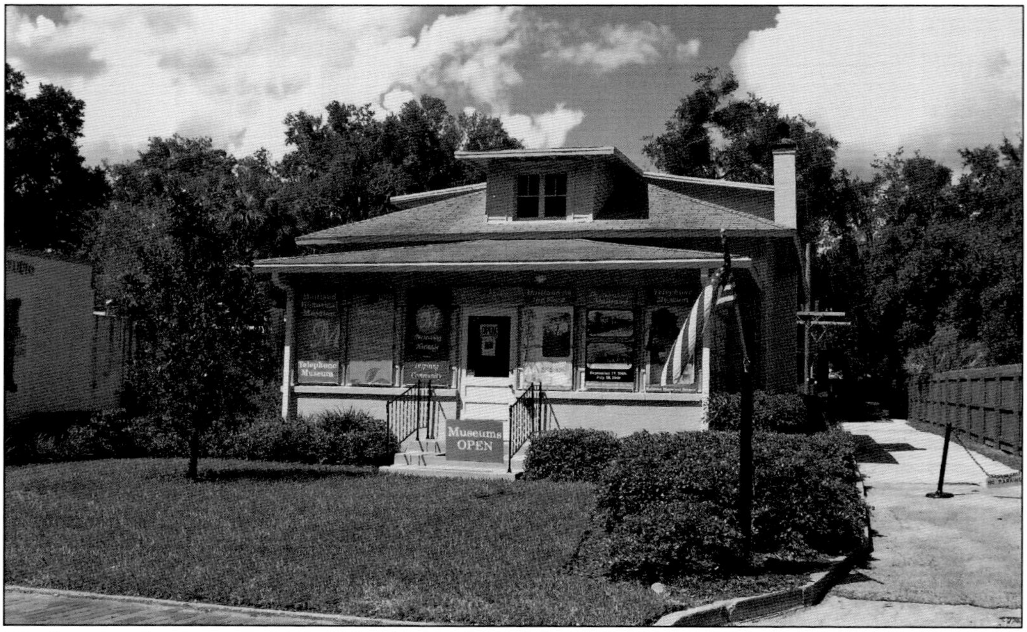

The historical museum operated by the Maitland Historical Society is located in this building at 221 West Packwood Avenue. It contains permanent and changing exhibitions as well as offices and storage space for the historical society's growing collection of archives. Its displays offer the public information and exhibits that trace Maitland's history from its founding to current events.

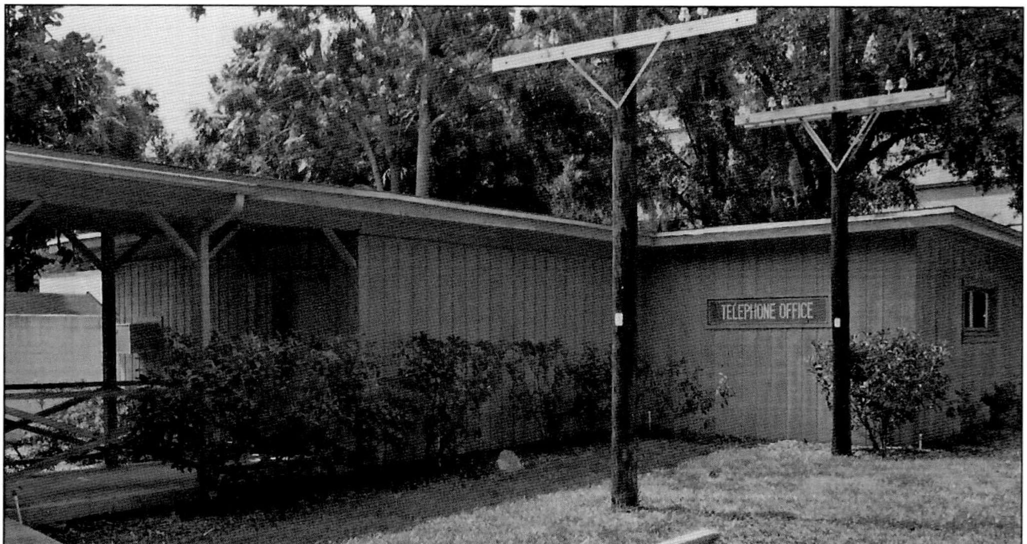

The Telephone Museum, located behind the historical museum, is one of the unique offerings of the Maitland Historical Society. Inside, visitors can look at memorabilia, a working switch station, and a variety of styles of telephones in use in the Maitland area since 1910. That year, Carl Galloway, a local resident, installed telephones in his father's grocery store and in the homes of several store customers so they could quickly place orders. Galloway's start became the Winter Park Telephone Company and eventually was absorbed by larger corporations. The museum attracts visitors interested in the early days of this technology.

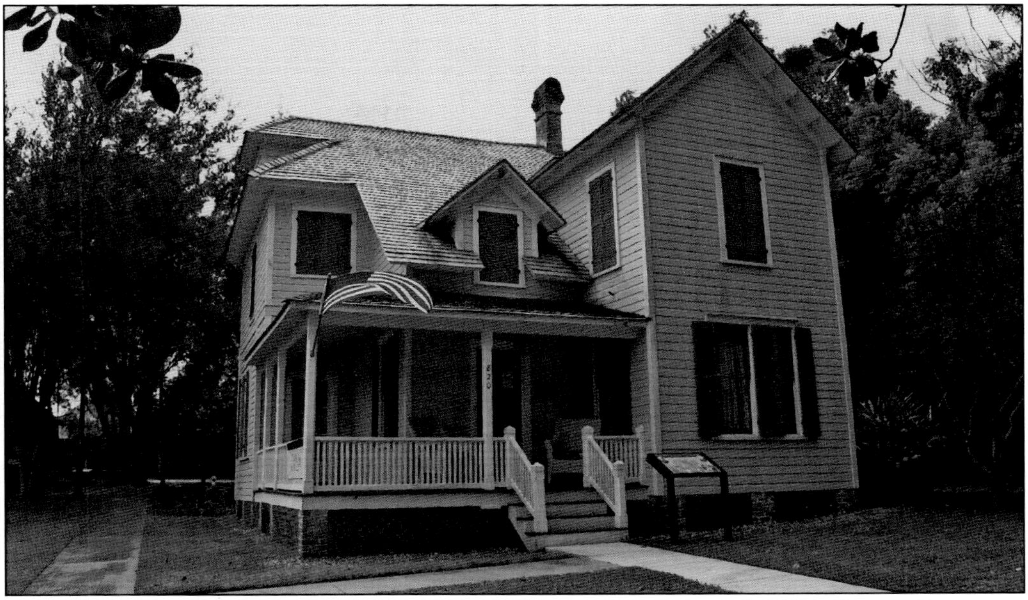

Pictured here are the Historic Waterhouse Residence Museum and the Waterhouse Carpentry Shop Museum. Located on the south shore of Lake Lily, the house and carpentry shop were built by pioneer settler William H. Waterhouse. The home, which dates to 1884, reflects the Victorian lifestyle of this pioneer family and features period furniture and a hand-turned heart-of-pine staircase. The carpentry shop was the site of Waterhouse's woodworking and construction business, responsible for many of the city's historic homes. Visitors can see displays of the tools and materials used by Waterhouse in his business, dating to the 19th century. Every holiday season, the house attracts hundreds of people who delight in its authentic decorations.

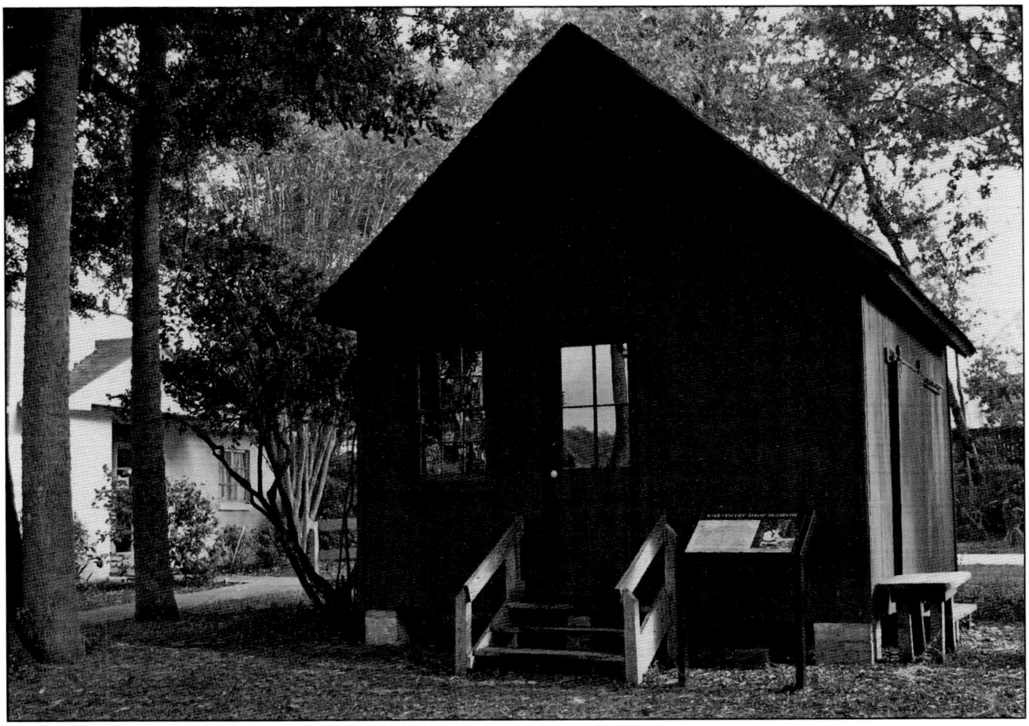

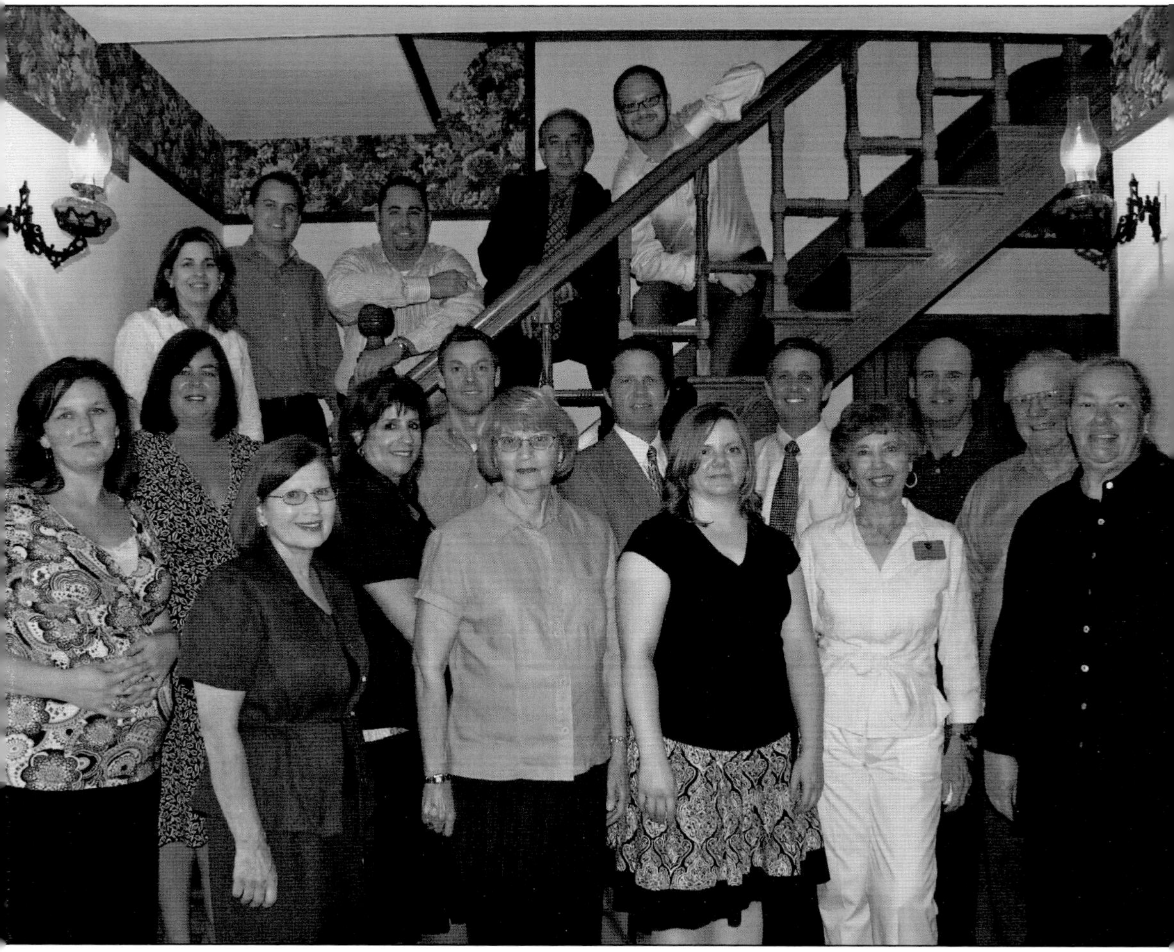

Maitland Historical Society staff and board members gather in the foyer of the Historic Waterhouse Residence Museum in summer 2008. Pictured from left to right are (first row) Andrea Bailey Cox, Betty Sample, Irene Logan, Jill Nash, Von Hancock, and Cathy Sandifer; (second row) Jacine Smallwood, Anita Blackwelder, Darrell DeVaney, Mayor Doug Kinson, Michael Culbertson, Larry Adams, and Jim Hancock; (on the stairs) Kathy Lapp, Jason Albu, Nate Morris, Bill Kavitch, and Doug Berger.

ABBREVIATED INDEX

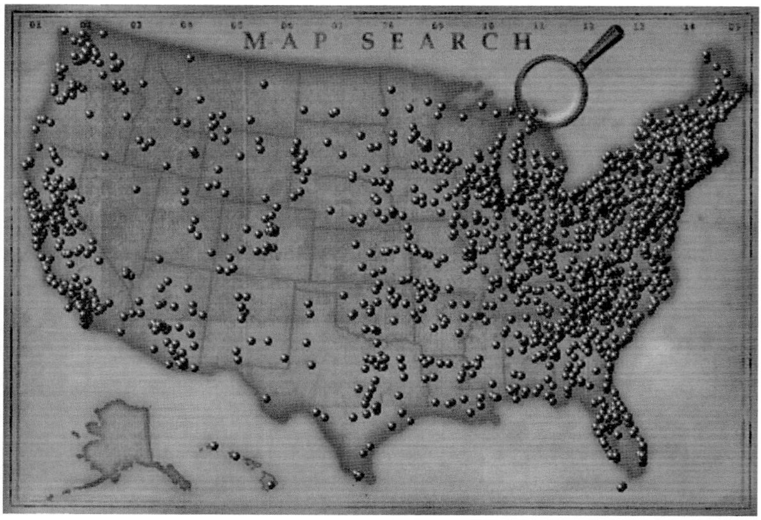
MAP SEARCH